The Number Sense
of Nineteenth-Century British Literature

The Number Sense of Nineteenth-Century British Literature

STEFANIE MARKOVITS

Great Clarendon Street, Oxford, OX2 6DP,
United Kingdom

Oxford University Press is a department of the University of Oxford.
It furthers the University's objective of excellence in research, scholarship,
and education by publishing worldwide. Oxford is a registered trade mark of
Oxford University Press in the UK and in certain other countries

© Stefanie Markovits 2025

The moral rights of the author have been asserted

All rights reserved. No part of this publication may be reproduced, stored in a retrieval system, transmitted, used for text and data mining, or used for training artificial intelligence, in any form or by any means, without the prior permission in writing of Oxford University Press, or as expressly permitted by law, by licence or under terms agreed with the appropriate reprographics rights organization. Enquiries concerning reproduction outside the scope of the above should be sent to the Rights Department, Oxford University Press, at the address above

You must not circulate this work in any other form
and you must impose this same condition on any acquirer

Published in the United States of America by Oxford University Press
198 Madison Avenue, New York, NY 10016, United States of America

British Library Cataloguing in Publication Data

Data available

Library of Congress Control Number: 2024943218

ISBN 9780198937791

DOI: 10.1093/9780198937821.001.0001

Printed and bound by
CPI Group (UK) Ltd, Croydon, CR0 4YY

Links to third party websites are provided by Oxford in good faith and
for information only. Oxford disclaims any responsibility for the materials
contained in any third party website referenced in this work.

The manufacturer's authorised representative in the EU for product safety
is Oxford University Press España S.A. of el Parque Empresarial San
Fernando de Henares, Avenida de Castilla,
2 – 28830 Madrid (www.oup.es/en).

For my children,

One, two, three: Nelly, Florence, Solly.

All equally beloved.

Acknowledgments

This book was written over the course of seven long and often hard years, a period that subtended trials both personal and global in nature, many of which inevitably colored my thinking about how to find meaning in numbers. Seven years: what Jacob labored for Rachel, it's also the span separating the various "chapters" in Jean Ingelow's *Songs of Seven* (1866), a giftbook comprised of seven poems that follow a girl from the age of seven to forty-nine, each lyric matched to a stage of life. A period, indeed, as Jane Austen might have said.

I couldn't have made it through those years, and this book couldn't have made it into the world, without help from many quarters. A work devoted to the power of numbers can't but instill anxiety in its author when it comes time to acknowledge the many who have contributed to its formation. There are fears of names forgotten—even worries of how best to order a series of acknowledgements: to rank or alphabetize? Yet into the breach I must go, so first my gratitude to all the friends, colleagues, and students who contributed in some way to this project—be it by asking a question during a conference panel or seminar, reading a draft of a chapter, sending me a curious citation or a useful reference, or reading the entire manuscript. These include Sarah Bilston, Alison Booth, Leslie Brisman, Ashley Duraiswamy, Tasha Eccles, Ben Glaser, Beatrice Goddu, Andrea Henderson, Linda Hughes, Aeron Hunt, Amy Huseby, Mark Knight, David Kurnick, George Levine, Naomi Levine, Maia McAleavey, Imogen Forbes-McPhail, John Durham Peters, Charles Rzepka, Talia Schaffer, Justin Sider, Emily Steinlight, Imani Tucker, Colton Valentine, and Ruth Yeazell. (Serendipity: My greatest debts are owed to the first and last named on this alphabetical list!)

Second, my thanks to the various editors, publishers, and anonymous readers who have helped bring out into the public sphere both this book and the articles that tested the waters with my ideas. Chapter 1 is derived in part from my article "*Don Juan's* Numerals," published in *European Romantic Review* 29.5 (October 2018), copyright Taylor & Francis, available online: www.tandfonline.com/doi.org/10.1080/10509585.2018.1511987. Parts of Chapter 2 first appeared as "Jane Austen, by *Half*" in *Eighteenth-Century*

Fiction 32.2 (Winter 2019/2020): 297–315. I thank the editors, the journal, and the University of Toronto Press for permission to republish it here. An earlier version of parts of Chapter 4 appeared as "But Who's Counting? Plotting Age in Trollope" in *Genre: Forms of Discourse and Culture*, 53.2 (July 2020): 111–33; it is republished by permission of the Publisher, Duke University Press. At Oxford University Press I have been lucky to work with Eleanor Collins, Jack McNichol, and Aimee Wright.

Third, and most, thanks to my family: my one and only husband, Ben; my two parents, Inga and Dick; my four siblings—Daniel, Ben (the other one), Julia, and Rebecca—and their four partners; and last (but not least) in this list, interrupting the tidiness of a serial progression, my three children, to whom the book is dedicated. I can tally all your numbers, but I can measure neither my gratitude nor my love for you.

Contents

Introduction	1
0.1 Number Sense	1
0.2 Three Threes	9
0.3 By the Numbers	19
1. Byron's Counts	25
1.1 Romantic Numbers	25
1.2 *Don Juan*'s Numerals	32
1.3 Counting	37
1.4 The One and the Many	43
1.5 Taking Measure	51
2. Jane Austen, by *Half*	57
2.1 Let's Do the Numbers	57
2.2 Thinking by Halves	66
2.3 Reserve, in lieu of a Coda: *The Odd Women*	80
3. Figuring Character in Dickens	91
3.1 Counting the Leaves	91
3.2 Name, Number, Character	98
3.3 Counting Heads in *A Tale of Two Cities*	115
3.4 Coda: Or Ouroboros?	130
4. Plotting Age in Trollope	137
4.1 Counting the Years	137
4.2 Liberal Time and the Narrative Now	147
4.3 Plotting Age	156
4.4 Counting Down	166
4.5 Afterlife: One More Count(down)	171
Conclusion	181
C.1 First Things First: *Three* Redux	181
C.2 Two Threes in *Armadale*	185
C.3 Third and Last: *Desperate Remedies*	193
Bibliography	205
Index	217

Introduction

0.1 Number Sense

A novel numberiness ranks high among the distinguishing characteristics of the nineteenth century.[1] The modern science of statistics that emerged in its early decades produced "an avalanche of printed numbers" throughout the period.[2] Forces composing this avalanche had been building up for some time, contributing to the long process whereby, as Mary Poovey has chronicled, numbers have "come to epitomize the modern fact."[3] To cite just a few examples, the Stamp Act of 1765 required the numbering of houses (think of William Blake's "charter'd street[s]"[4]). The first catalogue of stars was published in 1798—an effort to count what only God had heretofore known.[5] Then there were theoretical pressures: The publication of Thomas Malthus's *Essay on the Principle of Population* in the same year precipitated the ascendency of numerical ways of thinking. Jeremy Bentham's "felicific calculus" suggested how one might quantify what was previously described qualitatively.[6] And the imaginary digits of Adam Smith's "invisible hand" seemed to foreshadow a world dictated by the play of numbers.

When the first modern census was taken in Britain in 1801, the die was cast. It was followed by a parade of additional official numbery innovations. The Board of Trade instituted its statistical office in 1832. The 1832–4

[1] I owe the useful term *numberiness* to David Kurnick. See David Kurnick, "Numberiness," "Three Responses to 'Ulysses by Numbers,'" *Representations: Responses* (Jan. 13, 2015): n. pag. www.representations.org/response-to-ulysses-by-numbers-david-kurnick/. Accessed May 23, 2024. The term registers a general saturation with numbers, both as elements of the textual world and as a means used to organize experience.

[2] Ian Hacking, *The Taming of Chance* (Cambridge: Cambridge University Press, 1990), 2.

[3] Mary Poovey, *A History of the Modern Fact* (Chicago: University of Chicago Press, 1998), xii.

[4] William Blake, "London," in *Blake's Poetry and Designs*, ed. Mary Lynn Johnson and John E. Grant (New York: W. W. Norton, 1979), 53.

[5] Genesis 15:5 (*KJV*): "And he brought him forth abroad, and said, Look now toward heaven, and tell the stars, if thou be able to number them: and he said unto him, So shall thy seed be."

[6] See Bentham's *Introduction to the Principles of Morals and Legislation* (1781), which dedicated its fourth chapter to the "Value of a Lot of Pleasure or Pain, How to be Measured."

The Number Sense of Nineteenth-Century British Literature. Stefanie Markovits, Oxford University Press. © Stefanie Markovits (2025). DOI: 10.1093/9780198937821.003.0001

2 THE NUMBER SENSE

royal commission, which was appointed to investigate the poor law, collected numerical data on a scale sufficient to be useful for formulating—or at least defending—government policy. Charles Babbage (father of the difference engine and modern computing), Malthus, and others inaugurated the Royal Statistical Society in 1834. Moreover, liberal democracy—under consolidation through the Reform Acts of 1832, 1867, and 1884—depends on what John Stuart Mill called "the numerical theory of representation," as suggested also by his quoting Bentham's maxim: "Everybody to count for one, nobody for more than one."[7] Indeed, while the numbery advances may be beyond count, that last term was being deployed in innovative ways, indicating its pervasiveness as a method of making sense of the world. As Matthew Bevis has observed, "According to the OED, several new uses of the verb *count* come into being in the nineteenth century: to count as 'to mark the time or rhythm' (1848); to 'count out' (1833); to 'count in' (1857); to count as an intransitive, meaning 'to admit of being counted' (1845—from *Blackwood's Magazine*: 'An unimpeachable verse, for it counts right'); 'to count for' (1857); and 'to count out ... in children's games, with the words of a rhyme' (1842)."[8]

Such numerical saturation inevitably combined with cultural backlash. In *Sartor Resartus* (1833-4), Thomas Carlyle lamented the "Arithmetical Mill" that had "destroy[ed] Wonder, and in its stead substitute[d] Mensuration and Numeration."[9] The following year, when the journalist William Cooke Taylor defended the recent statistical data compiled from "tables of

---

[7] J. S. Mill, "Speech upon the Reform Bill," April 13, 1866, in *The Collected Works of John Stuart Mill*, ed. J. M. Robson (Toronto: University of Toronto Press, London: Routledge & Kegan Paul, 1963-91), 33 vols., XXVIII; https://oll.libertyfund.org/collection/the-collected-works-of-john-stuart-mill. Accessed Feb. 13, 2023. Hereafter *CW*. J. S. Mill, *Utilitarianism* (London: Parker, Son, & Bourn, 1863), 91 (in *CW* XVII). Poovey summarizes the increasing numberiness of politics: "The link between numerical representation and government—or, more specifically, centralized government bureaucracy—was forged by the seventeenth-century practice of 'political arithmetic.' By the mid-1830s, numbers had begun to play a prominent role in producing both a single 'imagined community' where various communities had once competed for loyalty and the government apparatus by which this national community could be governed." Mary Poovey, "Figures of Arithmetic, Figures of Speech: The Discourse of Statistics in the 1830s," *Critical Inquiry* 19.2 (Winter 1993), 264. See also Ronjaunee Chatterjee, *Feminine Singularity: The Politics of Subjectivity in Nineteenth-Century Literature* (Stanford: Stanford University Press, 2022): "If British liberalism's techne is the ballot and the census, then the resulting form of personhood made legible before the liberal state is a countable one, an assumption shared by Jeremy Bentham, John Stuart Mill, and other prominent figures of British liberal thought in the nineteenth century" (9).

[8] Matthew Bevis, "Poetry by Numbers," *Raritan* 37.2 (2017), 38.

[9] Thomas Carlyle, *Sartor Resartus*, Bk. I, ch. 10. In *The Collected Works*, Ashburton Edition, 17 vols. (London: Chapman & Hall, 1885-6), III.47. Hereafter, all references to Carlyle's works will be to volume and page in this edition unless otherwise noted.

mortality, the records of hospitals and police-offices, the registers of parishes and courts of justice," he complained that "there are still people in the world, who prefer the figures of speech to the figures of arithmetic, and the rules of Longinus to those of Cocker. Pathetic tales, more than sufficient to supply a whole generation of novelists, prevailed over a dull, dry parade of stupid figures."[10] See, for instance, Dickens, who channels such views through his bewildered Sissy Jupe in *Hard Times* (1854). Sissy tries to process her teacher M'Choakumchild's lessons in statistics (which she can recall only as "stutterings"). As she tells Louisa Gradgrind:

"he said, Now, this schoolroom is a Nation. And in this nation, there are fifty millions of money. Isn't this a prosperous nation? Girl number twenty, isn't this a prosperous nation, and a'n't you in a thriving state?"

"What did you say?" asked Louisa.

"Miss Louisa, I said I didn't know. I thought I couldn't know whether it was a prosperous nation or not, and whether I was in a thriving state or not, unless I knew who had got the money, and whether any of it was mine. But that had nothing to do with it. It was not in the figures at all," said Sissy, wiping her eyes.

"That was a great mistake of yours," observed Louisa.[11]

"Figures of arithmetic" have replaced more embodied forms of knowledge, much to Sissy's (and the novelist's) dismay. Taking the temperature of his times in *Dipsychus and the Spirit* (composed in the 1850s), the poet Arthur Hugh Clough described the narrowing sphere of action produced by a world governed by such characters:

> The modern Hotspur
> Shrills not his trumpet of "To Horse, To Horse!"
> But consults columns in a railway guide;
> A demigod of figures; an Achilles
> Of computation;
> A verier Mercury, express come down
> To do the world with swift arithmetic.[12]

---

[10] Quoted in Poovey, "Figures of Arithmetic," 260.

[11] Charles Dickens, *Hard Times*, ed. Paul Schlicke (Oxford: Oxford University Press, 2008), 59.

[12] Arthur Hugh Clough, *Dispychus and the Spirit*, in *Clough's Selected Poems*, ed. J. P. Phelan (London: Longman, 1995), 3.2.107–13.

4 THE NUMBER SENSE

His "demigod of figures" marks a fallen age.

If these attitudes also sound familiar to you, it may be, Dear Reader, because you are among the many members of our profession who share these Victorian writers' suspicion of the numberiness of modernity. James English has even claimed that a "negative relation to numbers" is "foundational" to literary studies, which views itself institutionally as the quintessential noncounting discipline.[13] Poovey has suggested that this antagonism arose—concurrently but not, I think, coincidentally with the modern academic field of literary study—in the late eighteenth century, as numbers became divested of moral significance. She observes the perceived "wedge" Thomas Malthus had "driven between numbers and morality," making numerical figures "seem immune from theory or interpretation"—that is, from most of what we do.[14] Others may find earlier origins for the contest; as John Durham Peters points out, "When Plato banished poets from his Republic and made mathematical knowledge the prerequisite for entering his academy, he started, in a way, the long battle between story and number."[15] Still, my opening account indicates that there are in fact many reasons for a literary critic of the nineteenth century to look at numbers. And the period's numbery atmosphere, with its cultural, scientific, and social elements, has garnered close attention from scholars of literature in recent years, as these pages will frequently attest. In our own knowledge economy, in which information is increasingly both generated and acquired digitally, numbers have been thrust to the very forefront of research, as method (the so-called Digital Humanities [DH]) and as subject.[16]

But while the historical and cultural background certainly inform my readings here, and while I will occasionally make use of some of the basic

[13] James F. English, "The Resistance to Counting, Recounted" *Representations*, January 2015, n.pag. www.representations.org/reponse-to-ulysses-by-numbers-james-f-english/. Accessed Feb. 16, 2023.

[14] Poovey, *History*, 293. See also Lorraine Daston and Peter Gallison's influential work on the emergence of objectivity in the nineteenth century, *Objectivity* (New York: Zone, 2007).

[15] John Durham Peters "'The Only Proper Scale of Representation': The Politics of Statistics and Stories," *Political Communication* 18.4 (2001), 437. The post-founding American focus of this essay's argument overlaps with the timeframe of my enquiry.

[16] The interest in statistics and in probability theory has been particularly strong, as Genie Babb has noted in her account of the intersection of this field with the methods of Digital Humanities: "Victorian Roots and Branches: 'The Statistical Century' as Foundation to the Digital Humanities," *Literature Compass* 15 (2018): 1–14. https://doi.org/10.1111/lic3.12487. She provides a useful summary of the literature, citing several instances from a 2017 special issue of *Genre* exploring "Narrative against Data in the Victorian Novel," edited by Jesse Rosenthal. That issue's title indicates the perceived antagonism between the literary and the numerical. The field of mathematics and literature offers a further numbery approach with which my own work engages at times. For recent work in this area, see R. Tubbs et al. (eds.), *The Palgrave Handbook of Literature and Mathematics* (London: Palgrave Macmillan, 2023).

INTRODUCTION 5

tools of DH, my point of departure in what follows is rather to follow *the effect produced by represented numbers* (be they ordinal or cardinal, printed as Arabic or Roman numerals or spelled out as words) when we encounter them in novels and poetry. It is primarily through the deployment of such figures that texts display what I call their *number sense*; similarly, we hone our own faculty of number sense by paying attention to their presence. And in this context, we might begin by taking note of much more ancient associations between numbers and the field of letters. The earliest forms of writing were used for accounting; in most alphabets the first three numbers tend to be denoted in a way that can be linked back to their tally, as in Roman numerals.[17] Moreover, letters in ancient Hebrew and Greek also signified numbers, possessing the double meaning of a sound and a count. As Tobias Dantzig explains in his foundational history of numbers, "The sum of the numbers represented by the letters of the word was the *number of the word*, ... [T]wo words were equivalent if they added up to the same number."[18] (In Tolstoy's *War and Peace* [1869], Pierre plays with this tradition when, after writing "the French alphabet out with the same numerical values as the Hebrew," he is able to calculate that by translating "the words *L'Empereur Napoléon* in numbers, it appears that the sum of them is 666, and that Napoleon was therefore the beast foretold in the Apocalypse."[19]) Sanskrit poetry uses the links between numbers and related objects to permit the replacement of number words to meet the demands of the meter; thus the number one can be represented by a unique object, such as the moon, while the word for teeth can stand in for the number thirty-two.[20] Friedrich Kittler argues for the transformative nature of the shift when we move from Greek or Roman or Hebrew numerals—interchangeable with letters—to Arabic, which aren't.[21] Both the

---

[17] See Stanislaus Dehaene, *The Number Sense: How the Mind Creates Mathematics*, rev. ed. (Oxford: Oxford University Press, 2011), 97.

[18] Tobias Dantzig, *Number, the Language of Science*, ed. Joseph Mazur (1930; New York: Plume, 2007), 40. Emphasis in original.

[19] Leo Tolstoy, *War and Peace*, trans. Louise and Aylmer Maude, rev. and ed. Amy Mandelker (Oxford: Oxford University Press, 2010), 713–14. Pierre goes on to play with the numbers of his own name, and (by fiddling with the spelling and calling himself *L'russe Besuhof*) he achieves the same result.

[20] See Sarah Hart, *Once Upon a Prime: The Wondrous Connections between Mathematics and Literature* (New York: Flatiron, 2023), 5.

[21] Friedrich Kittler, "Number and Numeral," in *Theory, Culture & Society* 23.7–8 (2006): 51–61 (London, Thousand Oaks, and New Delhi: SAGE). (First publ. 2003 as "Zahl und Ziffer.") With the 0s and 1s of computing, numbers and letters have again become interchangeable. Bits and bites—i.e., numbers as the stuff of information flow—didn't arise until the mid-twentieth century (telegraphs, for example, converted letters into signals or used Morse). But, as Richard Menke observes, "the emerging Victorian understandings of information anticipate

6 THE NUMBER SENSE

difference and the connections between numbers and letters were important to the development of mathematics: Dantzig describes how the discovery in the sixteenth century by the Frenchman Franciscus Vieta that one could use letters to symbolize unknown magnitudes (i.e., numbers) was one of the great mathematical "achievements" of the era because it allowed for algebraic operations to be performed, encouraging the creation also of new numbers, such as fractions and negative numbers.[22] In this basic sense—as in other, more complex ways that I will describe in what follows—the potential overlap between numbers and letters opened up new kinds of imaginative worlds.[23]

Yet the role of numbers *in literature* also stretches back to the very origins of linguistic artistic expression. Just think of the Book of Numbers in the Bible, which offers a census of the Tribes of Israel at its start when, obeying God's instructions to Moses, the Israelites "numbered"—that is, counted—all their men "from twenty years old and upward, all that are able to go forth to war."[24] Or consider the catalogue of ships in the *Iliad*, which includes not only the names of the leaders of each group but also the count of vessels in a given contingent.[25] These numbers matter to the varied meanings generated by these disparate texts. The *Iliad*'s counts

this vision [of numbery computation] in important respects" (*Telegraphic Realism: Victorian Fiction and Other Information Systems* [Stanford: Stanford University Press, 2008], 22).

[22] See Dantzig, *Number*, 88.

[23] Anna Kornbluh has argued that the advent of mathematical formalism in the nineteenth century, which "valued the power of signs to exceed experiential reality and even to project rigorously consistent hypothetical realities," offered writers of the period "utopian prospects." In her fourth chapter, she considers the potential of algebraic letters when reading the overlapping mathematical and political formalisms of Lewis Carroll's *Alice in Wonderland* (1865) (a text to which I will turn in Chapter 3). See *The Order of Forms: Realism, Formalism, and Social Space* (Chicago: University of Chicago Press, 2019), 7, 8, 115.

[24] Numbers 1:3 *KJV*.

[25] Homer, *Iliad*, trans. Robert Fagles (New York: Penguin, 1990), 2.494–759. Like the 1801 institution of the British national census, these two examples point to the long connection between numbers and soldiers. It thus makes sense that many texts dealing with war are numbery. Take *War and Peace*: Tolstoy's novel is preoccupied with the operations of numbers and chance—or probability—in the context of war. It opens with Marie's math lesson, and it not only includes repeated references to troop contingents but also cites the work of the remarkably numbery British historian Henry Thomas Buckle, whose unfinished *History of Civilization in England* (1857) attempted to integrate statistics with history in order to achieve a more "scientific" approach to the discipline—one that could comprehend society as a whole rather than focus on specific individuals and events (see *War and Peace*, 1271, 1278). As the mathematician Sarah Hart points out, Tolstoy's novel also includes an actual equation within the text (*War and Peace*, 1113; Hart, *Once Upon a Prime*, 136–8). I'll return to it in Chapter 1 when I discuss the relationship between war literature and numbers. The association between soldiers and counting is the subject of my chapter, "Making Soldiers Count: Literature and War in the 1850s," in *Nineteenth-Century Literature in Transition: the 1850s*, ed. Gail Marshall (Cambridge: Cambridge University Press, 2024), 179–200.

INTRODUCTION   7

(like those of the Book of Numbers) are often of combatant forces (or of the prizes they win), but most of the *Odyssey's* many, many numbers are calendrical in orientation (like the 350 Oxen of Helios, which represent the days in a year)—a fact reflecting that epic's obsession with counting the passage of time. The word *account* itself suggests a fundamental connection between narrative and numbers; one might think of Ian Watt's observation, writing of *Robinson Crusoe* (1719), of how Daniel Defoe's "innate reverence for book-keeping" contributed to the "rise of the novel," the paradigmatic nineteenth-century narrative form.[26] And we can trace the connection back even earlier: Franco Moretti refers to how in Medieval royal courts, "complaints" were made in French in what was termed a "*counte* (*narratio* in Latin), meaning a tale or a story. ... Before the middle of the thirteenth century a new profession of countors or narrators had emerged, whose business was to compose countes."[27] Not only the difference but also the similarity between storytelling and counting can be seen in the composition of annals and chronicles, early forms of historical narrative. For Stanislaus Dehaene, the very lines of print comprising a text link spatially to our number sense. He considers the number line to be a fundamental construct for grasping numerical quantity—for Westerners, one that works, like our reading, from left to right (thus we instinctively associate small figures with our left; large ones with our right).[28] Connections between the realms of numbers and words have been wired into our brains.[29]

So numbers can work together to tell a story. But even when numbers help narrate plot (a subject of my fourth chapter), they don't suffice. George Carlin tells a joke about an imaginary sportscaster who makes this error: "Folks, Nick here. Running out of time, so I'll have to rush with the scores— 4 to 2, 6 to 3, in a big blow-out, 15 to 3, 8 to 5, 7 to 4, 9 to 5, 6 to 2, and finally, in a real cliff-hanger, 2 to 1. And this just in, a partial score: 6."[30]

---

[26] Ian Watt, *The Rise of the Novel: Studies in Defoe, Richardson, and Fielding* (London: Penguin, 1983), 70.

[27] Quoting the legal historian J. H. Baker, in Moretti, *The Way of the World: The Bildungsroman in European Culture*, new ed. (London: Verso, 2000), 211.

[28] See Dehaene, *The Number Sense*, 69–71.

[29] Amanda Paxton has considered the effect of number–space synaesthesia (NNS)—a phenomenon first identified by Francis Galton in 1880 that involves the very personalized spatial visualization of numbers—on the poetry of Gerard Manley Hopkins. She argues that Hopkins's experience with this phenomenon aestheticizes his use of numbers, removing them from spheres of utility like measurement and counting. See Paxton, "The Hard Math of Beauty: On Hopkins and 'Spectral Numbers,'" *Victorian Studies* 63.2 (2021): 246–70.

[30] Quoted by John Allen Paulos, *Once Upon a Number: The Hidden Mathematical Logic of Stories* (New York: Basic Books, 1998), 142.

8   THE NUMBER SENSE

Of course, these aren't totally meaningless numbers. On the basis of their ranges, we can posit the most likely sports: hockey or baseball. Structurally, though, the joke's focus on the inadequacies of numerical representation makes it resemble one told toward the close of *Hard Times*, albeit this time with character rather than plot being signified through number. As they sit through a performance at Sleary's circus, biding their time until the proper moment for Louisa's brother Tom's escape, Sissy and Louisa experience the same mounting narrative tension as does the reader, especially when the performance

> stopped to afford the Clown an opportunity of telling Mr. Sleary (who said 'Indeed, sir!' to all his observations in the calmest way, and with his eye on the house) about two legs sitting on three legs looking at one leg, when in came four legs, and laid hold of one leg, and up got two legs, caught hold of three legs, and threw 'em at four legs, who ran away with one leg. For, although an ingenious Allegory relating to a butcher, a three-legged stool, a dog, and a leg of mutton, this narrative consumed time; and they were in great suspense.[31]

In the earlier schoolroom scene, M'Choakumchild had discoursed on the definition of a horse as, among its other numbery attributes, a "quadruped"; here the lesson is upturned by its circus environment.[32] But, surely, in addition to indicating that numbers can take us only so far, both these jokes also reveal the dependence of all forms of narrative—whether realist or fanciful, plot- or character-driven—on numbers.

I will often, in what follows, trace a series of varied numbers across a work, to see what kind of tale emerges from its patterning. But individual figures can hold real significance, too. They can resonate structurally and associatively, in ways that gesture outwards to other narratives and concepts. As Dehaene points out:

> Numbers have multiple meanings. Some "random" numbers such as 3,871 refer only to a single concept, the pure quantity they convey. Many others, however, especially when they are small, evoke a host of other ideas: dates (1492), hours (9:45 p.m.), time constants (365), commercial brands

---

[31] Dickens, *Hard Times*, 258. This "allegory" is itself a modern take on the famous riddle of the Sphinx: "What goes on four feet in the morning, two feet in midday, and three feet in the evening?"—to which Oedipus must answer, "man."

[32] Dickens, *Hard Times*, 9.

INTRODUCTION   9

(747), zip codes (90,210, 10,025), phone numbers (911), physical magnitudes (110/120), mathematical constants (3.14...; 2.718...), movies (2001), games (21), and even drinking laws (21 again!).[33]

Still—and this, after all, is their *raison d'etre*—not all numbers are created equal. So let me start simply here, by way of introducing both my methods and their potential payoff, with what is certainly one of the most symbolically charged of numbers, at least in Western literature: three.[34] In the spirit of my enterprise, I offer a trio of brief readings. In each instance, we will see how leaning into the numbers yields insights into how these very different works of literature make their meanings. We will also see how this specific number toggles between older and newer forms of signification—between mystical and factual realms—and, in the process, heralds the tensions between past and present. It thus highlights the peculiar ways in which, despite their ancient literary associations, numbers register distinctively in the nineteenth-century context.

0.2 Three Threes

First. To begin with what seems a fairly generic case: Tennyson's use of threes in *Idylls of the King* (1859–85). The figure punctuates this text. There are seventy-three *three*s in the work (and thirteen *third*s)—in contrast to only fifty-six *two*s (a dozen *second*s), twenty *four*s (six *fourth*s), and five *five*s (paired with a single *fifth*).[35] In Tennyson's work, *three* serves as a generic marker—to use the term this time in its more technical literary sense—pointing back to the threes of epic (recall the triple efforts of many a Homeric hero to grasp some aspect of his past or future), myth (three fates), and fairy tale or romance (three suitors, three sisters, three caskets, and one could go on).[36]

---

[33] Dehaene, *The Number Sense*, 178. Dehaene notes, though, that "the inferior parietal cortex seems to encode only the quantitative meaning of numbers ... Distinct brain areas must be involved in coding the other meanings" (178).

[34] Hart's delightful *Once Upon a Prime* recognizes this special status in both opening and closing her chapter "Fairy-Tale Figures: The Symbolism of Number in Fiction" with three (103–20).

[35] *One* is, of course, a number that stands alone in its frequency and importance, as I will have reason to remark elsewhere in the following pages.

[36] See also Vladimir Propp's observation of the motif: "Trebling is at the origin of the most ancient of all genres, namely, the folktale." Vladimir Yakovlevich Propp, *The Russian Folktale by*

10   THE NUMBER SENSE

In "Gareth and Lynette," for example, most things come in threes, even when other numbers initially seem important. Thus, Lynette is presented as living

> in Castle Perilous: a river
> Runs in three loops about her living-place;
> And o'er it are three passings, and three knights
> Defend the passings, brethren, and a fourth
> And of that four the mightiest, holds her stayed
> In her own castle ...[37]

That fourth "mightiest" brother with whom Gareth expects a fearful encounter proves harmless, though, a mere "blooming boy" who cries, "Slay me not: my three brethren bad me do it" (ll. 1373, 1375). Three is indeed the poem's magic number. After Gareth makes it past the first three challenges, Lynette sings to him in one of the poem's many intercalated lyrics, suggesting how the figure is coded into the very verse-form:

> "O trefoil, sparkling on the rainy plain,
> O rainbow with three colours after rain,
> Shine sweetly: thrice my love hath smiled on me."
>
> (ll. 1130–2)

Such "riddling triplets of old time," as they are elsewhere designated ("The Coming of Arthur," l. 401), underscore the *Idylls'* departure from a strict epic trajectory for something more lyrically regressive. And transgressive, since these threes also recall what is among the most basic of literary threesomes, the adultery plot, the corrupt heart of Tennyson's poem.

In this sense, the work's threes can seem modern as well as of "old time," can point to the European novel as well as to medieval *chanson*: they take the stamp of both times. Similarly, in "Geraint and Enid," when Geraint defeats a trio of marauding knights who had lain in ambush hoping to rob the travelling couple, he

> Stript from the three dead wolves of woman born
> The three gay suits of armour which they wore,

Vladimir Yakovlevich Propp, ed. and trans. Sibelan Forrester (Detroit: Wayne State University Press, 2012), 175. I will return to Propp's account in my Conclusion.

[37] Alfred (Lord) Tennyson, "Gareth and Lynette," *Idylls of the King*, in *The Poems of Tennyson*, ed. Christopher Ricks, 2nd ed., 3 vols. (Harlow: Longmans, 1987), ll. 596–601. Hereafter, all references to Tennyson's poems will be to this edition and will be internally documented.

INTRODUCTION 11

And let the bodies lie, but bound the suits
Of armour on their horses, each on each,
And tied the bridle-reins of all the three
Together ...

(ll. 94–9)

Rather than operate as trophies or talismanic objects, however, these suits (and the three more he acquires later) function more like money—something to be traded to support the pair through their trials.[38] The threes of epic or myth become currency.

Still, threes rule the action of the *Idylls*, something affirmed by the release of Excalibur in "The Passing of Arthur," which happens only after two false starts by Sir Bedivere, and only then with a further triple flourish:

So flashed and fell the brand Excalibur:
But ere he dipt the surface, rose an arm
Clothed in white samite, mystic, wonderful,
And caught him by the hilt, and brandished him
Three times, and drew him under in the mere.

(ll. 310–14)

There is, after all, a magic to the figure. Hence the old proverb, *third time's a charm*.[39] In the "Conclusion" to his dramatic lyric "New Year's Eve," Tennyson's May Queen anticipates her own death by listening out for "the music on the wind." As she tells her mother, who sits beside her sickbed: "But you were sleeping; and I said, 'It's not for them: it's mine.' / And if it come three times, I thought, I take it for a sign."[40] She sums up her position: "So now I think my time is near." The May Queen keeps count, and so do we, together finding meaning in the number.

Second. While Tennyson's invests his threes with traditional literary significance, he seems to avoid reference to the number's common association

---

[38] See also Herbert Tucker, "Trials of Fiction: Novel and Epic in the Geraint and Enid Episodes from *Idylls of the King*," *Victorian Poetry* 30.3–4 (1992): 441–61.

[39] Suggestively, while the *OED* does not include reference to this proverb, it does have a listing for the more secularized (or perhaps gambling-oriented) "third time('s) lucky" (A.1.e), which it first ascribes to a c. 1840 letter by Elizabeth Barrett Browning to R. H. Horne that might be read as a reflection on Tennyson's usage of threes: "The luck of the 'third adventure' is proverbial." The next example, while also from the nineteenth century, likewise indicates a longer provenance; it comes from Alexander Hislop's *The Proverbs of Scotland* (1862).

[40] In *Tennyson*, ed. Ricks, 422; 1842. Bevis also mentions this line in "Poetry by Numbers," 50.

12   THE NUMBER SENSE

in Christian culture with the Trinity of God, Son, and Holy Spirit. This three-some underscores the verse of perhaps the most numerological of European poets: Dante Alighieri, whose *Divine Comedy* (c. 1321)—composed of three canticles comprised of thirty-three cantos each, made up in turn by inter-locking tercets—rings changes on the number to remind us constantly of its foundational role in Catholic teaching.[41] It also provides the backdrop against which the poet's namesake Dante Gabriel Rossetti situates his own memorable threes in "The Woodspurge" (written 1856, published 1870). If Tennyson's threes seem part of the background pattern of his poem, Rossetti's demand—and have received—much consideration. Yet they also reward a fresh look.

In this poem the speaker, having attempted to escape an unnamed sorrow on a windswept walk through a natural landscape, finds himself seated with his head between his knees. The second half of the lyric records his view:

> My eyes, wide open, had the run
> Of some ten weeds to fix upon;
> Among those few, out of the sun,
> The woodspurge flower'd, three cups in one.
>
> From perfect grief there need not be
> Wisdom or even memory:
> One thing then learnt remains to me,—
> The woodspurge has a cup of three.[42]

These verses have long been read as reflecting the secularization of the Victorian age. Thus "three cups in one," which appears to imply the three-in-one of Trinitarian thought, transforms into a statement of bare fact: "The woodspurge has a cup of three." The act of numbering helps to numb the speaker's pain, one might say, offering a very modern kind of therapy that steps into the space previously occupied by more religious forms of conso-lation (critics disagree on the efficacy of this consolation).[43] The very limits

---

[41] *Inferno* includes a thirty-fourth canto, but the first in this canticle is generally considered to be a kind of preface. That additional canto also yields the perfection of the Comedy's full hundred.

[42] In D. G. Rossetti, *The Works of Dante Gabriel Rossetti*, ed. W. M. Rossetti (London: Ellis, 1911), 205.

[43] See, for example, Jerome McGann, who argues that the plant, with its numbered cup, becomes "a token of the magical potential in any objective datum." "Rossetti's Significant Details," *Victorian Poetry* 7.1 (1969), 46. For a counter-reading that continues to view the poem as invested in Trinitarianism, see John Holmes, *Dante Gabriel Rossetti and the Late Victorian Sonnet Sequence: Sexuality, Belief, and the Self* (Aldershot: Ashgate, 2005), 22. For a reading

INTRODUCTION   13

set by the parameters of the view caught between his legs allow for a loose count of "some ten weeds"—a kind of estimation—before settling into the reassuring precision of that *three*. I can't help but think of George Eliot's recognition in *Middlemarch* (1871–2) that we must set limits somewhere: Combine her awareness of the disabling roar that comes from "hearing the grass grow" with her focus on "this particular web" and her invocation of the microscope's enabling lens, and you get something akin to the speaker's attitude.[44] Like that of novel-writing, the process of counting generally requires a bounded set (as I will have reason to remark elsewhere, as well).

Behind the verse, though, lies a more fundamental kind of measure: that of meter. In this framework, the link between numbering and numbing—especially in the context of a plant that has medicinal uses—brings to mind Tennyson's reflections in *In Memoriam* (1850):

> But, for the unquiet heart and brain,
> A use in measured language lies;
> The sad mechanic exercise,
> Like dull narcotics, numbing pain.[45]

Tennyson's passage draws attention, however, to the surprising fact that the measures of "The Woodspurge" operate on a steady principle of fours, not threes: four iambic tetrameter quatrains constitute the poem. Rossetti's choice of verse form seems especially marked when we reflect that the most common tetrameter measure, the ballad stanza, would have incorporated threes into its rhythms. Thus, for example, Wordsworth's "We Are Seven" (which I will discuss in Chapter 1) offers an instance where a ballad's interlocking iambic tetrameter and trimeter lines overlap with the tally of seven within the poem. In "The Woodspurge," we find rather something out of step between the speaker's count and the poet's.

The discrepancy becomes more startling if—as I did, after decades of familiarity with this poem—you actually take the time to *look* carefully

refusing the recuperative turn and stressing rather the lyric's "disenchanted world" by linking it to "the dehumanized and dislocated status of poetic voice that sound recordings would soon accentuate and echo," see Veronica Alfano, "Technologies of Forgetting: Phonographs, Lyric Voice, and Rossetti's Woodspurge," *Victorian Poetry* 55.2 (Summer 2017), 141.

[44] George Eliot, *Middlemarch*, ed. David Carroll (Oxford: Oxford University Press, 1998), 182, 132.

[45] Tennyson, *In Memoriam A. H. H.* V.5–8. Bevis, who does not comment on this passage, does remark how the poetic practice of rhythm can in effect represent "numbing pain by numbering it" in the context of his reading of Tennyson's "Charge of the Light Brigade," which also centers on a much-remembered number: six hundred ("Poetry by Numbers," 53).

14   THE NUMBER SENSE

at a woodspurge. Because, it turns out, the woodspurge *does not have a cup of three*. Rather, it has multiple cups of two double-lobed bracts. The plant structure does incorporate threes in its central three-lobed stigma (the female pollen-accepting organ), but these have nothing concave about them, each part being Y-shaped. Hunting further afield for threes (or rather, escaping the field entirely), one might note, as Catherine Maxwell has done, that the botanical book Rossetti may have used while composing the verses, John Gerard's *Herball* (1597), records that the woodspurge's seed is "contained in three-cornered seed-vessels."[46] Yet these "vessels" are enclosed rather than cupped, again flouting the poem's description. I'm almost tempted to see in Rossetti's three-cupped spurge something like a four-leafed clover; if it existed, it would have done so only as a sport of nature (*this* woodspurge, not *the* woodspurge).

How much do the numbers matter here? What can they reveal? These are questions I will have frequent reason to ask as I proceed through my argument in this book. Maxwell does not mention the error in Rossetti's description of the plant.[47] But she does cite Gerard's language to argue that the poem's genesis is in book-learning, gleaned both from the *Herball* and Dante Alighieri's *Purgatorio*, rather than direct observation of nature; the two sources combine to suggest to her the woodspurge's powers to "purge" the speaker's "vision," so offering balm (since the *Herball* records the weed's purgative uses). At the very least, the numerical discrepancy between the actual plant and Rossetti's description lends support to such a claim by indicating limits to the poem's empiricist record of direct experience of nature. Yet the more botanically correct threes of seed and stigma also link the work to another modern phenomenon: that of classification. Carl Linnaeus's system (described in *Systema Naturae*, from 1735) is based on the number of parts in the reproductive structures of flowers; here they could play a role. The impulse to categorize—as anyone who has worked on genre recognizes—often requires enabling fictions. Rossetti's count exposes this impulse more than it does any empirical fact; in doing so, it also helps to highlight those fictions. So it seems that the "cup of three" won't easily consolidate its meaning into "*One* thing then learnt," the bare "remain[der]"

---

[46] Catherine Maxwell, "'Devious Symbols': Dante Gabriel Rossetti's Purgatorio," *Victorian Poetry* 31.1 (1993), 20.

[47] The only critic I have been able to locate who makes note of this fact is Mark William Brown, in "Language, Symbol, and 'Non-Symbolic Fact' in D. G. Rossetti's 'The Woodspurge,'" *Symbolism: An International Annual of Critical Aesthetics* 19 (2019): 243–63. Brown goes into the botanical details at great length, ultimately seeing the error as a sign of the poet's inadequacy (he's not a fan of the poem) and concluding that "the image evoked by Rossetti's formulation not only has distorted the perceptions of critics, but also is indicative of the speaker's own distorted perception of the world" (246).

INTRODUCTION 15

of the process of subtraction that the poem records. Rather, the numbers retain mysterious powers of signification.

We have noted how the woodspurge is but one of "some ten" weeds upon which the poem's speaker might have focused. In a way, I have been asking just how random—or how culturally predetermined—its selection was. With a sample size so small, perhaps this flower was as close as the speaker could come to the complexly salvific and symbolically charged *three* he desired. In this regard, we might also be tempted to see it as intersecting with the rise of statistical culture associated with such sampling (and its abuse). That culture is the source of the final three I myself want to sample here, perhaps the strangest of them all.

Third. It is three months after Jane Eyre's arrival at Thornfield, and some few days more following her abrupt initial encounter with the man who would only later reveal himself as her employer. Mr. Rochester subjects his new governess to an evening of interrogation. (A first such scene had shown him drawing out from her something like a vita, including his calculation of Jane's age as "eighteen" by adding her stay of "eight years" at Lowood to the "ten" she had lived before her arrival there: "Arithmetic, you see, is useful; without its aid, I should hardly have been able to guess your age," Mr. Rochester admits.[48]) Surprised by her "candour" in response to his own rude inquiries during this prolonged interview, he remarks: "Not three in three thousand raw school-girl-governesses would have answered me as you have just done" (*JE* 118).

I must have read over this statement half a dozen times at least before, having lately embarked on this book project, I found myself suddenly caught up short by it. But once noticed, it is hard to unsee. Why three? Is he thinking of some kind of shortlist of applicants for her position? Surely not! So why hasn't he simplified his figures? Why on earth not the more expected "one in a thousand"?

This last expression and its multiples of ten have a long history meriting its own consideration. The always-number-conscious Jane Austen could thus have Mary Crawford of *Mansfield Park* (1814) remark to her sister, "With all due respect to such of the present company as chance to be married, my dear Mrs. Grant, there is not one in a hundred of either sex who is not taken in when they marry."[49] Such taking measure was on the rise

---

[48] Charlotte Brontë, *Jane Eyre*, ed. Richard J. Dunn, 2nd ed. (New York: Norton, 1987), 108–9. Hereafter, internally referenced as *JE*, followed by a page number.

[49] Jane Austen, *Mansfield Park*, ed. James Kinsley (Oxford: Oxford University Press, 2003), 36.

16 THE NUMBER SENSE

when Charlotte Brontë published *Jane Eyre* in 1847, reflecting the increasing influence of statistical modes of thought. Mary's "one in a hundred," like Rossetti's "some ten," offers a rough estimate in place of the more precise figures of a text like Henry Mayhew's number-saturated *London Labour and the London Poor* (appearing in the *Morning Chronicle* in the 1840s, published 1851 in volume form). Consider this typical passage of Mayhew's work:

> One in every twenty-eight labourers, according to [the Criminal Returns of the metropolis], has a predisposition for simple larceny: the average for the whole population of London is one in every 266 individuals; so that the labourers may be said to be more than 9 times as dishonest as the generality of people resident in the metropolis.[50]

As Audrey Jaffe has argued, and as I will have reason to recall in Chapter 3, such moments show how statistics helped to shape conceptions of character by situating individuals in relation to collectives such as classes (Rochester's "raw school-girl-governesses") and the averages that they produced. (That being said, in *Uneven Developments* Mary Poovey points to the strange discrepancy between "the relatively small number of women affected by the governess's woes" according to the census lists and the "disproportionate" attention given to them in the literature of the 1840s and 1850s.[51] Might the tripling of Brontë's figures mirror such exaggeration?)

By the time Wilkie Collins writes *The Woman in White* (1859–60), when the family solicitor Mr. Gilmore declares Marian Halcome to be a "sensitive, vehement, passionate nature—a woman of ten thousand in these trivial, superficial times"[52]—he could almost be said to annex the expression to those times. Jaffe reads *Middlemarch* to demonstrate that novels of the

---

[50] Audrey Jaffe quotes this passage from "Skilled and Unskilled Labour," "The Coal Heavers." See Audrey Jaffe, *The Affective Life of the Average Man: The Victorian Novel and the Stock-Market Graph* (Columbus: Ohio State University Press, 2010), 28. Its focus on crime reflects the role of policing in the rise of statistics as a discipline, as evidenced in the work of Alphonse Bertillon, Adolphe Quetelet, and Francis Galton.

[51] Mary Poovey, *Uneven Developments: The Ideological Work of Gender in Mid-Victorian England* (Chicago: University of Chicago Press, 1995), 157.

[52] Wilkie Collins, *The Woman in White*, ed. John Sutherland (Oxford: Oxford University Press, 2008), 137. The statistical turn does appear to be particularly characteristic of the solicitor's legal reasoning, as well. A few pages later, he says of Marian's evasive response to a query, "When a sensible woman has a serious question put to her, and evades it by a flippant answer, it is a sure sign, in ninety-nine cases out of a hundred, that she has something to conceal" (141). Christopher Kent has shown how Collins's characters often view the world through a probabilistic lens, a topic to which I will return in my Conclusion. See Christopher Kent, "Probability, Reality and Sensation in the Novels of Wilkie Collins," *Dickens Studies Annual* 20 (1991): 259–80.

INTRODUCTION   17

period offer evidence of the ways in which "identity is already emptied out and filled with the collective: shaped by a formulation that, in the manner of the statistically-formed average man who becomes a part of common consciousness in the nineteenth century, situates the many within the one and makes of that one an element ... in a larger pool."[53] And David A. P. Womble has described how Anthony Trollope exploits this phenomenon of modern characterization to describe in the titular hero of *Phineas Finn* (1867–8) a kind of "statistical subjectivity," one that appears "far less interiorized and far more like an embodiment of collectivized thinking" than that we generally associate with the Victorian novel. In Trollope's political novel, which is set against the backdrop of the passage of the Reform Bill, such selfhood is produced via a kind of polling of Phineas's various constituencies.[54] To this end, both Trollope's narrator and his protagonist make repeated use of the "not one in X" formula, thereby gauging how unusual our representative hero actually is.[55]

Nevertheless, for Womble, Jane Eyre is different: "Jane transcends one unflattering social category after another by remaining true to something intrinsic about herself." *Jane Eyre* might even mark a watershed, "emerging from one of the last moments when any successful novel could ask its readers to believe in a heroine capable of existing independently of the social categories she transcends."[56] Such seems also to be the significance of a third scene of interrogation, in which Jane's relationship to other "thousands" is again adduced when Rochester, in the guise of a "gipsy" Sibyl, pretends to tell Jane her fortune. When the Sibyl declares her to be "cold," "sick," and "silly" (for insisting on her own emotional isolation), Jane remonstrates by pointing out the predictability of this diagnosis:

> "You might say all that to almost any one who you knew lived as a solitary dependent in a great house."
>
> "I might say it to almost any one: but would it be true of almost any one?"

---

[53] Jaffe, *The Affective Life of the Average Man*, 26. Michael Klotz has also considered this phenomenon in relation to Dickens's mode of characterization, as I will discuss at more length in Chapter 3.

[54] David A. P. Womble, "*Phineas Finn*, the Statistics of Character, and the Sensorium of Liberal Personhood," *Novel* 51.1 (2018), 20, 17.

[55] Examples of the formula (not something upon which Womble remarks, although he does include one such moment among his pieces of evidence) appear three times in this novel. See Anthony Trollope, *Phineas Finn*, ed. Simon Dentith (Oxford: Oxford University Press, 2011), 21, 58, 163.

[56] Womble, "*Phineas Finn*, the Statistics of Character," 19, 22–3.

18   THE NUMBER SENSE

"In my circumstances."

"Yes; just so, in your circumstances: but find me another precisely placed as you are."

"It would be easy to find you thousands."

"You could scarcely find me one."

(*JE* 173)

Notice how this scenario intertwines the mystical language of the seer—divinely inspired vision—with the language of secularized probability; after all, both modes can use numbers to forecast the future.

At stake in the contest is Jane's singularity. It is this characteristic that Mr. Rochester wishes to emphasize: "You could scarcely find me one." "By my word! there is something singular about you," he had said to her in the earlier interview (*JE* 114). Indeed then, as here, even "one" seems too high a figure; his *scarcely* echoes in the *not*s that so frequently introduce these statistical disclaimers. That's because, in a way, *one* isn't really singular at all. While we might want to attribute to *singularity* the designation of "a numerical *one*," we would do so "only under a concept of number that is non-additive and in that respect (maybe others too) analogous to the proper name."[57] The multiplication by three in Mr. Rochester's "not three in three thousand" thus ups the ante, openly acknowledging the degree to which, while Jane might be unusual, she is not actually singular. It takes what might have been a metaphor for the incommensurable, something akin to a proverbial unicorn, and subjects it to mathematical processes that expose such an order of being as a figment of the imagination, a matter of superstition.

Still, part of what makes the unicorn so magical is that its singular horn is also single: there is only one of them. Similarly, the choice of three as the multiplier for Jane's unusual nature simultaneously recognizes that she is not really alone in her circumstances or characteristics *and* brings with it a

---

[57] Marjorie Levinson, "Notes and Queries on Name and Number," *Romantic Circles*, "Romantic Numbers" (April 2013): n. pag. § 13. https://romantic-circles.org/praxis/numbers/HTML/praxis.2013.levinson. Accessed May 21, 2020. This essay has been republished in Levinson's *Thinking Through Poetry: Field Reports on Romantic Lyric* (Oxford: Oxford University Press, 2018). I will have frequent reason to consider the distinction between name and number in what follows, especially in Chapters 1 and 3. For recent reflections on a different idea of singularity, one countering liberal individualism by stressing rather the feminine subject's essential embeddedness, see also Chatterjee, *Feminine Singularity*. For Chatterjee, feminine singularity isn't solitary. As she puts it, "I offer the term 'singularity' to describe a model of subjectivity—particularly feminine subjectivity—grounded in what is partial, contingent, and in relation rather than what is merely 'alone'" (1), something both "irreducibly unique *and* in relation" (13; original emphasis).

INTRODUCTION   19

touch of the Sybil's aura of magic: "not four in four thousand" would have sounded differently. This double effect appears also when we compare it to other threes in the novel. On the mystic front, it might recall the three uncanny pictures Mr. Rochester had just singled (trebled?) out from Jane's portfolio as indicating special promise of originality and genius. Or, when Jane hears the spectral cry that takes her back to Thornfield, it naturally (that is, supernaturally) comes in the repeated form of a triple repetition of her name: "then vibrated thrice a cry on my startled ear" (the moment echoes the pattern I described in Tennyson's verse) (*JE* 369, 371). More threateningly, though, *many* of the novel's women come in groups of three. Take the Ingram ladies, "all three of the loftiest stature of women" (*JE* 150). Before his offer of marriage, St. John promises to consider Jane as a "third sister" (*JE* 350). And Mr. Rochester admits to three prior mistresses.[58] Most troublingly, the architecture of Thornfield Hall, with its id-like "fateful third storey," contains the woman who by rights should have been Mr. Rochester's one and only (*JE* 183). If we discount (as I think we must) both the abandoned Blanche Ingram and the multiplied Céline Varens from the list of his wives, Jane comes second. Rochester's "not three" might thus make us wonder of Jane's fate. Will there be a third story here, too?

0.3 By the Numbers

Using number sense to search a familiar text for meaningful figures can reframe one's perspective on it. Recently, I returned for an umpteenth reading to E. M. Forster's *A Room with a View* (1908) and noticed for the first time that of all the chapters, only two are designated solely by number (rather than by a descriptive title): Chapters 4 and 12 are named "Fourth Chapter" and "Twelfth Chapter." These contain, respectively, the murder in the Plaza and the scene of skinny-dipping ("come and have a bathe"). Are they numbered because unmentionable? In order to preserve their surprises? If the latter, why title the chapter containing the pivotal scene of the kiss by a full description that is simultaneously a circumlocution ("The Reverend Arthur Beebe, the Reverend Cuthbert Eager, Mr. Emerson, Mr. George Emerson, Miss Eleanor Lavish, Miss Charlotte Bartlett, and Miss Lucy Honeychurch

---

[58] "The first I chose was Céline Varens—another of those steps which make a man spurn himself when he recalls them. You already know what she was, and how my liaison with her terminated. She had two successors: an Italian, Giacinta, and a German, Clara" (*JE* 274).

20   THE NUMBER SENSE

Drive Out in Carriages to See a View; Italians Drive Them")?[59] Nothing (mere tautological numbers) and everything (an apparent litany of cast, character, and plot) represent equally baffling signposts; the more obviously pointed cues of the other chapter titles hover significantly in-between. I find myself stimulated again and again to observe and ask questions of such textual numbers, and I have felt, in places, the lure of the code breaker, of the numerologist, of the conspiracy theorist, of the Kabbalist.

Yet I can't help but keep thinking, also, of *The Hitchhiker's Guide to the Galaxy*. There, when Deep Thought (a computer) finally arrives at the answer to the "Ultimate Question of Life, the Universe, and Everything"— 42—a new supercomputer (Earth) must be designed to figure out the question.[60] The answers are everywhere; deciphering the questions to ask of them can be a harder proposition. As is deciding which numbers, in which works, will generate interesting questions. I have tried to sketch out here how *three* is a particularly loaded number. But if not all numbers are equal, neither are all texts—nor all writers—on par in their deployment of figures. When do the numbers really count, and when do they provoke us to keep count? Why are some texts especially numbery? What kinds of labor, intellectual and ethical, do they oblige or invite readers to perform? As we shall see in what follows, some figures fit into predictable but important categories: those pertaining to time, space, and money, say. Then we have counts of people: the proverbial one and many. And there are the distinctions between ordinal (first, second, third) and cardinal (one, two, three) numbers to consider. One might even wonder why authors choose to spell out integers rather than use a numeral, as Dickens does with the years in *A Tale of Two Cities*. (Rereading *Ulysses* [1922] recently, I noticed that Molly switches between *1* and *one* in her thoughts, even when counting. Why? "Do we use the same neuronal circuits to identify the Arabic digit 5 and the word *five*? Probably not," Dehaene has remarked.[61]) Paying attention to the number sense of these works reveals how such figures can serve both as valves, releasing cultural pressures, and as fulcrums, places where pressures coincide in ways that can create new forms of literary agency.

To phrase my central claim so broadly is simultaneously to acknowledge that much of this book's argument is to be found in its method. Numbers

---

[59] E. M. Forster, *A Room with a View*, intro. Wendy Moffat (London: Penguin, 2000).

[60] Originally a 1978 radio sci-fi comedy written by Douglas Adams and appearing on BBC Radio 4, the work has since appeared in many formats (including, since 1979, as a novel [London: Pan]).

[61] Dehaene, *The Number Sense*, 179.

matter, yes—but different numbers matter differently, and authors use them in diverse ways. The figures' distinctive meanings would be lost were I to try to add them into a tidy sum; even the discovery of a single pattern would need so much statistical "smoothing" as to result in serious distortion. But while I may be wary of trying to tie them into a bow, certain threads of enquiry will emerge over the course of my readings—threads that I hope will yield a mesh or fabric of argument (indeed, numerically implicated imagery of knitting and weaving will materialize as one such "thread"). Since I am mentioning method, I might start here by observing a metacritical strand: our discipline's use of numbers constitutes a recurring concern in what follows. My own way of generating a feel for numbers may usually be implemented by means of rather old-fashioned close reading, but even the fairly primitive word-searches and word-counts that I do throughout the book belong to the digital turn in the Humanities. That is to say, the close reading that notices a writer as peculiarly "numbery" frequently turns for support to more distant reading methods, ones that almost always involve forms of enumeration.

As the close is to the distant, so are small numbers to large ones. The difference in kind, rather than merely in degree, between small and large numbers will often arise in this study, both as a mathematical question (in statistics, the "law of large numbers"—the phrase is coined in 1835— allows probability to be applied to social questions, explaining also how there can be stability in social trends[62]) and a political one (I'll consider how texts use numbers to illuminate the struggles between individuals and the masses). Large numbers can be hard to discriminate among, but when it comes to small ones, certain figures will transpire to be especially worthy of attention. I've already hinted at *three*'s significance, but the *doubling* or *matching* (both these processes are important) implied by *two* and the sin- gularity of *one* are even more laden with meaning, not only literary but also ethical.[63] And I will keep following the number line down, contemplating also the fraction that is *half* (what might it mean to take this term seriously as a number?) and touching occasionally on the cipher that is *zero*. Indeed, such a practice not only of *counting* but of *counting down* will prove to be a regular feature of literary texts, a way in which they encourage readers to exercise their number sense.

---

[62] See Hacking, *The Taming of Chance*, Chapter 12 (95–104).

[63] Chatterjee, for example, distinguishes "an ideological oneness that is both patriarchal and racially violent" and develops her ideas of *singularity* in opposition to this force (*Feminine Singularity*, 11).

22 THE NUMBER SENSE

Sarah Hart points out that three is smallest number of iterations allowing us to see both a pattern (repetition) and its breaking; it is suggestive of the beginning, middle, and end required by any story.[64] It establishes a bare minimum for narrative. At the other extreme, numbers can help us consider questions of seriality, the method—so vital to publishing practices and reading experiences in the nineteenth century—that often created the period's "large loose baggy monsters," as Henry James famously described Victorian novels.[65] It is a telling irony that on the very first page of the working notes for *Hard Times*—the novel he considered satirically titling *Two and Two are Four*, hoping to highlight thereby the imprisonment by number it describes—Dickens fills the left side of the paper with calculating how many of his own manuscript pages he will need to produce an installment for *Household Words*.[66] Lingering over texts' figures can thus help us notice how numbers contribute to shaping works of literature into the recognizable forms we call *genres*. How do numbers relate to questions of metrical measure or to aspects of the novel such as plot and character (in regard to the latter, the relationship between names and numerals will be a recurring motif)? What varieties of service do they perform in various literary environments and against specific historical backdrops? What affordances do they wield?[67] *One*, for example, operates very differently from within the context of a Victorian *Bildungsroman* and a Romantic lyric poem, yet it might be said to mark both these forms. Using number sense to track the figures can

[64] See Hart, *Once Upon a Prime*, 116, 119.

[65] Henry James, Preface to the New York edition of *The Tragic Muse*, 2 vols. (New York: Scribner, 1908), I.x. In *Serial Forms: The Unfinished Product of Modernity, 1815–1848* (Oxford: Oxford University Press, 2020), Clare Pettitt considers the concept of seriality as a defining one of Modernity. Her version of this concept is not particularly numbery, but her argument nevertheless resonates with mine here. Chatterjee's usage of *serial* explicitly avoids the kind of "one-after-another structure" that is linked with serial fiction, offering something that is instead akin to Modernist serial typology: "By serial, I mean a horizontal and contiguous arrangement of subjects who are similar but not the same" (*Feminist Singularity*, 130). See also Daniel Williams's conception of "serial thinking" in Thomas Hardy's work, which he defines as "an approach to representation and cognition that emphasizes repetition, enumeration, and aggregation," and which is "animated by the concept of 'series' in the work of the nineteenth-century logician John Venn." Williams calls this concept "unrelated to serialized publication," but the centrality of enumeration to both ideas does seem to me to indicate some relevant overlap, and I will return to it in my Conclusion ("Slow Fire: Serial Thinking and Hardy's Genres of Induction," *Genre* 50.1 [2017]: 19–38; 19). For a pathbreaking account of Victorian serial fictions that is frequently attentive to numbers within the texts, see Linda K. Hughes and Michael Lund, *The Victorian Serial* (Charlottesville: University Press of Virginia, 1991).

[66] See Dickens, *Hard Times*, 276, 275.

[67] *Affordances* is of course Caroline Levine's immensely useful term for the specific agencies of form. See *Forms: Whole, Rhythm, Hierarchy, Network* (Princeton: Princeton University Press, 2015), 11.

INTRODUCTION   23

help us to notice fresh aspects of familiar forms and to understand better the sets within which we place them.

I begin with Romantic poetry, not only because it allows me to reflect on the long association between the term *numbers* and poetry but also because it is in the field of Romanticism that much of the earliest scholarship on the role of numbers in literature first took root. Chapter 1 starts with Wordsworth, a renowned poet of number. The broad employment of measures and counts in his verse generally reveals a distrust of counting in keeping with the idea of a separation between the two cultures. I then shift to Byron, arguing that while *Don Juan*'s numbers may mislead at times, they also yield positive forms of meaning. Byron uses the generic affordances of narrative verse to encourage counting in order to manage the challenge that experiences of proliferation pose to a sympathy-based, Enlightenment ethics—especially in the case of collective disasters such as war. *Don Juan* teaches us how to get a *feel* for counting, for a process that can lead us from the one toward the many. This lesson is delivered formally, through the workings of the *ottava rima*, as it addresses issues of number, genre, and naming.

Chapter 2 turns to prose, to the notoriously numbery Jane Austen, focusing on her use of a particular figure: her novels exhibit a surprising preponderance of the fraction *half*. I consider this "rational number" as kind of generic marker of the courtship plot and as a measure of her ontology. Looking at Austen's interest in halves reveals her ambivalence regarding the perfect fit of wholes, which, while the *telos* and ultimate source happiness in her writing, also represent structures of disciplinary containment (broadly social and, via the novel, generic) that arise in response to a scarcity economics that Austen knows well to fear. The chapter ends by watching these same forces at play in George Gissing's *The Odd Women*, another peculiarly *half*-rich text from later in the century.

Chapters 3 and 4 concentrate on two Victorian novelists, Charles Dickens and Anthony Trollope, famous for their serialized fictions, one kind of "writing by number" strongly associated with the period. I consider how the frequent use of actual numbers within their works can illuminate their attitudes toward perhaps the most Victorian division of aspects of the novel (and of the novelists): character versus plot. Chapter 3 focuses broadly on how numbers have intersected with characterological description before homing in on how Dickens's treatment of name, number, and character offers a novel rejoinder to the numberiness of democracy. Dickens's fictions have long been recognized as testing grounds for ideas of character

24 THE NUMBER SENSE

(minor and major, flat and round), but *A Tale of Two Cities* has proved especially fertile in this regard in recent years. I highlight how this fact relates to this novel's unusual numerical saturation. *A Tale* reveals that the politics of character is always, on some level, a politics of number. My coda turns to Lewis Carroll's *Alice in Wonderland*, reflecting on its modes of characterization in relation to those of Dickens's revolutionary novel—and to the preeminent genre of individualist singularity, the *Bildungsroman*.

In Chapter 4, I explore Trollope's habitual use of integers to describe his characters' ages. "X was now Y years of age" is a favorite locution, and all Trollope's novels measure the gap between adjacent *now*s by watching characters grow older. But while Trollope's numbers describe his characters, they also bear heavily on his form of plotting. Narrative generally depends on keeping track of numbers, but not all genres of narrative count in the same ways. Numbers also structure more plot-driven fictions (like detective fictions and sensation novels), and I consider how novelists working in these genres deploy counts of years. Trollope's age-related numbers show what happens when plot is not so much subordinated to but rather embodied in character. A coda to this chapter moves from Count Fosco of Wilkie Collins's *The Woman in White* to Bram Stoker's Count Dracula of the novel that bears his name to see how numbers describe age in a novel of the Un-Dead.

Finally, my Conclusion reprises the Introduction via an exploration of two more sets of threes, in Collins's *Armadale* and Thomas Hardy's *Desperate Remedies*—both sensation novels that use this number to think through ancient ideas of fate, chance, and agency against the numbery backdrop of modernity.

Working on this project, I have tried to keep in mind Samuel Beckett's somewhat derogatory designation of literary critics as "chartered recountants" (his pun on chartered accountants): "The chartered recountants take the thing to pieces and put it together again. They enjoy it."[68] I *have* enjoyed playing with the numbers, seeing how they might be arranged and rearranged to make meaning out of a text. But in putting the thing together again, I have endeavored to see something new about how it works—and to avoid introducing errors into the system. I hope the kinds of reading I do here will encourage you, Dear Reader, to use *your* number sense to look at everything you encounter with fresh eyes. Numbers are, after all, everywhere—and never more so than in our own numbery times.

---

[68] He contrasts this with the artist's approach: "The artist takes it to pieces and makes a new thing, new things. He must." Samuel Beckett, "An Imaginative Work!" *Dublin Magazine* xi, n.s. (July–Sept. 1936), 80.

1
Byron's Counts

1.1 Romantic Numbers

"Ours is a numbery historical moment," it has been declared.[1] This condition arises from the marked "technicist (and digital) bent" of contemporary life. While our actual collective literary-critical practice may fail fully to display the trend (*pace* Franco Moretti's advocacy of "distant reading" and the rise of stylometric methods enabled by the Digital Humanities), our experiential immersion in the world means we can't help but be affected by it.[2] But the scope of the interest in numbers also grows out of a pressing ethical need to make sense of how to negotiate the gap separating what Alex Woloch has termed "the one" and "the many."[3] In the wake of today's resurgent populisms, both on the right and on the left, the stakes of the contest between individualism and mass experience have risen. And, as Woloch demonstrates so powerfully, works of literature can articulate and illuminate those stakes.

Woloch shows through his analysis of "character space" that novels—especially the "large, loose, baggy monsters" of high-Victorian fiction—offer one technology by which to approach the issue. Caroline Levine, whose scholarship has forcefully declared the need for literary studies to speak in the political arena and the ability of formalist methods to bridge the divide between aesthetic and ethical discourse, agrees. She believes that Victorian novelists show a surprising resistance to the pervasive new discipline of statistics. In the era of works like Henry Mayhew's *London Labour and the London Poor*, writers of fiction nevertheless tended to eschew the citation of large numbers. Instead of such "counting," the novelists "develop a discursive

---

[1] David Kurnick, "Numberiness," n. pag. Web. Jan. 4, 2017.

[2] Andrew Goldstone and Ted Underwood have counted the use of "number words" in literary scholarship over the decades to arrive at the surprising recognition that (at least, a decade ago) they have been on the decrease, rather than the increase. See Goldstone and Underwood, "The Quiet Transformations of Literary Studies: What Thirteen Thousand Scholars Could Tell Us," *New Literary History* 45.3 (2014): 359–84.

[3] See Alex Woloch, *The One vs. the Many: Minor Characters and the Space of the Protagonist in the Novel* (Princeton: Princeton University Press, 2003).

The Number Sense of Nineteenth-Century British Literature. Stefanie Markovits, Oxford University Press.
© Stefanie Markovits (2025). DOI: 10.1093/9780198937821.003.0002

26   THE NUMBER SENSE

strategy that draws on the tradition of the sublime to train readers to extrapolate a vast world beyond the frame of the fiction, to glimpse the vastness
of a reality that cannot be conveyed by the novel form in any direct or literal way."[4] Levine dubs this method the "enormity effect," and she sees in
it an implicit "critique of the mastery implied by statistical knowledge—a
mastery that to many nineteenth-century thinkers seemed to promise not
only reliable knowledge but also the ground for political, moral, and social
action."[5]

I will myself get to the novelists soon, whom I believe to be both more
statistically oriented and more interested in keeping count than Levine suggests. But I want to start further back in time, and in a different mode. The
"tradition of the sublime" cited by Levine is most readily associated with
the Romantic period. And, in fact, the statistical science to which the enormity effect responds also has its roots in that earlier era. Thomas Malthus's
Essay on the Principle of Population went through six editions between 1798
and 1826, just when the most famous works of British Romantic poetry were
composed. The first modern decennial census was gathered in 1801, spurred
both by Malthus's claims in the *Essay* and by the need to ascertain the number of men available to be conscripted into fighting the Napoleonic Wars.
As the century progressed and the movement to extend suffrage gained in
momentum, the census took on further representational significance; as
Jeremy Bentham's "Essay on Representation" (composed 1788–9) states the
principle, "Everybody to count for one, nobody for more than one."[6] Against
such a backdrop, numbers themselves became highly charged. So perhaps it
is predictable that Romanticist scholars have been at the forefront of the turn
to numbers in literary criticism. Maureen McLane, who considers Malthus's
influence on Shelley's conception of an "arithmetic of futurity" in *Romanticism and the Human Sciences* (2000), also edited a special volume of *Romantic Circles* titled *Romantic Numbers* (2013).[7] The essays in that collection

---

[4] Caroline Levine, "The Enormity Effect: Realist Fiction, Literary Studies, and the Refusal
to Count," *Genre* 50.1 (April 2017), 62.

[5] Levine, "Enormity Effect," 70.

[6] As mentioned in my Introduction, John Stuart Mill quotes this line from Bentham in *Utilitarianism*, 91. For a related interrogation of name and number in Victorian fiction that is closely
attuned to the question of who gets counted, see Hensley, *Forms of Empire: The Poetics of Victorian Sovereignty* (Oxford: Oxford University Press, 2016), 85–133. Hensley points out that
the census takers were called *enumerators*.

[7] As McLane's introduction notes, the volume is the outcome of an MLA panel in 2012
that (rather fittingly) doubled in size after the initial response to the call for papers proved

range across poets (Wordsworth and Coleridge), novelists (John Galt), and scientists and social scientists (including Malthus and Charles Babbage).

Nevertheless, the order of my own list here is not random: when it comes to Romantic numbers, it is pretty clear that William Wordsworth stands first. Almost a decade before McLane's volume appeared, Charles Rzepka had observed "the sheer enumeration of 'things' in the world" of Wordsworth's poems: "'three score and ten,' 'eighty,' 'not twenty paces from the door'; 'one summer day'; 'a single blow.'" "Is there, in fact, any collection of poems in any language," he asked, "conveying as many acts of enumeration and quantification as *Lyrical Ballads*?"[8] And in his exploration of Tennyson's poetic numbers, Matthew Bevis begins by calling Wordsworth "the century's first and most audacious counter in poetry."[9] Bevis cites the preface to the 1815 *Poems*: "the Imagination also shapes and *creates*; and how? By innumerable processes; and in none does it more delight than in that of consolidating numbers into unity, and dissolving and separating unity into number."[10] Still, the poet's chiasmus suggests a commutability (to turn from a poetic lexicon to a mathematical one) that I think misleading: Wordsworth, as many have felt, seems more invested in the former operation than the latter. His is an "egotistical sublime," to use Keats's oft-repeated formulation. That is to say, no number figures as prominently in his verse as *one*.

Just think of "one, the fairest of all Rivers," that nurses the poet of *The Prelude*.[11] Or the "one dear nook / Unvisited" of "Nutting." Lucy of "She dwelt among the Untrodden Ways" is described as "—Fair, as a star when only one / Is shining in the sky!" Here's someone who can't see the forest for the tree: "But there's a tree, of many, one," Wordsworth insists in the Intimations Ode. Indeed, he doubles down on the phenomenon: "A single field which I have look'd upon." And then, to round things off: "Both of them speak of something that is gone." In the Wordsworthian arithmetic, one plus one equals one. One, though, also equals many, as the preface suggests. After all, the Old Cumberland Beggar teaches us that "we have all of us one human heart."

---

overwhelming. The phrase "arithmetic of futurity" is taken from Thomas Love Peacock's portrait of Malthus as Fax in *Melincourt* (1817). Maureen McLane, "Romantic Number(s): A Brief Introduction," *Romantic Circles* (April 2013): n. pag. Web. Accessed Jan. 4, 2017.

[8] Charles Rzepka, "Sacrificial Sites, Place-Keeping, and 'Pre-History' in Wordsworth's 'Michael,'" *European Romantic Review* 15.2 (2004), 207.

[9] Matthew Bevis, "Poetry by Numbers," 39.

[10] Quoted in Bevis, "Poetry by Numbers," 39; original emphasis.

[11] *Prelude* I.272, in *William Wordsworth: The Major Works*, ed. Stephen Gill (Oxford: Oxford University Press, 1984), 381. Hereafter, all references to Wordsworth's poems will be to this edition, unless otherwise cited, and will be given internally.

28 THE NUMBER SENSE

It's this number-fact that allows for the paradox Wordsworth experiences in France when he feels "How bright a face is worn when joy of one / Is joy of tens of millions" (*Prelude* VI.359–60). The math behind such a picture is ontological as well as affective, indicating a universe composed by and reflecting the

> workings of one mind, the features
> Of the same face, blossoms upon one tree,
> Characters of the great apocalypse,
> The types and symbols of eternity,
> Of first, and last, and midst, and without end.
>
> (*Prelude* VI.568–72)

These processes of consolidation are, however, not without their tensions. Consider Michael's request to his one-and-only son Luke that, before departing, he "lay one Stone" of the sheepfold they had been building together. For Michel Foucault, the sheepfold is an icon of governmentality, an essentially biopolitical form of pastoral power. That's because part of what is at stake for the shepherd is population control. Such control incorporates a paradox regarding number, versions of which will plague many of the writers with whom I am concerned in this book. As Foucault observes, pastoral power is simultaneously "individualizing" and consolidating; "the shepherd directs the whole flock, but he can only really direct it insofar as not a single sheep escapes him."[12] How can one care simultaneously for the individual and for the flock? In "Michael," the dilemma makes its way into the poetry through its count not of sheep but of stones. When Luke's absence proves permanent, both construction and poem end; the lyric concludes by declaring how Michael "never lifted up a single stone."

Still, it is no coincidence that this poem uses a pile of stones to think through questions of singularity. The gesture invites thoughts about a second paradox of number: the sorites paradox. This ancient thought puzzle asks one to consider: When does the heap become a heap, rather than a discrete count? In the context of Wordsworth's poem, we might also recall that

---

[12] Michel Foucault, *Security, Territory, Population: Lectures at the Collège de France, 1977–78*, trans. Graham Burchell, ed. Michel Senellart (New York: Picador, 2009), 128. Foucault views such pastoral governmentality as a symptom of (especially) Christian systems, arguing that it is rare in the Greco-Roman tradition (115–30). Regarding the paradox, we might compare Jacques Derrida's observation of the "countable singularity" at the heart of Democratic Liberalism (*The Politics of Friendship*, trans. George Collins [London: Verso, 2005], 22). I will return to this problem in Chapter 3.

BYRON'S COUNTS   29

the term *calculation* is derived from the Latin for stones. Again, one senses an investment in a multiplicity that can't be expressed as, and thereby reduced to, a large number—in an "innumerable" that is simultaneously a "unity." In this sense, the sheepfold resembles another structure in Wordsworth's poems that has been read as hovering between the one and the many: the cloud of "I wandered lonely as a cloud." After all, *cumulus* means *heap*; the clouds and stones that dot the landscapes of Wordsworth's poems thus emerge as tests of the concept of number.[13] In her influential reading of "I wandered lonely," Marjorie Levinson has invited readers to deconstruct the apparent binary the poem presents between the singular "cloud" that is Wordsworth and the "crowd" of "Ten thousand" daffodils that confronts him, "so as to model singularity as a way of being numerous."[14]

In the same essay, Levinson turns toward the end to what is no doubt the most famously numbery of Wordsworth's poems: "We Are Seven." It is her brief discussion of this ballad that elicits her observation, "Everyone knows there's something screwy about number in Wordsworth."[15] Recent readings of "We Are Seven" often reference how the little girl of the poem seems to resist the activity of counting imposed upon her by her questioner, one that critics have seen as anticipating the kind of mathesis soon to be represented by census-takers (the ballad was composed just three years before the inaugural 1801 census). Aaron Fogel, for example, sees in the verses Wordsworth's effort to "oppose [poets'] numbering"—that is to say, the kind of numbering intrinsic to the measures that make up verse, about which I will have more to say when I turn to Byron—"to the state's."[16] But the girl's

---

[13] Perhaps responding unconsciously to his reading of Wordsworth, Tennyson pairs these two things in an early poem, "The How and the Why," read by Bevis as one of the poet's "dalliances" with both meter and arithmetic ("Poetry by Numbers," 48). In the verse, the phrase "Why two and two make four?" is followed in the next line with, "Why the rock stands still, and the light clouds fly?" (Ricks, ed., 186).

[14] Marjorie Levinson, "Of Being Numerous," *Studies in Romanticism* 49.4 (Winter 2010), 634. Her title references George Oppen's *Of Being Numerous*, to which I will return. She anticipates here elements of Chatterjee's argument in *Feminine Singularity*.

[15] Levinson, "Of Being Numerous," 652.

[16] Aaron Fogel, "Wordsworth's 'We Are Seven' and Crabbe's *The Parish Register*: Poetry and Anti-Census," *Studies in Romanticism* 48 (Spring 2009), 52. See also Hollis Robbins, "'We Are Seven' and the first British Census," *English Language Notes* 48.2 (Fall/Winter 2010): 201–13; and Miranda Burgess, "How Wordsworth Tells: Numeration, Valuation, and Dwelling in 'We are Seven,'" *English Language Notes* 54.1 (Spring/Summer 2016): 43–57. Burgess notes Frances Ferguson as the first (followed by Levinson) to "identify mathematical questions as a crucial way in which" Wordsworth "explored the vexed relations between individual and groups" (44). Ferguson sees the poem as expressing the "pitting of numbering against number." Frances Ferguson, *Solitude and the Sublime: Romanticism and the Aesthetics of Individuation* (New York: Routledge, 1992), 168. For Bridget Keegan, "if the girl is a figure for poetry, it is a poetry that

30   THE NUMBER SENSE

insistent refrain that her siblings comprise an indissoluble unit—that "we are seven," regardless of deaths or dispersals—might also be reconfigured as 7=1.[17] That is to say, like the "ten thousand" daffodils of "I wandered lonely as a cloud," the number signifies a heap rather than a count, an experience of unity.[18] "Of course they can't understand each other," Levinson explains of the poem's interlocutors, "she speaks a language of similitude, he speaks *representation*. His language creates an order of independent free-standing things—numbers, the grid. Hers conjures up the mesh."[19]

What makes it odd, though, both for the reader and for her interrogator, is not only the fact, often noted, that the girl does not distinguish between presence and absence, whether locational (see Miranda Burgess) or onto-logical (as critics have long asserted), but also that the figure at stake here is of an order associated with precision. These features both anticipate Lewis Carroll's joke in his final novel, *Sylvie and Bruno Concluded* (1893) (recall that Charles Lutwidge Dodgson was a mathematician):

> "Don't imperrupt!" [Bruno] said as we came in. "I'm counting the Pigs in the field!"
>
> "How many are there?" I enquired.
>
> "About a thousand and four," said Bruno.
>
> "You mean 'about a thousand,'" Sylvie corrected him. "There's no good saying '*and four*': you *ca'n't* be sure about the four!"
>
> "And you're as wrong as ever!" Bruno exclaimed triumphantly. "It's just the *four* I *can* be sure about; 'cause they're here, grubbling under the window! It's the thousand I isn't pruffickly sure about!"[20]

---

works according to a different numerical order." Keegan, "'Another Still! and Still Another!': A Poverty of Numbers in Wordsworth's 'We Are Seven' and 'The Last of the Flock,'" *Friend: Comment on Romanticism* 2.1 (Wordsworth Trust, 1993), 16.

[17] See also Ronjaunee Chatterjee's reading of the ballad, which foregrounds what she calls "the disruptive count of girl femininity," so stressing the child's gender as well as her age (*Feminine Singularity*, 38). As Chatterjee puts it, the girl's "alternative count" is "more attentive to the rift of subjectivity away from the neutralized contours of a preexisting 'one'" (39).

[18] See also Ferguson, who argues that the girl "uses number as if it were a name"—as opposed to her interrogator's "insistence upon counting what is there ... and not ... what isn't. ... Counting, that is, always takes numbers to have references that are available to be pointed to" (*Solitude and the Sublime*, 166). As I mentioned in the Introduction, the relationship between name and number will occupy me repeatedly throughout this study, including in the closing section of this chapter. Levinson turns to Georg Cantor's set theory of the 1870s and '80s and the distinction between matching and counting to think through this dynamic ("Of Being Numerous").

[19] Levinson, "Of Being Numerous," 652.

[20] Lewis Carroll, *Sylvie and Bruno Concluded* (London: MacMillan, 1893), 77–8.

BYRON'S COUNTS   31

Unlike a thousand—much less ten thousand—seven is also a number regarding which one should be able to be perfectly sure. I'm reminded, too, of the old joke about animal husbandry: "Did you hear about the rancher who had 97 cows in his field? When he rounded them up he had 100!" As Larry McMurtry has also shown, a cattleman expresses his "sense" through what I might call his number sense: his ability keep count of livestock.[21]

And so we return to another numbery Lyrical Ballad, one that might be read as a pendant to "Michael": "The Last of the Flock."[22] Sheep are perhaps the most countable of animals, so much so that "counting sheep" is proverbial. This ballad counts both up and down. We first follow the speaker's fortunes from his acquisition of one to fifty sheep: "And from this one, this single ewe, / Full fifty comely sheep I raised, / As sweet a flock as ever grazed!" I have already mentioned Foucault's paradox of the shepherd: his simultaneous duty to each individual sheep and to the collective flock. Foucault recognizes that the technology of both this responsibility and the power through which it is met is the *count*: "The shepherd counts the sheep; he counts them in the morning when he leads them to pasture, and he counts them in the evening to see that they are all there, and he looks after each of them individually."[23]

But if sheep weren't tricky enough on their own, Wordsworth's numbers don't stop at livestock: to fifty sheep, add the "Ten children, Sir! had I to feed"—suddenly, we seem to have reentered the human terrain of "We Are Seven," with its auguries of Malthusian population dynamics. This doubling means that to add here requires the speaker to subtract, to count down, as he must sell off his beloved flock to feed his children. They, in the process, lose in his affections, which are transferred over to the diminishing flock. Until we come to the final stanza:

> "They dwindled, Sir, sad sight to see!
> From ten to five, from five to three,
> A lamb, a weather, and a ewe;

[21] See Larry McMurtry, *The Streets of Laredo* (New York: Simon & Schuster, 1993), 108–10. In this scene in the novel, the livestock in question are sheep that had died while being transported by train.

[22] Noting the rock upon which the last of the flock is found, Keegan observes the connection in Wordsworth's imagination between mathematics and stone or rock: "The lamb is here 'sacrificed' on a rock, the altar of society's numbers and empirical calculations that would make the shepherd unable to attain assistance. This stone site of sacrifice ... looks toward the sheepfold at the end of *Michael*." She also adduces the biblical *Akedah*, the sacrifice of the ram in place of Isaac ("Another Still," 19).

[23] Foucault, *Security, Terror, Population*, 128.

32 THE NUMBER SENSE

> And then at last, from three to two;
> And of my fifty, yesterday
> I had but only one,
> And here it lies upon my arm,
> Alas! and I have none;
> To-day I fetched it from the rock;
> It is the last of all my flock."

The "ten" with which we begin the stanza seems initially to suggest the ten children. But we learn, with a rather strange shock of combined relief and horror, that the lament is instead for the diminishing flock.[24] The exchangeability introduced by number thus incites an ethical quandary: Which is to be preferred? How many sheep equal one child? This question breeds thoughts of related ethical dilemmas introduced by ranking: Sophie's choice, or even the trolley problem—all of them scenarios from which, one might argue, one can be rescued only by refusing to deliberate (as Bernard Williams maintains). That is to say, on some level, such problems demand the refusal of counting or ordering, the refusal of mathesis. Considered in this light, one might leave "The Last of the Flock" with the sense that numbers provoke the crisis here, as they did in "We Are Seven." So much better to think in terms of singularities that are also numerous (as, indeed, the word *sheep* connotes both the one and the many). Only by avoiding a count can a heap—or, for that matter, a flock—preserve this paradox.[25]

1.2 *Don Juan*'s Numerals

The original preface to *Don Juan*'s first two cantos begins by ridiculing Wordsworth's "mensuration" in yet another of that poet's numbery verses,

---

[24] I quote here from the 1798 text of *Lyrical Ballads*; by 1800 there are only "six" children (as in the version used in Gill's edition). Yet surely, we miss the uncomfortable echo, which seems central to the ballad's argument. Keegan surmises that the switch may have been made in subtle allusion to Malthus, whom she believes Wordsworth may have read in the interim. She cites a passage from Chapter 5 of the *Essay* about the suffering of the six children of a laborer who is unable to keep them nourished ("Another Still," n. 9, 22).

[25] Mario Ortiz-Robles turns to Hardy's Wessex novels to consider how they portray sheep as countable creatures against the backdrop of a statistically governed culture. As he concludes, "*Far from the Madding Crowd* can thus be understood as an extended meditation on the biopolitical condition [i.e., one in which events arise through 'chance as a statistical probability'] in which humans are counted as the sheep we always were." Ortiz-Robles, "Hardy's Wessex and the Natural History of Chance," *Novel: A Forum on Fiction* 49.1 (2016), 93.

BYRON'S COUNTS   33

"The Thorn."[26] Yet the numbers of *Don Juan* are also inescapable, not least because of Byron's system of numbering cantos and stanzas to keep track of its growing chain of *ottava rima*. Scholars writing about the work will inevitably find themselves counting—often as they translate Byron's expanding and contracting Latin numerals into more transparent Arabic forms.

Byron himself did a lot of tallying as he wrote his epic, as evidenced by the repeated comments in his correspondence concerning the lines and stanzas he had produced and his remarks to friends and publishers about the different ways to calculate the poem's extraordinary length. "Why—man— I could have spun the thoughts of the four cantos of [*Childe Harold*] into twenty—had I wanted to book-make—& it's [*sic*] passion into as many modern tragedies—since you want *length* you shall have enough of *Juan*, for I'll make 50 cantos," he wrote in 1819 to his publisher, John Murray, who had been eager to capitalize on the popularity of the earlier work.[27] Later, when he found himself bifurcating a runaway canto to produce a couple of more manageable length (a fact he rather disarmingly records in the verse itself: "I must cut down / (In copying) this long canto into two" [3.111.2–3]), he warned Murray that the true measure of the poem could be taken only by counting stanzas or pages, not cantos, which were of arbitrary rather than intrinsic length (*Letters and Journals* 226).[28] Regardless of this disclaimer, critics have explored the work's "numerology," as Gordon Potter does in his essay claiming Byron's place in "the tradition of central-line symbolism," where he discovers in the poet a tendency to place particularly important observations at the midpoints of his cantos. The effort strikes me as strained, but the ambition nevertheless recognizes that Byron's numbering methods invite us to seek meaning in counting. After all, Byron more than once evokes Dante, the great bard of numerology, in the epic, as when he describes how the Florentine's "more abstruse ecstatics" were "Meant to personify the mathematics" (3.11.7–8).

---

[26] "The pond near [the thorn] is described according to mensuration: 'I measured it from side to side, 'Tis three feet long and two feet wide.' Let me be excused from being particular in the detail of such things, as this is the sort of writing which has superseded and degraded Pope in the eyes of the discerning public." George Gordon Byron, *Don Juan*, ed. T. G. Steffen, E. Steffen, and W. W. Pratt (London: Penguin, 1986), 37. Hereafter internally documented by canto, stanza, and line numbers rather than by page.

[27] George Gordon Byron, *Lord Byron: Selected Letters and Journals*, ed. Leslie A. Marchand (Cambridge, MA: Harvard University Press, 1982), 190. Hereafter, *Letters and Journals* internally referenced.

[28] Byron's comments recall his account of Lambro's division of his prisoners into "numbered lots" that are described as being "like chapters" (3.15.6–7).

34 THE NUMBER SENSE

Numbers figure prominently within the verse, as well. For that matter, when it comes to centers, Dante also shows up in *Don Juan* as the poet of "That horrid equinox, that hateful section / Of human years, that halfway house" designated by Byron as the "most barbarous" "middle age / Of man": "thirty-five" (10.27.4–5, 12.1.2–3, 12.2.1). The narrator of *Don Juan* obsesses over age (a quality, as I will show, he shares with the novelist Anthony Trollope, the subject of my fourth chapter). Many of the poem's figures register that obsession. The first canto delivers a case in point, offering sufficient age-oriented numerals to provide the word questions for a very respectable third-grade math exam (although perhaps, given the subject, not quite an age-appropriate one). Thus, we are introduced to Julia, "married, charming, chaste, and twenty-three" (1.59.8),

> Wedded she was some years and to a man
>> Of fifty, and such husbands are in plenty;
> And yet, I think, instead of such a one
>> 'Twere better to have two of five and twenty
>>>> (1.62.1–4)

Instead, she meets Juan and befriends him:

> Quite innocently done, and harmless styled,
>> When she had twenty years, and thirteen he;
> But I am not so sure I should have smiled
>> When he was sixteen, Julia twenty-three.
>>>> (1.69.3–6)

While Juan's mother Inez, whose "favourite science was the mathematical," may be styled "a walking calculation" (1.12.1, 1.16.1), Byron's narrator seems to be playing a similar game as he "rattle[s] on exactly as [he'd] talk / With anybody in a ride or walk" (15.19.7–8), judiciously assessing the age of practically every character we meet even while counting the lines and feet of his verse (recall that *numbers* has for centuries been a synonym for measured verse).[29] Given the poet's fixation on his own age, the fascination hardly surprises: "At five-and-twenty, when the better part of life is over,

---

[29] Inez's portrait has long been recognized as drawing on Byron's characterization of his wife, Annabella Milbank, whom he labeled "the amiable *Mathematician*" and "Princess of Parallelograms" in his correspondence (*Letters and Journals* 63–5). The use of *numbers* for measured verse goes back to the Renaissance (see, for example, Thomas Campion, *Observations in the Art of English Poesie* [1602]). Fielding references it in *Tom Jones* when he remarks

one should be *something*;—and what am I? nothing but five-and-twenty," Byron recorded in his journal (*Letters and Journals* 84). Byron's final poem is "On This Day I Complete My Thirty-Sixth Year." In a manner that, as we shall see, again anticipates Trollope, he was constantly taking chronological measure of his productivity: "Awoke, and up an hour before being called; but dawdled three hours in dressing. When one subtracts from life infancy (which is vegetation),—sleep, eating, and swilling—buttoning and unbuttoning—how much remains of downright existence?" (*Letters and Journals* 93). In other words, the forms of Byronic numbering I have thus far isolated should be viewed as parts of a single phenomenon: as efforts to account for generativity.

Despite the concern for age, *Don Juan* is subject to some notable chronological confusion.[30] N. E. Gayle has attempted to track the poem's temporal arc from the precise numbers we are given. We know that at its start Juan is sixteen (as the lines quoted above indicate); by its conclusion he is the twenty-one-year-old Adeline's "junior by six weeks" (14.51.8, 14.54.7–8). But when Gayle tries to fit the events of the cantos around these points—to "do the sums," as he puts it—he finds that "they reveal a temporal hole": the action can't fill the five years allotted it. As Gayle remarks, Byron was "clearly not" "thinking chronologically."[31] And yet he was, after a fashion. Consider the comedic specificity of the one calendrical date he gives, that of Juan's initial tryst with Julia, from which all else flows:

> 'Twas on a summer's day, the sixth of June:—
> I like to be particular in dates,
> Not only of the age, and year, but moon.
> They are a sort of post-house, where the Fates
> Change horses, making history change its tune,
> Then spur away o'er empires and o'er states,
> Leaving at last not much besides chronology,
> Excepting the post-obits of theology.
>
> (1.103.1–8)

---

that "Poetry"—according to him, unlike novels and romances—"demands numbers, or something like numbers." Henry Fielding, *Tom Jones*, ed. John Bender and Simon Stern (Oxford: Oxford University Press, 1996), 423.

[30] Once more, there's a resemblance between Byron and Trollope, whose own chronological confusions will be the subject of Chapter 4.

[31] N. E. Gayle, "Don Juan and the Dirty Scythe of Time," *The Byron Journal* 41.1 (2013), 32, 33.

36   THE NUMBER SENSE

The stanza's final three lines actually offer a fair plot synopsis of the ensuing poem. But the joke of the number here is partly a joke about genre, about how the kind of writing we call *history* can be made to "change its tune"—shift its generic register—through the manipulation of such figures. One might compare the effect of the single date provided by the sixteen-year-old Jane Austen—that of the execution of her heroine, Mary, Queen of Scots—in her youthful send-up of Whig histories, *The Brief History of England, ..., by a partial, prejudiced, and ignorant Historian* (1791).[32] Both gestures mock the proliferation of meaningless numbers punctuating historical accounts as they select the one that really matters. Thus, while Gayle has figured out a year to add to *Don Juan*'s sole date and month—the memorably revolutionary 1789, arrived at by computing back from the historical sack of Ismail on December 22, 1790 (the subject of Cantos 7 through 9)—he recognizes that such computation misses the point.

That point concerns not strict chronology but the experiential place of age: the 6th of June represents Juan and Julia's youthful promise, as the euphony among all three and the overlapping sixes in Juan's age and the month and day suggest. Byron rhymes the month with *tune*; as the tryst had the potential to produce other forms of offspring, the date promises to generate song.[33] It does so partly through the iterative operations of the poem's enormously generative rhymes, which propel its narrative forward as the poet works to meet the complex requirements of the *ottava rima* despite his medium of rhyme-impoverished English. But the specific date's tuneful promise would eventually play itself out over a longer historical arc than Byron could have predicted. Walter E. Anderson surmises that Byron's ur-point spurred Joyce in selecting June 16th as the temporal setting for *Ulysses*. While Bloomsday (as it has since been christened) was in fact the date of James Joyce's first tryst with Nora Barnacle, Byron's influence appears when Bloom gives Molly a volume of the poet's verses during their courtship.[34] And while Gayle doesn't mention the Joycean link, I find it curiously fitting—indeed (Harold) Bloomian, given we are talking of influence—that his essay, even as it attempts to account strictly for the

---

[32] See Jane Austen, *Catharine and Other Writings*, ed. Margaret Anne Doody (Oxford: Oxford University Press, 2009), 141.

[33] Although Julia's lack of children may not suggest generativity, and Juan's only known progeny dies in Haidée's womb, the poem's Malthusian context nevertheless encourages the reader to link sexuality to productivity, as I hope what follows will show.

[34] James Joyce, *Ulysses*, ed. Walter Gabler (New York: Vintage, 1986), 612.

chronological inconsistencies of the poem, at one point misidentifies the date in *Don Juan* as the 16th.[35]

Gayle for the most part resists attributing specific meaning to Byron's miscalculations. David Kurnick, with whose declaration of numberiness I began, is less reticent in his response to Eric Bulson's numerical reading of *Ulysses*, which prompted the thoughts on our numbery times. He asks the question directly:

> Does it matter that Joyce's numbers [in the Ithaca episode] don't work? (By my calculation, when Stephen reaches 1190, Bloom would be 20,230 ...). Barry McCrea, commenting recently on these errors, has read them as indicating that "the world is neither perfectible nor fully describable ... [T]he mistaken calculations serve as a reminder that this is a novel" and not a mathematical formula.[36]

So yes, it matters. But while Byron would no doubt agree that "the world is neither perfectible nor fully describable," his numbers perform work that goes beyond their signaling of this fact, which in any case merely manifests the poet's more general abhorrence of systemic thinking. And unlike Wordsworth, he is not fundamentally suspicious of counts. In fact, while *Don Juan*'s numerals may mislead at times, they also yield positive forms of meaning. "Why not count?" Levine asks of the Victorian novelists.[37] "Why count?" is my question of Byron. Even as *Don Juan*'s numbers result from its fundamental embrace of generativity, Byron's poem uses the generic affordances of narrative verse to encourage counting. It does so to manage the challenge experiences of proliferation pose to a sympathy-based, Enlightenment ethics—especially when faced with collective disasters such as war.

1.3 Counting

We can start to see these competing aspects of the poem's mathematics by observing a couple of characteristics of Byron's numbers in *Don Juan*. First,

---

[35] Gayle, "Dirty Scythe," 29. In a historical echo that I suspect Byron would have appreciated, June 6th also happens to be the date of the Allied invasion of Normandy in 1944, thus joining the two themes of love and war that will serve as recurring loci in my account of Byron's numbers.

[36] Kurnick, "Numberiness," n. pag.; Barry McCrea, *In the Company of Strangers: Family and Narrative in Dickens, Conan Doyle, Joyce and Proust* (New York: Columbia University Press, 2011), 143.

[37] Levine, "Enormity Effect," 70.

38   THE NUMBER SENSE

with some notable exceptions, they tend to be rather human in scale, most often fitting within the range of the plausible span of a life in years even when applied to objects or people rather than age. In this regard, they contrast with the (much rarer) numbers of *Childe Harold*, where orders of magnitude organize the figures as they move from ones to hundreds to thousands and, in the Waterloo passages, to millions (3.XX.7, 3.XXXV.5). The distinction recalls the difference between ten thousand and seven I discussed in relation to Wordsworth.

Second, many of *Don Juan*'s numbers are implicitly *ordinal*, rather than *cardinal*, even if they are articulated in their cardinal forms. That is to say, they usually make sense of position in a series—first, second, third, and so on—rather than outright size. Here, we should distinguish Byron's attitude toward the ordinal from Wordsworth's. As Marjorie Levinson shows in relation to "We Are Seven," where the speaker counts (uses ordinal numbers) and the child matches each sibling to a place (uses cardinal numbers), Wordsworth mistrusts ordinal numbers. This fact underlies Levinson's argument about the girl's treatment of number as forming a "mesh" rather than a systematic and systematizing order of things;[38] Frances Ferguson doesn't use the terminology, but the same difference causes her to compare the girl's numbering to naming and her questioner's methods to census-like counting.[39] But Byron does not appear to share in such misgivings concerning the ordinal. In his case, numerical age again offers a good example of his contrasting tendencies. He seems more invested in the fact that a twenty-six-year-old woman like the "ripe" Gulbayez (5.98.2) will soon become twenty-seven than he is in the twenty-six years she has completed thus far (although twenty-seven would represent a limit of feminine "ripeness," being the most advanced age, according to the narrator, which need not "dread the enumeration" [14.54.2, 14.52.4][40]). Byron's ordinally functioning figures also differ from many of Dante's, whose threes and hundreds have symbolic resonance even when isolated from their serial context.

Yet his numbers also resist some standard mathematical applications. While counting is normally understood as an activity applied to a finite set, Byron seems to believe in counting in the face of infinities (hence, perhaps, his indifference as to whether the count is strictly accurate: small

[38] See Levinson, "Of Being Numerous," 634, 652.
[39] See Ferguson, *Solitude and the Sublime*, 168.
[40] Looking forward to my next chapter, on Austen, we might also recognize it as the threshold for marriageability that has been reached by Charlotte Lucas in *Pride and Prejudice* and Anne Elliot in *Persuasion*.

BYRON'S COUNTS   39

inconsistencies are trivial—mathematically speaking—in the grand scheme of things).[41] Jerome McGann implies as much when he points out that if Coleridge, in the famous formulation, wants narrative verse "to convert a series into a whole," Byron's poem tries "to convert the whole (i.e., the human world) into a series."[42] The poem, that is, privileges the process of counting over the end of summation. It keeps on adding without ever resolving the problem. In McGann's terms, "*Don Juan* is not a poem that develops, it is a poem that is added to. *Don Juan* attacks the organic concept of *development*—a word which never appears, in any form, in the poem. The words *add*, *added*, and *adds*, on the other hand, occur with great frequency, and they locate a crucial quality in the form and style of the *Don Juan* manner."[43] In fact—returning to a term I used earlier in relation to the poem's rhyme-scheme—the effect might be called *iterative* rather than strictly additive, given the recurring patterns, although the mathematical sense of that word is a twentieth-century invention.[44]

Versions of development may be missing from the work. Versions of *growth*, however, are not (as in, for example, "Don Juan grew" [10.21.1, 10.23.3]). The poem successfully accumulates meaning (implied, after all, by *add*), even if we are far from the world of the *Bildungsroman*, where development inheres within the protagonist and serves as an engine for novelistic closure. *Don Juan's* additive quality appears unmistakably in those ever-growing stanza and canto designations that actually lead McGann, rather uncharacteristically, to start counting (which he does in terms of both stanzas-per-canto and -per-"episode") at the end of the chapter in which he turns his attention to form—including, as it happens, the increasingly

---

[41] The idea of the infinite features in Levinson's discussion of Wordsworth's use of cardinal and ordinal numbers; she discusses how "[George] Cantor's astonishing claim—that infinity comes in different sizes—relies on the difference between cardinal and ordinal numbers" and on processes of matching sets rather than counting ("Of Being Numerous," 653–4). In a reading of George Eliot's "large" novels that resonates with my treatment of Byron's long poem, Jesse Rosenthal also points out that Cantor's work on set theory in the 1870s would actually prove the existence of a "countably infinite" set. Coincidentally, Rosenthal notes a connection to Byron: the poet's grandniece provided the germ for the opening scene of Gwendolen's gambling in *Daniel Deronda*. See Jesse Rosenthal, "The Large Novel and the Law of Large Numbers; or, Why George Eliot Hates Gambling," *ELH* 77. 3 (Fall 2010): 777–811; 784, 801.

[42] Jerome McGann, *Don Juan in Context* (Chicago: University of Chicago Press, 1976), 109.

[43] McGann, *Don Juan in Context*, 60.

[44] This interest in iteration is a notable aspect of the neo-Victorian genre of steampunk. William Gibson and Bruce Sterling's *The Difference Engine* (New York: Ballantine, 1990), often considered the foundational text of the genre, is a novel written by a computer in "iterations" rather than "books." It tells of an alternative history in which Lord Byron becomes prime minister and in which Babbage's design of the "analytical engine" (his second-generation improvement on the "difference engine") is realized and proliferated.

40   THE NUMBER SENSE

novelistic register of the English cantos.[45] Similarly, Byron's most obvious stylistic tic in *Don Juan* may be his use of lists, as in the many asyndetons and polysyndetons that encouraged Thomas Rommel to select the work for an early trial of computer-assisted quantitative literary analysis that concentrated on those two varieties of word cluster.[46] Julia's description as "married, charming, chaste, and twenty-three" offers a nice example of the work's overlapping additive and numerical tendencies.[47]

Of course, the poem's expanding architecture depends most clearly on the list generated by stringing together Juan's many lovers, as its cantos take us from Julia, to Haidée, to Gulbayez and her maidens, to Catherine, and to the trinity of English beauties—Adeline, Aurora, and the Duchess of Fitz-Fulke—with which *Don Juan* abruptly breaks off. This series yields a variety of numbery formulations, as the narrator speaks, for instance, of "the third canto—and the pretty pair" (3.81.6) or "Our hero and third heroine" (6.7.1). Such an accretive process is premised on the recognition that the number *one* implicitly represents a *first*: that, as the narrator succinctly puts it, "there are some, they say, who have had none, / But those who have ne'er end with only one" (3.4.7–8). As Byron observes, once coupling occurs, counting becomes inevitable. Considering the "first love" of women, Byron's narrator explains, "One man alone at first her heart can move; / She then prefers him in the plural number, / Not finding that the additions much encumber" (3.3.6–8) (much as the verse plows on through the additional metrical syllable in "the additions").[48]

The poem's opening stanza obliquely introduces this premise as the narrator himself searches—not for a true love but for a true hero:

> I want a hero: an uncommon want,
>> When every year and month sends forth a new one,
> Till, after cloying the gazettes with cant,

---

[45] McGann, *Don Juan in Context*, 128–9.

[46] Thomas Rommel, "'So soft, so sweet, so delicately clear.' A Computer-assisted Analysis of Accumulated Words and Phrases in Lord Byron's Epic Poem *Don Juan*," *Literary and Linguistic Computing* 9.1 (1994): 7–12.

[47] I will return to this type of formulation in my treatment of character in Chapter 3.

[48] Somewhat shockingly, given her reputation, Jane Austen's Colonel Brandon suggests the same basic number fact in *Sense and Sensibility* when recalling his attempt to locate his beloved Eliza after her fall into adultery: "I could not trace her beyond her first seducer." A much younger Austen sounds even more like Byron when making a mathematical joke of this tragic phenomenon in an early story, in which an experienced lady advises her young friend of the inverse claim: "Preserve yourself from a first Love & you need not fear a second." Jane Austen, *Sense and Sensibility*, ed. James Kinsley (Oxford: Oxford University Press, 2004), 154; "Jack and Alice," in *Catharine and Other Writings*, 15.

BYRON'S COUNTS   41

> The age discovers he is not the true one;
> Of such as these I should not care to vaunt;
> I'll therefore take our ancient friend Don Juan ...
>
> (1.1.1–6)

The quest for a "true one" emerges against the backdrop of the never-ending proliferation of "new one[s]"—of seriality. Moreover, in a manner that will prove characteristic, this search yields not only the poem's first triple-rhyme but also the bastardized pronunciation of Don Juan's name. To reinforce the links among expanding numbers, strophic verse, and names, the triple-rhyme reappears in feminized form when, in the second canto, Juan encounters his second love, Haidée:

> But Juan, had he quite forgotten *Julia*?
> And should he have forgotten her so soon?
> I can't but say it seems to me most *truly a*
> Perplexing question, but no doubt the moon
> Does these things for us, and whenever *newly a*
> Strong palpitation rises, 'tis her boon, ...
>
> (2.208.1–6; emphasis added)

Notice how temporality, whether registered by the chronicle of the masculine gazettes' lists or the feminine moon's fluctuating face, inevitably yields the experience of seriality (and recall that *moon* had earlier been made to rhyme with *June* in the narration of Juan and Julia's first sexual encounter).[49]

The serial mode of *Don Juan's* publication amplifies one's sense of the additive principle undergirding both subject and stanzaic measure.[50] It is further accentuated by the work's incomplete state, which has encouraged many readers—and writers—to keep going beyond the bounds of the narrative. Samuel Chew celebrated *Don Juan's* centenary by putting together a list of its spurious sequels; he was able to enumerate and describe twenty-eight examples—and that without computers and digitalization.[51] Still, McGann

---

[49] The same triple rhyme appears twice in the opening canto (stanzas 48 and 86) and again when introducing one of the poem's final heroines, Adeline (14.91.1–6). I discuss this phenomenon in the context of adultery in *The Victorian Verse-Novel: Aspiring to Life* (Oxford: Oxford University Press, 2017), 92–3.

[50] *Ulysses's* serial publication forms the basis for Eric Bulson's argument about Joyce's numbers ("Ulysses by Numbers," *Representations* 127.1 [Summer 2014]: 1–32).

[51] Samuel C. Chew, "The Centenary of Don Juan," *American Journal of Philology* 40 (1919): 117–52.

42   THE NUMBER SENSE

is surely right in saying that, unlike Charles Dickens's *The Mystery of Edwin Drood*, *Don Juan* is not "seriously weakened by being a fragment."[52] Even before the poem's premature end, brought about by Byron's early death at Missolonghi, *Don Juan*'s method had rendered it oddly immune to incompleteness, precisely by virtue of its infinitely iterative nature. Notably, the continuations started to turn up immediately, long before Byron's demise may have been claimed to create a need. Four days after the quarto of the first two cantos appeared in 1819, William Hone published a false third canto; in his correspondence, Byron somewhat wryly records the arrival of "*two* new *third* Cantos" (*Letters and Journals* 223, original emphasis). Still, his own uncertainty regarding the poem's limits can be seen not only in the promise of fifty cantos, cited above, and the oft-quoted letter to Murray in which Byron wonders whether Juan will end in an unhappy marriage or in hell (*Letters and Journals* 252), but also in the improvisational narrator's fluctuating claims regarding the number of cantos to come (1.200.1–2, 2.216.5). Yet while the work's many illegitimate offspring suggest the limitless quality to Don Juan's tale, they also—once again—seem to encourage a paradoxical urge to count. When G. W. M. Reynolds produced an anonymous *Sequel to Don Juan* in 1843 (the year before his most famous book, the weekly serial *The Mysteries of London*, began its incredibly long run), his second stanza blithely asks the muse to inspire his song "of horns unnumbered."[53] Still, as his Advertisement announces, Reynolds offered only five initial cantos, with a promise of precisely eleven more to follow, should the public approve—thus matching Byron's own sixteen completed cantos.[54]

We count in the face of infinity. Such counting may sometimes provide an expedient solution to a practical problem: Where should I stop for now? But in Byron's poem, it addresses a deeper ethical quandary, as well. Rather than claiming the epistemological "mastery" of the statistician, counting can serve as a gesture of defiance, a fist raised in the face of the incomprehensible. It can also represent a quieter effort to find a measure of meaning in some corner of existence: The poem may be limitless, but the stanza has eight lines, two triple-rhymes, one couplet. As Susan Stewart has observed, it is "keeping time, the work of intended care in meter" that "makes infinity

---

[52] McGann, *Don Juan in Context*, 4.

[53] [G. W. M. Reynolds], *A Sequel to Don Juan* (London: Paget & Co., 1843), 1.2.2.

[54] *The Mysteries of London* (1844–8) had its own sequel in the even longer *Mysteries of the Court of London* (1848–55); Reynolds's novels also have close ties to Mayhew's statistically oriented work.

BYRON'S COUNTS   43

bearable."[55] The *moral* "ecology of number" (extending a phrase used by Kurnick) in Byron's *Don Juan* can thus be identified by focusing on both the endlessly generative nature of the verse and the counterbalance provided by what I want to call Byron's ethics of counting, an ethics formalized in *Don Juan*'s aesthetic practices.

1.4 The One and the Many

When Byron selected Horace's declaration "*Difficile est proprie communia dicere*" ("It is difficult to speak in your own way of common things") for his motto to *Don Juan*, he was no doubt mocking society's tendency toward prudery and announcing the threat to truth posed by censorship. Yet the difficulty partly involves number: When something becomes too "common," when the figures at stake become too large—whether they be numbers of lovers or the volume of the war dead—it can be hard not only to keep count (think of Carroll's thousand and four) but also to write of the persons affected in a manner occasioning sympathy. In fact, love and war both resonate numerically in *Don Juan*: The reproductive promise of sex stands in opposition to the poem's discourse of death, which climaxes in the cantos treating the sack of Ismail. The mathematical connection between the two appears in the narrator's apostrophe, following the war cantos and apropos Catherine the Great, to the female genitalia—"Thou gate of life and death— thou nondescript! / Whence is our exit and our entrance"—as the "*teterrima causa* of all *belli*" (9.55.2–3, 9.55.1). Yet while to some, a woman's vagina may be "the most foul cause of war," to Byron's narrator, it is "the best," because the sexual organs contain the ability to "replenish worlds both great and small" (9.56.1, 9.55.2, 9.55.6). It is even tempting to translate Byron's initial apostrophic "Oh" (9.55.1) into a zero—a "nondescript," perhaps, but one that holds the power to convert ones (phallic "all things at a stand" [9.56.7]) into Malthusian millions.[56]

Here we are again: the one and the many. In a compelling discussion of the contemporaneous response to the vast scale of casualties in the Napoleonic

---

[55] Susan Stewart, *Poetry and the Fate of the Senses* (Chicago: University of Chicago Press, 2002), 197.

[56] Contrast the Fool's account of Lear: "[T]hou art an 0 without a figure. I am better than thou art now, I am a Fool, thou art nothing." *The Tragedy of King Lear*, in *The Riverside Shakespeare*, ed. G. Blakemore Evans (Boston: Houghton Mifflin, 1974), 1.4.192–4. Hereafter, all references to Shakespeare's plays will be cited by act, scene, and line numbers in this edition.

44 THE NUMBER SENSE

Wars, Mary A. Favret has described the need to create a "feeling for numbers" in the face of what Adam Smith recognized as the limited nature of human sympathy. If we sympathize by putting ourselves in someone else's shoes, how are we to fathom the suffering of the many? Favret quotes Josef Stalin's claim, "One death is a tragedy, a million deaths ... a statistic," as a gloss on Napoleon's purported admission that "A man like me does not give a shit about the lives of a million men."[57] Byron may have been thinking of Napoleon when he observed of the Russian General Suwarrow (his spelling) that he "saw things in the gross" and "calculated life as so much dross," so long as "The work of glory still went on" (7.77.1, 7.77.3, 7.78.1). Still, Suwarrow is temporarily arrested by Juan's request for assistance in protecting the two sobbing women who helped him escape the harem:

> for however habit sears
> Men's hearts against whole millions, when their trade
> Is butchery, sometimes a single sorrow
> Will touch even heroes, and such was Suwarrow.
>
> (7.69.5–8)

Note how the narrator silently blends even two women into a "single sorrow." As the psychologist Paul Bloom puts it in *Against Empathy: The Case for Rational Compassion*, empathy "is innumerate, favoring the one over the many." Bloom explains that "This perverse moral mathematics is part of the reason why governments care more about a little girl stuck in a well than about events that will affect millions."[58]

Or why readers care more about a little girl saved from the sack of Ismail. Although we may be as quick as Suwarrow to forget Dudu and her comrades, Leila's case presents a special appeal to sympathy that must be understood within the dynamics of the one and the many. Byron admits as much in describing the occasion of her rescue:

---

[57] Mary A. Favret, "A Feeling for Numbers: Representing the Scale of the War Dead," in *War and Literature*, ed. Laura Ashe and Ian Patterson (Cambridge, UK: D. S. Brewer, 2014), 185. Favret is particularly interested in the peculiar nature of sympathy for a dead person and in "numbers that straddle the bar separating the living from the dead" (192). Her poetic readings center on Wordsworth's Salisbury Plain poetry, although she does mention that a variety of other writers of the age, including Byron, might offer as fertile terrain for enquiry (189).

[58] Paul Bloom, *Against Empathy: The Case for Rational Compassion* (New York: Ecco, 2016), Prologue.

BYRON'S COUNTS   45

Upon a taken bastion where there lay
　　Thousands of slaughtered men, a yet warm group
Of murdered women, who had found their way
　　To this vain refuge, made the good heart droop
And shudder; while, as beautiful as May,
　　A female child of ten years tried to stoop
And hide her little palpitating breast
Amidst the bodies lulled in bloody rest.

(8.91.1–8)

"Thousands of slaughtered men" and a "group / Of murdered women" barely register in the balance when compared to the emotional impact of this single ten-year-old girl's sufferings. Yet "The drying up a single tear has more / Of honest fame, than shedding seas of gore," according to the narrator's somewhat self-justifying calculation (8.3.7–8).

Juan's rescue of Leila embodies an anomaly in the poem's number dynamics. Her singularity puts her outside of Don *Juan*'s iterative logic, even as her age—at least for now—renders her safe from the generative imperative implied by its serial treatment of love as sexuality.[59] Nevertheless, Byron's focus on the singular presents a familiar trope, that with which I began this chapter: "there's a tree, of many, one," as Wordsworth put it in the Intimations Ode. Still, Leila is no lyrical Lucy.[60] This despite the high seriousness with which her salvation is treated in a poem that otherwise fluctuates consistently between moods of deep feeling and more satiric and detached registers. Indeed, for all the episode's emotional intensity, Byron may have appreciated that Leila's singularity could suggest a different conventional literary response to the problem of numbers, one that we generally associate with the novel.

If a novelistic moral calculus is effective, a *one*—or so goes the generic logic, which I find very potent—should be able to represent *many*, should stand in for the work's myriad readers even as the form emphasizes the protagonist's individuality. Such is the power of identification. Compare

[59] Although Byron supposedly told Medwin that in a later episode Leila was to become enamored of Juan, he also indicated that the love would remain unrequited. See Chew, "Centenary," 130.

[60] Marjorie Levinson's reading of "She dwelt among th'untrodden ways" highlights the centrality of singularity to lyric by focusing on the relation posited between the number *one* and the name *Lucy*: "By *fantasy*, I mean that the proper name—the *one*, the singularity—set forth by lyric unleashes a dream of individuation or determination without negation." Levinson, "Notes and Queries on Names and Numbers," 33; republished in Levinson's *Thinking Through Poetry: Field Reports on Romantic Lyric* (Oxford: Oxford University Press, 2018).

46   THE NUMBER SENSE

Leila's function with Estella's in *Great Expectations* (1861). (I am tempted to observe a certain nominative kinship among these three heroines: *Lucy* means light and *Estella* means star, while *Leila* means dark or night.) Reading Dickens's novel against the backdrop of the census and of contemporary articles regarding its implementation published in *All the Year Round*, Michael Klotz has described how

> in narrating Estella's history prior to her introduction into Pip's life, Jaggers emphasizes that to him Estella was merely one of the "great numbers" of children destined to commit criminal acts and to be imprisoned for their actions. For Jaggers they were the "fish that were to come to his net" bound for "certain destruction"... His decision was to alter the fate for this one anonymous child: by bringing her to Miss Havisham, he effectively turned her from the statistical path that she would otherwise have pursued. Estella is envisioned as the "one pretty little child" who has been taken "out of the heap."[61]

And Dickens follows Jaggers in using many of the novel's formal affordances to highlight Estella's individuality. But while Leila's literal fate resembles Estella's, her *literary* fate feels quite different. She hovers in a kind of generic limbo, in a realm neither fully lyrical nor fully novelistic. Although Byron may temporarily make space for an affective response to the one, he is not writing a novel. He never enters into Leila's consciousness.[62] He also seems to recognize the limitations of her uniqueness; the narrator quite happily dispenses with Leila upon Juan's arrival in England. "But first of little Leila we'll dispose," he announces, before promptly dispatching her to the margins of the character-space (12.41.1).

Moreover, as an alternative to Leila's singularity, Byron's narration of the siege includes an episode that instead emphasizes the ethical power of counting past one: the story of the "brave Tartar khan," "a good, plain, old, temperate man, / Who fought with his five children in the van" (8.104.5, 8.105.7–8). Those "five brave sons" are identified as the product of the

---

[61] Michael Klotz, "Manufacturing Fictional Individuals: Victorian Social Statistics, the Novel, and *Great Expectations*," *Novel* 46.2 (2013), 229.

[62] As I will discuss at more length in Chapter 3, such delving below the surface is a marker of "round" novelistic characterization. See also Levine, "Enormity Effect," on a related novelistic phenomenon, the *type*: "one classic strategy for the novel is to scale up from one or two instances to uncountable examples that extend beyond the frame" (67). The *type* (such as the "fallen woman") offers a "strategy for the novel to imply the many through the one" (68). But Byron's Leila hovers uneasily between these two novelistic modes rather than falling neatly into either. There is nothing typical about her, for all that she represents an innocent victim of war.

BYRON'S COUNTS   47

same polygamy that so fascinates Byron in the harem scenes, a system that "spawns warriors by the score, where none / Are prosecuted for that false crime bigamy" (8.105.1–3), where a single Sultan can bear "fifty daughters and four dozen sons" (5.152.1). They raise a collective fist against the Malthusian doctrine that Byron subjects to increasing mockery in *Don Juan* (11.30, 12.14, 12.21, 15.37–8). In fact, Byron implies that the khan's multiple sons should provide some protection from the threat of extinction represented by the only children that somewhat paradoxically seem to proliferate through the poem: Juan, "An only son left with an only mother" (1.37.7); Julia, a "single one," the "only daughter" of an "only son" (1.59.3–4); Haidée, "only daughter / Of an old man" (2.124.7–8), who on her deathbed also "held within / A second"—yet nevertheless only—"principle of life" (4.70.1–2); Leila; Aurora Raby, "an orphan; left an only / Child" (15.44.1–2). Even the final, incomplete canto opens with an excursus on "orphans" and so-styled "only-children" (17.1–2).[63]

But if Byron (himself an only son) thumbs his nose at Malthus, when set against such singularities, his portrait of the five sons also takes some measure of the vast scale of the war dead. It reminds us again of the close relationship between numbers and war, of the fact that the 1801 census was justified in part by the need for the British to man their armies to fight against Napoleon. War literature naturally reflects this numberiness: think again of the *Iliad*'s numbered boats. Or consider this remarkable passage from Tolstoy's *War and Peace*, one of many moments in the novel where reflections on battle shift into mathematical musings:

> Ten men, battalions, or divisions, fighting fifteen men, battalions, or divisions, conquer—that is, kill or take captive—all the others, while themselves losing four, so that on the one side four and on the other fifteen were lost. Consequently the four were equal to the fifteen, and therefore $4x = 15y$. Consequently $x/y = 15/4$. This equation does not give us the value of the unknown factor but gives us a ratio between two unknowns. And by bringing variously selected historic units (battles, campaigns, periods of war) into such equations, a series of numbers could be obtained in which certain laws should exist and might be discovered.[64]

---

[63] I am tempted to see the peculiar "General Boon" passage of 8.60 ff. as an effort to describe a kind of Goldilocks effect: the ideal degree of sociability and the proper number of offspring. "Nor yet too many nor too few their numbers," the narrator remarks of Boon's "sylvan tribe" of children (8.67.3).

[64] Tolstoy, *War and Peace*, 1113. This equation, as an earlier passage makes clear, is implicitly underwritten by developments in calculus that take into account not only "disconnected units"

48   THE NUMBER SENSE

Before focusing on perhaps the most famous number in Victorian verse—the noble "Six hundred" of Tennyson's "The Charge of the Light Brigade"— Matthew Bevis observes that the poet uses "numbers" as a noun only thrice in his poetry, always in the context of warfare (the Latin *numerus* is also a term for a body of troops), noting also that "The word 'numberless' appears only once ... (when he's counting the dead at the Battle of Brunanburh— 'numberless numbers')."[65] This military context supports Bevis's reading of the notoriously imprecise body count of "The Charge" as evidence that "poetic numbers may be implicated in a process that turns individuals into approximations."[66] Recall also the millions of the Waterloo passages of *Childe Harold*. Or how the "crowd" of "ten thousand" daffodils in "I wandered lonely as a cloud" is called a "host," a word that has distinctly Miltonic and martial overtones.

Five, though, like Wordsworth's *seven* and Carroll's *four*, is a figure we can conjure. In a manner that may initially bring to mind "The Last of the Flock," Byron offers us a count that is implicitly a kind of countdown, as the sons are slaughtered one by one before their father's eyes:

> At last they perished:
> His second son was levelled by a shot;
> His third was sabred; and the fourth, most cherished
> Of all the five, on bayonets met his lot;
> The fifth, who, by a Christian mother nourished
> Had been neglected, ill-used, and what not,
> Because deformed, yet died all game and bottom,
> To save a sire who blushed that he begot him.
>
> (8.110.1–8)[67]

The eldest, "a true and tameless Tartar," survives longest, lasting through four more stanzas until finally succumbing with multiple "houris in his sight" (8.111.1, 8.114.1). None but the father now remains; he, "like a felled

---

but also "continuous movement." It thus attempts to calculate the force of an army in a manner registering the movement of history in its collective "spirit" (rather than assuming everything depends on the "genius" of its leaders or on its size) (*War and Peace*, 881–2). In this way, the novel uses modern mathematics to attack the "great man" theory of history (see also Hart, *Once Upon a Prime*, 136–8).

[65] Bevis, "Poetry by Numbers," 51.

[66] Bevis, "Poetry by Numbers," 52. See also my chapter, "Making Soldiers Count: Literature and War in the 1850s," in which I consider the various maneuvers around the counting of soldiers in the period (both literary and actual), including in Tennyson's ballad.

[67] The countdown here anticipates a temporal feature of Trollope's writing that I will discuss at more length in Chapter 4.

BYRON'S COUNTS 49

tree, / Paused for a moment from the fight and cast / A glance on that slain son, his first and last," "And felt, though done with life, he was alone" (8.116.6–8, 8.117.8). That *though* sums up the full burden of the father's loss: so great as to matter beyond life, making even a dead man feel his solitude. A stark contrast with his son's vision of houris, we seem weirdly to be transported into a nightmarish reversal of the girl's enmeshed life in "We Are Seven." Yet if the scene also recalls, as I have hinted, the vision of Wordsworth's shepherd, whose tally at poem's close has fallen similarly from "one" to "none," the effect here is rather different. Wordsworth's counting felt like the source of the ethical dilemma in "The Last of the Flock"; Byron's appears to carry, albeit heavily, a more positive form of moral significance.

While the overall number of deaths may be largest here in the war cantos, the principle of the countdown enters earlier, in Canto 2's narrative of the shipwreck.[68] The death of the khan's sons before his very eyes reprises one of that episode's most moving parts, in which "two fathers" must witness the demise of their "two sons," one who goes quickly, the other who lingers.[69] Such doubling of what seems single, if not singular, suggests already a strange toggle between the one and the many (as we will see again when we come to Dickens in Chapter 3):

> There were two fathers in this ghastly crew,
> 　And with them their two sons, of whom the one
> Was more robust and hardy to the view,
> 　But he died early; and when he was gone,
> His nearest messmate told his sire, who threw
> 　One glance at him, and said, "Heaven's will be done!"
>
> 　　　　　　　　　　　　　　(2.87.1–6)

---

[68] Clare Pettitt looks at this shipwreck scene in *Serial Forms*. Perhaps surprisingly, though, she makes no mention of what I take here to be the key element of seriality in the episode: the diminishing numbers. This silence likely results from her interest in the passage's "visual effects," especially in comparison to panoramas and Géricault's contemporary *Raft of the Medusa* (1819). Painting, which captures a moment in time, can't easily record this particular version of serial narrative (in general, Pettitt's view of seriality deemphasizes simple temporal progression). Her chapter instead "considers the history of the shipwreck as (impossibly) 'live' performance, and analyses the strong sentiments of disgust elicited by both Byron's poem and Géricault's picture, concluding that it is both their reference to a 'real' news item, and their creation of virtual bodies to represent catastrophic death, that triggered such strong critical reactions" (25).

[69] Favret points to a place in David Hume's *Treatise of Human Nature* in which the philosopher considers how a father's response to a letter announcing the death of an unnamed son changes depending upon the number of sons he possesses ("Feeling for Numbers," 190–3). Such uncertainty stands in marked contrast to the experience of Byron's witnessing fathers—and of his witnessing readers, as well.

50 THE NUMBER SENSE

In this dark take on "one-and-done," in which *gone* uneasily mediates the significance of the stanza's B-rhyme, we see both the ominous side of the formula and its fallacy: the circumstances are about to be multiplied in the other father–son pairing. These deaths are also reckoned within a longer account of depleting numbers, as the "thirty" (2.63.1) who are rescued from the sinking ship in which "near two hundred souls" perished (2.55.1) gradually find "Their numbers ... much thinned," until they are finally "reduced to four" (2.80.1, 2.101.4), of whom one is devoured by a shark and "two" "could not swim" (2.106.7). And then there was one—Juan: "So nobody arrived on shore but him" (2.106.8). That this has been a numbers game finds literal support in the fact that the "one oar" (2.70.5) that had been so useless for propelling the craft—and thus saving the many—now becomes a life-preserving flotation device for the singular Juan (2.107.1–6).[70]

Marjorie Levinson's account of number in Wordsworth, "Of Being Numerous," takes its cue from George Oppen's 1968 collection of the same name, in which the title poem, itself comprised of forty short lyrics (the duration of the biblical flood?), emerges out of a scenario that Byron's hero's predicament summons up:

> Obsessed, bewildered
>
> By the shipwreck
> Of the singular
>
> We have chosen the meaning
> Of being numerous.[71]

"The shipwreck / Of the singular" describes Juan's position perfectly.[72] Oppen, a combat veteran of World War II, wrote these verses while living in New York City during the Vietnam War, and they are driven by wartime reflections on humanity's essentially social nature. Byron also turns to serial poetry—albeit of a very different form—and to the experience of war to think through the meaning of being numerous. Regardless of the challenges, he determines, we still need to keep count.

---

[70] It might also remind us of Odysseus—another only son from a line of only sons—washing ashore alone on the coast of Scheria.

[71] "Of Being Numerous," lyric 7. In George Oppen, *New Collected Poems*, ed. Michael Davidson (New York: New Directions, 2002), 163–208 (from stanzas 6 and 7).

[72] Pettitt suggestively cites Hans Blumenberg's argument "that the shipwreck becomes the core metaphor for modern subjectivity in 'the newly emerging [in the nineteenth century] historical consciousness'" (*Serial Forms*, 109).

1.5 Taking Measure

I have argued that despite Leila's rescue, *Don Juan* doesn't really teach us empathy. Nor does it teach us how to respond rationally to the sufferings of millions. What it does teach is how to get a *feel* for counting, for a process that can lead us from the one toward the many without succumbing to the hard logic of statistical enumeration. And part of the lesson is delivered formally. I am struck in the episode of the five sons, for example, by how Byron accentuates the count when suggesting meaningful overlap between the poem's *ottava rima* and the five sequential deaths with which that form must reckon. Four of the five sons perish during a single stanza (8.110, quoted above): the second son dies in the second line, the third in the third, the fourth in the fourth. Then the *ottava rima* lingers with the final (and eldest) son's death, which occurs over the course of a series of stanzas; like the old khan, we move from many to one and feel the increasing emotional stakes as the numbers diminish. But, by the same token, the episode as a whole begins to build a sense for larger numbers: if this is what it means to count down from five, try to extrapolate from the experience to imagine what it might mean to count down from a thousand. Or, perhaps, try to picture this serial episode's being replicated (iterated?) in scores of locations across the field of battle.

Repeatedly, the narrator makes it clear that Byron is thinking about the affordances of his chosen form. Consider how his extended serial verse contrasts with the poetry of Suwarrow. Byron records the notorious fact that the Russian general announced his victory to Catherine in a couplet: "She smiled at mad Suwarrow's rhymes, who threw / Into a Russian couplet rather dull / The whole gazette of thousands whom he slew" (9.60.2–4). Such condensation stands in stark opposition to Byron's expansive efforts to measure the scale of the losses through his poetic measure. Yet *Don Juan* is a countertext not only to Suwarrow's couplet but also to the lists that constitute the *Gazette*. Recall the opening stanza, with its dismissal of the endless record of heroes whose names are "cloying the gazettes with cant": it was against this generic backdrop that Juan had first emerged as an alternative. In fact, like Suwarrow's couplet, the *Gazette's* long list also represents a form of "contraction" that threatens to erase the many from historical memory:

> Thus even good Fame may suffer sad contractions
> And is extinguished sooner than she ought.
> Of all our modern battles, I will bet
> You can't repeat nine names from each *Gazette*.
>
> (7.34.5–8)

52 THE NUMBER SENSE

Note once more the emphasis on names, those supposed bastions of individuality, which here may be forgotten or else falsely transcribed. This dual danger catalyzes the narrator's rescue of his singular "hero":

> But here I leave the general concern,
> To track our hero on his path of fame,
> He must his laurels separately earn;
> For fifty thousand heroes, name by name,
> Though all deserving equally to turn
> A couplet, or an elegy to claim,
> Would form a lengthy lexicon of glory
> And what is worse still a much longer story.
>
> And therefore we must give the greater number
> To the *Gazette*, which doubtless fairly dealt
> By the deceased, who lie in famous slumber
> In ditches, fields, or wheresoe'er they felt
> Their clay for the last time their souls encumber.
> Thrice happy he whose name has been well spelt
> In the dispatch; I knew a man whose loss
> Was printed Grove, although his name was Grose.
>
> (8.17.1–18.8)

Of course, while he may have spelled it correctly, Byron had anglicized the proper pronunciation of his hero's name in the first stanza of *Don Juan*—as, for that matter, he surely mangles "Grose" in the final couplet quoted here.

Such passages show how intimately Byron associates questions of naming with issues of number and genre. His narration of the sack of Ismail repeatedly invokes the *Gazette* as the appropriate text for recording the deeds of the "greater number" (the *Morning Post* performs an analogous function in the English Cantos [13.53–4]). Yet the "thrice happy" of these lines reminds us that another form has long attempted to account for the heroics—and the deaths—of the battlefield: the epic. While Byron had declared his poem an epic in the first canto (1.200.1), and while the episode of the shipwreck may harken back to the diminishing numbers of Odysseus's shipmates, the Ismail cantos most forcefully insist on this generic lineage. Thus, the episode of the (unnamed) "brave Tartar khan" recalls both the *Iliad* and the *Aeneid*, in which sons must die in order to register the intense emotional cost of warfare (the *Iliad* closes with the return of Hektor's body to Priam, who also must witness his son Politës's murder towards the start of the *Aeneid*). As

BYRON'S COUNTS   53

it happens, Alex Woloch opens *The One vs. the Many* with a reading of the *Iliad* that describes a contest waged between his titular categories on the very field of epic battle: "Achilles' honor is produced through this destruction of the many, but such destruction can always potentially wrest attention away from the protagonist."[73] Names are crucial to the process of articulating this contest:

> The distinction between counting and naming occurs precisely at the fault line where an individual ceases to command attention as a qualitatively distinct being and begins to be viewed as a quantitative unit, absorbed into a larger number even as the ordinary soldiers are encompassed by the "lords of the ships" who represent them and do get named.[74]

For Woloch, moreover, names help identify his "two extreme modes of characterization": "the protagonist, whose identity rests on a narrative centrality that always threatens to take the form of wrath (erasing or absorbing all the other persons who surround him), and the minor characters who, simply through their subordinated multiplicity, hover vulnerably on the borderline between name and number."[75]

Nothing in Homer, though, can describe this "borderline" state "between name and number" with the precision of Byron's rhymes, which often make use of the malleability of names to create a kind of "multiplicity" that nevertheless seems to escape subordination. Rhyme's literal "borderline" position, most often standing on the brink between one line and the next, helps emphasize this fact. Byron takes advantage of the way that the designatory power of names doesn't lie in any preordained spelling or pronunciation. This feature allows for a peculiar form of poetic license, which Byron uses to stress not the individuality of a name but rather its shared nature. Indeed, even those names that Byron places in the middle of his lines seem crafted to remind us that we are somewhere in the center, between the one and the many.[76] Unlike novelistic names, which often enshrine individual identity, Byron's names offer neither such promise of particularity nor the solution to the dangerous threat to singularity posed by statistical information that

---

[73] Woloch, *The One vs. the Many*, 3.

[74] Woloch, *The One vs. the Many*, 5.

[75] Woloch, *The One vs. the Many*, 7.

[76] My sense of the poem's preference for middles resonates with Peter J. Manning's declaration that the poem "is all middle" ("*Don Juan* and Byron's Imperceptiveness to the English Word," *Studies in Romanticism* 18.2 [1979], 221).

54 THE NUMBER SENSE

Nathan K. Hensley identifies as part of their power in Victorian fiction.[77]
Consider the following attempt to account for the Russian heroes:

> How shall I spell the name of each Cossack—
> Who were immortal, could one tell their story?
> Alas, what to their memory can lack?
> Achilles' self was not more grim and gory
> Than thousands of this new and polished nation,
> Whose names want nothing but—pronunciation.
>
> Still I'll record a few, if but to increase
> Our euphony: there was Strongenoff, and Strokonoff,
> Meknop, Serge Lwow, Arseniew of modern Greece,
> And Tschitsshakoff, and Roguenoff, and Chokenoff,
> And others of twelve consonants apiece;
> And more might be found out, if I could poke enough
> Into gazettes; but Fame (capricious strumpet),
> It seems, has got an ear as well as trumpet
>
> And cannot tune those discords of narration,
> Which may be names at Moscow, into rhyme.
> Yet there were several worth commemoration,
> As ere was virgin of a nuptial chime,
> Soft words too fitted for the peroration
> Of Londonderry, drawling against time,
> Ending in ischskin, ousckin, iffskchy, ouski,
> Of whom we can insert but Rousamouski, ...

$$(7.14.3-16.8)$$

These lists, which start out by recording the names—albeit with proto-
Dickensian comical transliteration—of real Russian military men mentioned in Byron's source text (by Gabriel de Castelnau), are soon reduced by
the needs of Byron's "narration" to the record of common "ending[s]" that
could facilitate the poet's "euphony" and "rhyme." Singularities thus make
way for the larger numbers implied by the rhyming patronymic suffixes.

If you are tempted to proclaim this confusion a function of the strangeness
of those Russian names, something very similar happens when Byron turns
his attention to the lists of English soldiers. Once again names, which should
identify individuals, appear to point to many. Byron's narrator pauses over

---

[77] See Hensley, *Forms of Empire*, 131.

BYRON'S COUNTS 55

a group of mercenaries, including "several Englishmen of pith, / Sixteen called Thomson and nineteen named Smith" (7.18.7–8). And if you think that Christian names may help discriminate among these, the narrator soon dispels this illusion: while the Thomsons include a "Jack Thomson and Bill Thomson—all the rest / Had been called 'Jemmy,' after the great bard" (note the nod to poetry as a force behind the confusion). Similarly, while "Three of the Smiths were Peters," "The rest were Jacks and Gills and Wills and Bills" (7.19.1–2, 7.19.5, 7.20.1) (note here how they metastasize via superfluous internal rhyme). When it comes to the fortunes of war, both Russians and Englishmen succumb in the numbers implied within their names, as when the same bombardment becomes "The cause of killing Tchitchitzkoff and Smith, / One of the valorous Smiths whom we shall miss / Out of those nineteen who late rhymed to pith" (7.25.4–6).

But what of "our hero," Juan? Far from providing a backdrop against which he might emerge like Achilles (or Tom Jones) in all his glorious singularity—as Byron's narrator suggests Juan will do when announcing his intention to "leave the general concern, / To track our hero on his path of fame"—this litany of shared and similar names brings out his resemblance to all these other figures. In this regard, it multiplies the doubling effect produced by Juan's friendship with John Johnson, whose own name not only reproduces itself but also anglicizes and harmonizes with Juan's (as Johnson's serial marriages anglicize Juan's continental adulterous loves). Byron's poetry reinforces the connection both by verbal pairings (such as "Juan and Johnson" [8.19.1]) and by placing the names in proximate and parallel places within his stanzas (7.75.1, 7.75.3). Thus, like one of Woloch's minor characters, Juan, despite his centrality, stands precariously on the borderline between a name and a number. While Juan may initially occupy a privileged position as the poem's "true one," the vocal distortion required to fit him to this measure is a product of a more significant literary distortion: the dissolution of the one, if not into the many, at least into the several.

So we start to count beyond the one. Early in his poem, Byron's narrator pauses to apologize for what he admits to be a particularly unprofitable digression:

> Sure my invention must be down at zero,
>   And I grown one of many "wooden spoons"
> Of verse (the name with which we Cantabs please
> To dub the last of honours in degrees).
>
> (3.110.5–8)

56 THE NUMBER SENSE

The reference here is to the Mathematical Tripos at Cambridge, at the time a required exam from which Byron himself was exempted only by virtue of his aristocratic standing. But far from being a "'wooden spoon' / Of verse," Byron develops in *Don Juan* into a genuine "poet[] of arithmetic" (his scathingly applied term for the Chancellors of the Exchequer, who demonstrate such flexibility with their numbers) (16.99.1).[78] By the final but incomplete canto, even the narrator admits his own singularity to be a fallacy, his inconsistencies so significant "that I almost think that the same skin / For one without has two or three within" (17.11.7–8). It is a lesson Byron has learned from his "only" yet plural hero and from the mathematical operations of the rhymed verse that contains him. By inviting us to count, *Don Juan* offers an antidote not just to the kinds of indifference prompted by the larger numbers of modern statistical experience but also to novelistic full immersion in a singular experience. In place of these alternatives, we keep adding: zero, one, two, three ...

---

[78] It is apt that Byron's only legitimate child, his daughter Ada Lovelace, is celebrated as a mathematician; she lived up to the promise of her given name. The friend and pupil of Charles Babbage, Lovelace was dubbed "the enchantress of numbers" and has been credited with writing the first algorithmic computer program for Babbage's "analytical engine." A computer language has been named in her honor. She also served as an inspiration for Tom Stoppard's portrayal of Thomasina Coverly, the doomed young protagonist of *Arcadia* (1993). Stoppard's play about sex, death, and poetry, over which Byron hovers as a kind of invisible muse, alternates between a Regency past and a present in which a pair of dueling academics try to recover the truth of that past (at times resorting to stylometric analysis)—in particular, the events of a visit Byron paid to the Coverlys shortly before his first departure from England in 1809. See also Imogen Forbes-MacPhail, "The Enchantress of Numbers and the Magic Noose of Poetry: Literature, Mathematics, and Mysticism in the Nineteenth Century," *Journal of Language, Literature and Culture* 60.3 (2013): 138–56. Tina Young Choi also briefly considers Babbage and Lovelace's relationship in *Victorian Contingencies: Experiments in Literature, Science, and Play* (Stanford: Stanford University Press, 2012), 36–8.

2

Jane Austen, by *Half*

2.1 Let's Do the Numbers

Despite their contemporaneity, prim Aunt Jane seems to occupy a very different cultural space from the author of *Don Juan*'s serial loves. When he features her in his "Letter to Lord Byron," however, W. H. Auden implies a resemblance:

> You could not shock her more than she shocks me;
>   Beside her Joyce seems innocent as grass.
> It makes me most uncomfortable to see
>   An English spinster of the middle-class
>   Describe the amorous effects of "brass",
> Reveal so frankly and with such sobriety
> The economic basis of society.[1]

This "economic basis of society" is, obviously, also a numbers game. Austen's persistent—nay, notorious—attention to "Money" is enough to merit its own thus-bluntly-titled chapter in the *Cambridge Companion* to the novelist's work. Here, Edward Copeland observes that, since "the heartbeat of romance lies in a good income," we almost always know how many thousands a year an Austenian hero will bestow upon his lucky bride.[2] It makes perfect sense, then, that since 2017 her portrait has graced the British ten-pound banknote. Even the "BabyLit" *Pride and Prejudice* board book takes the form of "a counting primer" progressing from "1 english [*sic*] village," through "2 rich gentlemen" and "5 sisters" ... not to 10, but to "10,000 pounds a year."[3]

---

[1] W. H. Auden, "Letter to Lord Byron," in *The English Auden*, ed. Edward Mendelson (London: Faber & Faber, 1986), 171. Notice again how, as through Bulson and Kurnick in my previous chapter, the numbery Joyce also finds his way into this mix.

[2] Edward Copeland, "Money," in *The Cambridge Companion to Jane Austen*, ed. Edward Copeland and Juliet McMaster (Cambridge: Cambridge University Press, 2010), 129.

[3] Jennifer Adams, *Pride and Prejudice* (Layton, UT: Gibbs Smith, 2011).

The Number Sense of Nineteenth-Century British Literature. Stefanie Markovits, Oxford University Press. © Stefanie Markovits (2025). DOI: 10.1093/9780198937821.003.0003

58 THE NUMBER SENSE

In other words, the frequently acknowledged truth of Jane Austen's unusual numberiness rests largely with her tendency, as in *Pride and Prejudice* (1813), to soon depart from the abstractions of the "single" and the "universal" into the relative specifics of Mr. Bingley's "four or five thousand a year" and Mr. Darcy's "ten."[4] News of the latter figure is "in general circulation within five minutes after [Darcy's] entrance" at the ball at which our protagonists meet. But that information had itself been anticipated by an earlier numerically oriented rumor:

> a report ... that Mr. Bingley was to bring twelve ladies and seven gentlemen with him to the assembly. The girls grieved over such a number of ladies, but were comforted the day before the ball by hearing, that instead of twelve he brought only six with him from London—his five sisters and a cousin. And when the party entered the assembly room it consisted of only five altogether—Mr. Bingley, his two sisters, the husband of the eldest, and another young man.
>
> *(PP 6)*

While these final odds may seem rather more favorable for our five Bennet sisters, we are reminded of the risks posed by the bigger picture when we learn that at the ball, "Elizabeth Bennet had been obliged, by the scarcity of gentlemen, to sit down for two dances" (*PP* 7).

So, as we keep the pounds in mind, we must also consider the populations among which they will circulate. If her novels testify to how ballrooms encourage such tallying, Austen's correspondence does, too. "Our Ball was very thin, but by no means unpleasant.—There were 31 People, & only 11 Ladies out of the Number, & but five single women in the room. Of the Gentlemen present You may have some idea from the list of my Partners," the twenty-three-year old Austen wrote happily to her sister on Christmas Eve, 1798.[5] Two years later, she displayed rather less satisfaction when describing another dance, using an expression that is replicated in *Pride and Prejudice*: "There was a scarcity of Men in general, & a still greater scarcity of any that were good for much" (*Letters* 53). The opening chapters of *Pride and Prejudice* thus show how numbers determine the marriage market that constitutes Austen's courtship plots.

---

[4] Jane Austen, *Pride and Prejudice*, ed. James Kinsley (Oxford: Oxford University Press, 1998), 1, 6. Hereafter *PP*, followed by a page reference.

[5] Jane Austen, *Jane Austen's Letters*, ed. Deidre Le Faye, 3rd ed. (Oxford: Oxford University Press, 1997), 29. Hereafter *Letters*, followed by a page reference.

Hence the odd-couple romance between this Regency-era novelist and modern economists. Thomas Piketty begins *Capital in the Twenty-First Century* by admiring how Austen "grasped the hidden contours of wealth and its inevitable implications for the lives of men and women, including their marital strategies," "depict[ing] the effects of inequality with a verisimilitude and evocative power that no statistical or theoretical analysis can match."[6] Regardless of such warnings, Michael Suk-Young Chwe's game-theoretical approach to Austen attempts to translate her characters' complex motives, including economic ones, into numbers. Chwe must even introduce additional figures, generated imaginatively from the details of Austen's text. He explains how "The core model of rational choice theory is payoff maximization: a person has numerical payoffs for each alternative and chooses the one with the highest payoff." While "Assigning payoff numbers to outcomes might seem artificial and crude," it is nevertheless, according to Chwe, "a convenient way to notate a person's ranking from best to worst."[7] His processes highlight how, for all their ostensible facticity (see Poovey), numbers often serve as a site in which fact and fiction combine.

But despite the recent concern for her keen financial eye, Austen is (like Byron) a creature of her own day in her regard for figures; her era was broadly numbery, as I have been arguing. Think of how her term for the paucity of men at the ball—*scarcity*—triggers competition in eighteenth-century economic theory. Karen O'Brien has even suggested that as the daughter of a rector, Austen may well have been involved with the collection of information for the 1801 census, which "required local clergymen to trawl through their parish registers and record numbers of baptisms and burials at ten-year intervals from 1700, along with the annual numbers of marriages from 1754."[8] As I have mentioned, Thomas Malthus's *Essay on the Principle of Population* went through six editions between 1798 and 1826: roughly the same period, that is, in which Austen composed her six novels. O'Brien surmises that Austen would have been acquainted with the *Essay*. Moreover,

---

[6] Thomas Piketty, *Capital in the Twenty-First Century* (Cambridge, MA: Harvard University Press, 2014), 2.

[7] Michael Suk-Young Chwe, *Jane Austen, Game Theorist* (Princeton: Princeton University Press, 2013), 11. William Stanley Jevon's earlier efforts (in the 1870s) to think through economic preferences in mathematical terms did not rely on assigning numbers to the utility of a given choice; instead, his metaphor was of an imagined balance, teetering according to preferences. See Audrey Jaffe, *The Affective Life of the Average Man*, 11. The metaphor actually aligns neatly with the Austenian number on which this chapter will come to rest: half.

[8] Karen O'Brien, "The Cultural and Literary Significance of the 1803 Essay," in *Thomas Robert Malthus, An Essay on the Principle of Population: The 1803 Edition*, ed. Shannon Stimson (New Haven, CT: Yale University Press, 2018), 549.

60   THE NUMBER SENSE

she observes that Austen's views of the marriage market reflect the "national resonance" issues of marriage had gained in the wake of Malthus's theories.[9]

Still, not all Austen's numbers refer to money and populations: many refer to time. Consider Anne Elliot's musings at the start of *Persuasion* (1818) on the "eight years" that "had passed" since her initial romance with Wentworth, which, by the novel's end, have become "Eight years and a half," "a period, indeed!"[10] Other figures track space: Precise distances locate the homes of the "3 or 4 Families in a Country Village" comprising the novels (*Letters* 275)—quintessentially, *Emma* (1815), where the plot is launched by the "half a mile" separation occasioned by Mrs. Weston's marriage and departure for Randalls.[11] Given that each novel narrates the removal of the heroine from one home to another (somewhat poignantly, with the single exception of *Emma*), such geographical precision often records the locational implications of the term *plotting*.[12] As Yoon Sun Lee has argued, "Austen emphasizes abstract, uniform units of measurement that can be used to calculate distance and coordinate actions in time. Small-scale synchronization is her hallmark."[13]

This attention to precision seems in tension, however, with a paradoxical awareness of numbers' failure to signify consistently across various kinds of experience. That is to say, numbers stage a contest between subjective and objective versions of knowledge. Recall Elizabeth's irritated response to Darcy's claim that the "nearly fifty miles" separating Charlotte Collins from her family in Hertfordshire must have been among the attractions of her marriage: what he may call a "*very* easy distance"—"Little more than half a day's journey"—seems more like an expedition to others (especially women of lesser means). As Elizabeth punningly remarks, "I do not mean to say that a woman may not be settled too near her family. The far and the near must

---

[9] O'Brien, "The Cultural and Literary Significance," 560. For more on connections between Austen and the field of political economy in her day, see Sheryl Craig, *Jane Austen and the State of the Nation* (New York: Palgrave Macmillan, 2015).

[10] Jane Austen, *Persuasion*, ed. James Kinsley (Oxford: Oxford University Press, 2004), 53, 181. Hereafter *P*, followed by a page reference.

[11] Jane Austen, *Emma*, ed. James Kinsley (Oxford: Oxford University Press, 2003), 6. Hereafter *E*, followed by a page reference.

[12] See Peter Brooks's account of "The Musgrave Ritual" in *Reading for the Plot: Design and Intention in Narrative* (Cambridge, MA: Harvard University Press, 1992), in which he shows how Sherlock Holmes must literally retrace the steps of the criminal to uncover the story (23–8). In Chapter 4 I will consider at more length how temporal numbers intersect with plot.

[13] Yoon Sun Lee, "Austen's Scale-Making," *Studies in Romanticism* 52.2 (Summer 2013), 173, 175, 176. See also Janine Barchas's *Matters of Fact in Jane Austen* (Baltimore: Johns Hopkins University Press, 2012), which argues for the novelist's "cartographic exactitude," comparing the mapping of *Northanger Abbey* to that executed by James Joyce in *Ulysses* (60).

be relative" (*PP* 137). In contrast with her narrator's methods of "abstract, uniform measurement," Austen's characters frequently show how "the far and the near" are indeed "relative." Edmund Bertram and Mary Crawford's argument concerning the distance they have covered while wandering about the wilderness at Sotherton reflects such ambiguity. When Edmund points to his watch ("We have been exactly a quarter of an hour here") and the impossibility of their "walking four miles an hour" to prove that they have gone "not half a mile," Mary retorts, "A watch is always too fast or too slow. I cannot be dictated to by a watch."[14] Or think of how John Thorpe maneuvers the numbers to impress Catherine with the speed of his horses when discussing his journey from Tetbury with her brother, who had bluntly stated the distance travelled to be "twenty-three miles":

> "Three and twenty!" cried Thorpe. "Five and twenty if it is an inch." Morland remonstrated, pleaded the authority of road-books, innkeepers, and milestones; but his friend disregarded them all; he had a surer test of distance. "I know it must be five and twenty," said he, "by the time we have been doing it. It is now half after one; we drove out of the inn-yard at Tetbury as the town clock struck eleven; and I defy any man in England to make my horse go less than ten miles an hour in harness; that makes it exactly twenty-five."

When Morland corrects him, "it was only ten o'clock when we came from Tetbury," Thorpe persists in his claim: "Such true blood! Three hours and a half indeed coming only three and twenty miles! Look at that creature, and suppose it possible if you can."[15]

If, in both these instances, we may be primed to mistrust those characters who tamper with the objective measures, Austen's novels at times appear to encourage awareness of how many reckonings involve acts of

---

[14] Jane Austen, *Mansfield Park*, ed. James Kinsley (Oxford: Oxford University Press, 2003), 75–6; hereafter *MP*, followed by a page reference. And this despite the fact that—as I mentioned in my Introduction—Mary Crawford often processes her experience of the people around her through statistically oriented numbers: "about any three sisters just grown up ... one knows, without being told, exactly what they are: all very accomplished and pleasing, and one very pretty. There is a beauty in every family; it is a regular thing. Two play on the pianoforte, and one on the harp; and all sing" (*MP* 226); or, as she writes to Fanny of Edmund, "Mrs. Fraser (no bad judge) declares she knows but three men in town who have so good a person, height, and air; and I must confess, when he dined here the other day, there were none to compare with him, and we were a party of sixteen" (*MP* 326).

[15] Jane Austen, *Northanger Abbey, Lady Susan, The Watsons, Sanditon*, ed. James Kinsley and John Davie (Oxford: Oxford University Press, 2003), 30. Hereafter *NA*, followed by a page number.

62   THE NUMBER SENSE

imagination for which the form of her own fiction provides an almost ontological support. Consider the scene in *Sense and Sensibility* (1811) in which "one subject only engaged the ladies till coffee came in, which was the comparative heights of Harry Dashwood, and Lady Middleton's second son William, who were nearly of the same age." As Austen notes, "Had both the children been there, the affair might have been determined too easily by measuring them at once; but as Harry only was present, it was all conjectural assertion on both sides; and every body had a right to be equally positive in their opinion, and to repeat it over and over again as often as they liked" (*SS* 176). Of course, in a novel, the things being measured are never actually "there."

Such balance between numbers' subjective and objective resonances seems almost to be condensed and reified by Jane Austen's own favoring within her fictions of one figure over others—to be more specific, her favoring of one figured over two, or *half* (1/2). Austen's unequal partiality for a number that stands for equality has intrinsic ironies; as defined by Dr. Johnson's *Dictionary*, a *half* represents "A moiety; one part of two; an equal part."[16] But once noticed, the penchant is hard to ignore. How else explain the odd extravagance of the description of Miss Lambe, the West Indian heiress who makes a brief, tantalizing appearance in Austen's final, incomplete novel, *Sanditon*, as "half Mulatto, chilly and tender"?[17] And while I was not (at least not intentionally) selecting them for this purpose, the preference also appears in the examples listed above: "Eight years and a half," "half a mile," "half a day's journey." As it happens, Bingley's reported yearly income is also half Darcy's, although Lizzy, as her mother asserts in the novel's opening exchange, "is not a bit better than the others; and I am sure she is not half so handsome as Jane, nor half so good-humoured as Lydia" (*PP* 1). By her measure, then, Austen's marriage plot reckoning in *Pride and Prejudice* fails to add up.[18]

The word *half* does not appear often enough to have made it into J. F. Burrows's early stylometric approach to the novels, *Computation into Criticism*, but it does grace his opening take on the famous first line of *Pride and*

---

[16] Samuel Johnson, *Dictionary of the English Language*, 5th ed. (London, 1785).

[17] Jane Austen, *Sanditon*, in *NA* 341.

[18] The resulting probabilistic unlikelihood is emphasized by the novel's take on statistical formulas to consider character (in a manner related to my discussion of *Jane Eyre* in the Introduction). Charlotte Lucas warns Elizabeth of the dangers of Jane's modest self-presentation to Bingley, observing that "In nine cases out of ten, a woman had better show *more* affection than she feels" (*PP* 16). One way to consider the plot of *Pride and Prejudice* is to note that Darcy and Lizzy are the tenth case!

Prejudice, intimating the happy marriage between statistical methods and Austen's numberiness: "It is a truth not generally acknowledged that, in most discussions of works of English fiction, we proceed as if a third, two-fifths, a half of our material were not really there. For Jane Austen, that third, two-fifths or a half comprises the twenty, thirty or fifty most common words of her literary vocabulary."[19] Building upon Burrows's "experiment in method," Victorina González-Díaz and Janine Barchas have contemplated the novelist's employment of the "degree words" *quite* and *very*.[20] *Half* may be rarer than these, but it appears more regularly in Austen's novels than in those of almost all of her best-known contemporaries. Thus, *Emma*, just above the middle of Austen's range of *half*-richness, turns to it roughly once every 1,300 words. Maria Edgeworth deploys the number at about three-quarters this rate in *Belinda* (1801), and Frances Burney uses it less than half as often in *Evelina* (1778). While one might presume Sir Walter Scott to have found fertile ground for *half* in *Waverley* (1814), given Edward's split Scottish-English loyalties, *Emma* resorts to it more than twice as frequently. Ann Radcliffe is even less fond of *half*. Of the contemporary authors I surveyed, only Samuel Richardson shares Austen's consistent predilection for the fraction[21]—especially in her favorite novel, *Sir Charles Grandison* (1753), where

---

[19] J. F. Burrows, *Computation into Criticism: A Study of Jane Austen's Novels and an Experiment in Method* (Oxford: Clarendon Press, 1987), 1.

[20] Janine Barchas, "Very Austen: Accounting for the Language of *Emma*," *Nineteenth-Century Literature* 62.3 (2007): 303–38; Victorina González-Díaz, "'I *quite* detest the man': Degree Adverbs, Female Language, and Jane Austen," *Language and Literature* 23.4 (2014): 310–30.

[21] Here is a list of the frequencies tested (the number of times *half* occurs in the text divided by the total word count), calculated from word searches on Project Gutenberg editions of the novels. These numbers are no doubt imprecise, and I did not always check each instance of the word (I did, however, deduct occurrences of *behalf*). One could most likely locate other authors who share Austen's predilection; indeed, I do so in the final section of this chapter. The purpose of this quick survey was to confirm my sense that Austen's usage was unusual in her own time.

Northanger Abbey: .00079676
Sense and Sensibility: .00046904
Pride and Prejudice: .00057996
Emma: .00076337
Mansfield Park: .00086506
Persuasion: .00068199

Belinda: .00054554
Evelina: .00035842
The Romance of the Forest: .00022401
The Mysteries of Udolpho: .00024796
Pamela: .00057334

64 THE NUMBER SENSE

it shows up with much the same regularity as in *Emma*.[22] In contrast to the generous usage of the measure in her novels, Austen's letters—although otherwise fully as numbery as her books (witness the above quotations)—fail to exhibit the taste for this one.[23] The relative paucity of *half* in the correspondence suggests that its proliferation in the novels is not merely what Barchas calls "an unconscious seeping-through of Austen's own idiolect."[24] Instead, it appears a deliberate response to the pressures of her particular version of novelistic form.[25]

In her own rumination on reading Austen numerically, "Jane Austen at 25: A Life in Numbers," Mary Favret has observed that the oeuvre itself splits in half: The early books are set apart from the later Chawton novels, "two sets of three" whose "division is underwritten by the logic—and further numbers—of chronological time."[26] The tendency to halve thus appears to parallel Austen's life experience. But might it not also express some of her fundamental ideas, as already hinted by my introduction to it via the crux it creates between objective and subjective takes on number? What does it mean that

Clarissa: .00047265
Sir Charles Grandison: .00074587
Waverley: .00033184
The Heart of Midlothian: .00049111

[22] The resemblance is noteworthy, although a few stock phrases contribute greatly to it; as Sir Charles's sister Lady L. explains, "The words *half a score* run as glibly off the tongue as *half a dozen*." Samuel Richardson, *The History of Sir Charles Grandison*, 2nd ed., 6 vols. (London: 1753–4), I.415 (L51).

[23] Similarly, the use of the word *half* in the shorter juvenilia is unremarkable, a fact to which I will return. That said, the famous letter to her nephew comparing her own work to that of a miniaturist working upon a "little bit (two Inches wide) of Ivory"—a rather half-like measure—occurs in response to his lament at losing "two Chapters and a half " of his manuscript (*Letters* 323).

[24] Barchas, "Very Austen," 320.

[25] For a related case, consider Elizabeth Barrett Browning's *Aurora Leigh* (1856), in which unusual half-richness (higher than in any Austen novel: .00095192, based on a rough word count) combines with the formal hybridity of a "novel-poem" (at one point, Romney even ranks Aurora among the "Half-poets" [IV.315]). Suggestively, both the work's discomfort with the marriage plot and its series of *Emma*-like romantic (self-)recognitions overlap with themes and structures I will highlight in Austen's novels. Take Aurora's description of Lady Waldemar as woman of the world:

> Like her I'm meaning,—centre to herself,
> Who has wheeled on her own pivot half a life
> In isolated self-love and self-will.
>
> (IV.513–16)

Here the reader may sense the portrait reflecting mirror-like back onto Aurora herself (as the protest of "like her I'm meaning" hints). In Elizabeth Barrett Browning, *Aurora Leigh and Other Poems*, ed. Bolton and Holloway (London: Penguin, 1995).

[26] Mary A. Favret, "Jane Austen at 25: A Life in Numbers," *English Language Notes* 46.1 (2008), 9–10.

JANE AUSTEN, BY *HALF* 65

she likes to think by halves? I'll suggest here that looking at Austen's interest in halves reveals her ambivalence regarding the perfect fit of wholes, which, while the *telos* and ultimate source happiness in her writing, also represent structures of disciplinary containment (broadly social and, via the novel, generic) that arise in response to a scarcity economics that Austen knows well to fear. Yet while the last sentence might serve as this chapter's thesis claim, my approach will be less teleological than ruminative—rather than having parts of an argument add up to a final sum, I will keep dancing around the implications of Austen's use of the figure *half*, substituting terms where necessary, trying to maintain my balance around the central pivot of an equals sign.[27]

In taking this tack, I am engaging in my own kind of half-thinking, as the metaphor implies (there are two halves to every equation). I might in defense cite J. S. Mill's observation concerning the value of such thought (he's considering Bentham): "Almost all veins of original and striking speculation have been opened up by systematic half-thinkers: although whether these new thoughts drive out others as good, or are peacefully superadded to them, depends on whether these half-thinkers are or are not followed in their track by complete thinkers. ... [N]o whole truth is possible but by combining points of view of all the fractional truths, nor, therefore, until it has been fully seen what each fractional truth can do by itself."[28] But the shift in focus to process over product is perhaps in some ways closer to a version of Keatsian "*Negative Capability*, that is when man is capable of being in uncertainties, Mysteries, doubts, without any irritable reaching after fact & reason." Keats berates those who, like Coleridge, "would let go a fine isolated verisimilitude caught from the Penetralium of mystery, from being incapable of remaining content with half knowledge."[29] *Half knowledge* is, after all, what I am seeking here. So, if pursuit comes at a price,

---

[27] While she is not interested in the presence of the term *half* in authors' works, Sarah Hart (*Once Upon a Prime*) looks at how the fraction has been used by recent novelists to impose structure. Thus, in Eleanor Catton's *The Luminaries* (2013) (set, as it happens, in the 1860s), each chapter is half the length of the previous one. Hart shows how this pattern "is sewn into the very fabric of the book" via a number: 4096, the value of the stolen gold, the discovery of which sets the plot in motion. In a series of complicated equations emerging from a process of halving, Hart demonstrates that this same figure features in an equation that determines the length of the entire novel (42–9). In her reading of Amor Towles's *A Gentleman in Moscow* (2016) (also historical fiction, although this time set during the rise of the Soviet state, between 1922 and 1954), Hart explains how the halves work chronologically: Each time period we visit roughly doubles the span of the previous episode, until its midpoint (set during the summer solstice of the middle year in the sequence, 1938), when the process reverses itself (51).

[28] J. S. Mill, "Bentham," in *Collected Works* X.94.

[29] John Keats, Letter to George and Tom Keats, Dec. 21, 27 (?), 1817, in *Letters of John Keats: A Selection*, ed. Robert Gittings (Oxford: Oxford University Press, 1992), 43.

66 THE NUMBER SENSE

I hope to demonstrate that Austen would have understood this fact—and that the pleasures of discovering "fine isolated verisimilitude[s]" offer if not superfluous at least adequate compensation for my focus on this particular figure.

2.2 Thinking by Halves

The processes of halving and doubling have long been central to mathematics. Tobias Dantzig describes how in the Middle Ages, before the discovery of place that occurred with the innovation of the zero, long multiplication was performed by trained accountants who would work via a series of *duplations*, while division worked via *mediation*, that is, splitting a number in half.[30] As a mathematical concept, *half* also holds more recent suggestive affinities with Austen. Today, such fractions of two integers are termed *rational numbers*; although the expression was introduced only at the start of the twentieth century, it seems appropriate to an author whose approach to romance has been deemed unusually rational.

But *half* is an essentially ambivalent term, as registered by the "glass half-full" versus "glass half-empty" distinction used to discriminate between constitutional optimists and pessimists (Mr. Woodhouse's reluctance to offer guests even "A small half-glass [of wine], put into a tumbler of water" puts him firmly in the latter camp [*E* 20]). Such ambivalence appears as well in the odd discrepancy between the idioms "by half" and "by halves." While the former phrase, *OED* 7e, is defined as "by a great deal; much, considerably, far. Esp. in phr. too clever by half," the latter, *OED* 7b, instead signifies deficiency: "to the extent of a half only; imperfectly, in part; half-heartedly, with half zeal." Similarly, while "half eight" denotes 8:30 in the British vernacular, "*halb acht*" means 7:30 in German. As I hinted earlier, the proliferating *half*s thus seem to concentrate the effects of some of Austen's other supposedly objective figures, pointing toward a fundamental instability in the novels. We may think we know where we stand with this novelist, but in fact the terrain often proves as unsettling as that of the lane, "half rock, half sand," that causes the carriage at the start of *Sanditon* to overturn (*NA* 295).

Most crucially, thinking by halves entails not only ambivalence but also the recognition of lack. In Austen's imaginative universe, to speak of a *half* is simultaneously to conjure forth imaginatively the half that is missing. On

---

[30] Tobias Dantzig, *Number*, 26.

JANE AUSTEN, BY HALF   67

the most basic level, this is marriage plot math, by which two halves join at the end of the story. It is premised on the procedure of matching—again, a fundamental mathematical concept. Historians of math surmise that matching predated counting: As Dantzig explains, first, our ancestors assigned to every object of one collection an object of another, recording their flocks through tally marks, for example; then, they created "*model collections*, each typifying a possible collection" ("the wings of a bird may symbolize the number two, clover-leaves three, the legs of an animal four ..."); finally, these collections were abstracted by number words.[31] But when it comes to love stories, the idea of the missing half is as old as Plato's *Symposium*, where Aristophanes offers an etiology for love. He explains how primeval man, initially whole, was divided. In consequence, man spends his life "looking for his other half," "And when one of them meets [this] other half, the actual half of himself, ... the pair are lost in an amazement of love and friendship and intimacy."[32] Hence the achievement of what *Emma*'s final words describe as the "perfect happiness of the union" (*E* 381). The perfect match.

Yet it is worth recalling that before Plato there was Zeno, whose paradox of Achilles and the tortoise also represents a kind of thinking by halves—one that may leave readers uncertain of arrival at that desired *telos*. This version of the fraction participates in the developing mathematical conception of infinity, as Dantzig also shows.[33] So while Austen's narrator may have affirmed earlier, during *Emma*'s climactic proposal scene, that Mr. Knightley had passed "Within half an hour"—observe the time-frame, to which I will return—"from a thoroughly distressed state of mind, to something so like perfect happiness, that it could bear no other name" (*E* 339), this very affirmation betrays the truth that the state remains a fiction: a *name* rather than a fact. The use of *half* aligns, then, with what Zelda

---

[31] Dantzig, *Number*, 7. See also Marjorie Levinson's account of "We Are Seven," discussed in Chapter 1 ("Of Being Numerous"). Matching is essential to how the girl in that poem performs a kind of arithmetic that steers clear of "counting": she matches her siblings to their locations.

[32] Plato, "Symposium," in the *The Dialogues of Plato*, trans. Benjamin Jowett, 3rd ed., 5 vols. (Oxford: Oxford University Press, n.d.), I.561, 562 (§191–3). Jane Austen would have had access to a 1752 edition of *Platonis Dialogi* in the library at Godmersham. See Gillian Dow and Katie Halsey, "Jane Austen's Reading: The Chawton Years," *Persuasions On-Line* 30.2 (Spring 2010); and the 1818 catalogue of Godmersham Park Library, available online at https://chawtonhouse.org/_www/wp-content/uploads/2012/03/Godmersham-catalogue.pdf.

[33] As Dantzig explains, "There are an infinite number of stages in [Achilles's] traversing of the race-course, and each one of these stages requires a finite time. But the sum of an infinite number of finite intervals is infinite. The runner will therefore never attain his goal" (*Number*, 129). See also his later discussion of how the concept of the infinite "bridges the chasm between the inescapable conception of a world which *flows with the stream of time*, and the number concept which was born in *counting the discrete*" (*Number*, 257).

68   THE NUMBER SENSE

Boyd has pointed to as the function of Austen's modal verbs (like "must" or "should"), words that negotiate the terrain indicated in *Sense and Sensibility* by Elinor Dashwood's lament at the pull of relativism: "Are no probabilities to be accepted, merely because there are no certainties?"[34] While its status as a number may make it seem a certainty, *half* more often registers Austen's desire to maintain belief in probabilities. Or rather—to return to my earlier half-rich examples highlighting characters' subjective experiences of presumably objective numbery measures ("Little more than half a day's journey")—halves mediate experience in a way that registers both perspectives.

I first noticed Austen's thinking by halves in *Sense and Sensibility*, the novel that, perhaps surprisingly, least frequently makes use of the word itself. It initially struck me when reading the early exchange between the Dashwood sisters' half-brother John and his grasping wife Fanny, a debate about John's promise to his dying father not to forget his sisters' and stepmother's needs. This scene in Chapter 2 shows the dangerous possibilities of second thoughts—a reverse narrative to *Pride and Prejudice*'s argument against "first impressions." In fact, in many ways, the scene's mathematical mode and operations anticipate those of the opening of *Pride and Prejudice*. Only here the numbers diminish both more emphatically and less hopefully by a process of halving that—*pace* Zeno—somehow manages to get all the way down to zero.

Chapter 1 closes with John Dashwood's solitary thoughts: "he meditated within himself to increase the fortunes of his sisters by the present of a thousand pounds a-piece. He then really thought himself equal to it" (*SS* 5). But when Fanny's voice enters at the start of Chapter 2, turning his internal monologue into a dialogue, this doubling ironically encourages, in place of John's initial state of being "equal to" largesse, a process of division by half:

> "Perhaps, then, it would be better for all parties, if the sum were diminished one half.—Five hundred pounds would be a prodigious increase to their fortunes!"

---

[34] Jane Austen, *Sense and Sensibility*, ed. James Kinsley (Oxford: Oxford University Press, 2004), 60; hereafter *SS*, followed by a page reference. See Zelda Boyd, "The Language of Supposing: Modal Auxiliaries in *Sense and Sensibility*," in Janet Todd (ed.), *Jane Austen: New Perspectives, Women and Literature* ns 3 (New York: Holmes & Meier, 1983), 142–54; and Margaret Anne Doody's Introduction to the edition of the novel used here (*SS* xxx).

"Oh! beyond anything great! What brother on earth would do half so much for his sisters, even if *really* his sisters! And as it is—only half blood!— But you have such a generous spirit!"

(*SS* 8)

Half blood demands a half legacy; the reasoning has the semblance of perfect logic. Yet once introduced, the halves prove hard to contain. Soon, John's thoughts turn to an annuity for Mrs. Dashwood: "A hundred a year would make them all perfectly comfortable," he considers. Again, his wife steps in to interrogate his sums: "'To be sure,' said she, 'it is better than parting with fifteen hundred pounds [that is, thrice five hundred, since he has three sisters] at once. But, then, if Mrs. Dashwood should live fifteen years we shall be completely taken in.'" John's appalled response indicates that his intent had been to halve the number once more: "Fifteen years! my dear Fanny; her life cannot be worth half that purchase" (*SS* 8–9). By the end of the exchange, the couple deems the women sufficiently rich as-is: "Five hundred a year! I am sure I cannot imagine how they will spend half of it" (*SS* 10). John's liberal first intention has been split so often that all that remains is a plan to perform "neighbourly acts" (*SS* 10)—which dissolves into nothing when the Dashwoods leave the county.

This stunning indictment of one form of thinking by halves owes much to the scene in *Lear* where Goneril and Regan whittle away at the King's retinue of a hundred knights.[35] That moment is the product of the foolish division of the kingdom with which *Lear* opens (a scene Austen may also have been channeling in Chapter 1, when "the old Gentleman" leaves almost all of his fortune to the four-year-old John Dashwood [*SS* 3]). Lear's realm should have been shared into thirds, but Cordelia's insistence that she can promise her father only a due proportion of love, "no more nor less," since she must reserve "half" for her future husband, results in Regan's and Goneril's husbands each receiving a "moi'ty" of the inheritance (I.i.93, I.i.102, I.i.7). Like Austen's, Shakespeare's subsequent scene parodies this fractional logic. When Goneril "abate[s]" Lear of "half [his] train" (II.iv.159), he turns to Regan, reminding her of the earlier division: "Thy half o' th' kingdom hast thou not forgot, / Wherein I thee endow'd" (II.iv.180–1). But Regan has learned that *half* is not just a fixed number but a process, shifting easily

---

[35] Cecil C. Seronsy observed the connection to *Lear* in "Jane Austen's Technique," *Notes and Queries* ns 3.7 (1956): 303–5. Jocelyn Harris (*Jane Austen's Art of Memory* [Cambridge: Cambridge University Press, 1989]) and Paula Byrne (*Jane Austen and the Theatre* [London: Bloomsbury Academic, 2007]) have both explored Austen's larger debt to Shakespeare.

70   THE NUMBER SENSE

from noun to verb. When she counters with the threat of yet another split in two, we already know that Lear will keep doing the math. "Thy fifty yet doth double five and twenty, / And thou art twice her love" (II.iv.259–60), he says to Goneril, again insisting on "the bond between numerical and affective value."[36] As in *Sense and Sensibility*, however, division feeds off its own energy. Thus Goneril responds with further figures: "What need you five and twenty, ten, or five, / To follow in a house where twice so many / Have a command to tend you?" (II.iv.261–3). And Regan pursues the logic to its inevitable conclusion: "What need one?" (II.iv.263). Only at this stage does Lear recognize that calculation has its limitations, if not its limits: "O, reason not the need" (II.iv.264), he pleads.[37]

Austen similarly uses halves in her opening sequence to expose the shortcomings of rationalism. A number bearing the promise of equality thus illuminates the persistence of fundamental social inequality, especially where women are concerned. Nevertheless, Austen doesn't deny the inevitability, perhaps even the necessity, of such reasoning: We often feel compelled to understand the world through numbers. In this very novel, Elinor exhibits her "sense," with apparent narratorial approval, by insisting that her own need is but half her sister's. When Marianne, privately weighing up Willoughby's habits, figures that a "competence" would entail an income of "About eighteen hundred or two thousand a-year; not more than *that*," Elinor responds with laughter: "*Two* thousand a-year! *One* is my wealth! I guessed how it would end" (SS 69). I, too, guessed how it would end: by half. The number seems at home in a work that does so much of its reasoning by ones and twos. As Margaret Anne Doody notes, "the book is itself divided into two"—between Elinor's and Marianne's plots—even as "Almost everything and everyone must arrive in pairs": first and second attachments, two Elizas, two Ferrars brothers (SS xxxv, xxxvii).

Perhaps, then, the word *half* occurs comparatively rarely after the early scene because the logic implied by the term can subsequently go without saying. Nevertheless, a related Austenian locution might be considered as

---

[36] Paula Blank, "Shakespeare's Equalities: Checking the Math of *King Lear*," *Exemplaria* 15:2 (2003), 494. Despite the play's apparent support of her position, Cordelia's opening insistence that she reserve half her love for her future husband betrays the same belief. Neither father nor daughter seems to feel that "love is like a magic penny," in the words of the song: something that can be split among many without diminution.

[37] On the page, this "O" again tempts me again to think numerically, in terms of the "nothing" (a loaded Shakespearean word) that is zero. For more on the number zero, see Dantzig, *Number*, 31–3.

JANE AUSTEN, BY HALF 71

standing in place for the fraction: "of the two" (it implies "one of the two"—
or half). Elsewhere, Austen often uses this phrase to select the favorite from
a pair of women, most frequently (and rather movingly, given Austen's own
biography) a pair of sisters (*MP* 282, *MP* 371, *P* 64). But in *Sense and Sensibility*, both the male and female pairings seem up for grabs (see *SS* 224).
The trend culminates in Mrs. Dashwood's remarkable statement to Elinor,
on hearing of Colonel Brandon's love for Marianne: "Had I sat down to wish
for any possible good to my family, I should have fixed on Colonel Brandon's
marrying one of you as the object most desirable. And I believe Marianne
will be the most happy with him of the two" (*SS* 255). The situation makes it
momentarily unclear to which "two" people Mrs. Dashwood refers: Elinor
and Marianne, or Colonel Brandon and Willoughby (who has just paid his
fleeting exculpatory visit to the perilously ill Marianne)? The moment thus
compounds the widespread sense created by the novel that the final pairings
are less than ideal, that the lovers are at best interchangeable—at worst, that
Elinor and Colonel Brandon, Marianne and Willoughby, would have been
the more suitable matches. We are far from the world of Plato's *Symposium*.[38]
Until, that is, the novel's conclusion, where *half* reappears in the negative to
assert its governing logic in the narrator's rather forced and dubious assertion: "Marianne could never love by halves; and her whole heart became, in
time, as much devoted to her husband, as it had once been to Willoughby"
(*SS* 288).

If both *Sense and Sensibility* and *Pride and Prejudice* argue through
the dialectics of paired titles that, as Favret observes, show an authorial
mind "obsessed with conjuring multiples"—or, I might add, divisions—"of
two,"[39] *Emma* seems less divided; after all, D. A. Miller reminds us how
"'Emma' means *whole*."[40] Still, as Dr. Johnson suggests, *half* implies equality, thus suiting *Emma*'s compulsive interrogation of rank in both courtship
and friendship. Aristotelian friendship demands full parity of condition
and capacities, but Highbury "afford[s] [Emma] no equals" (*E* 7), leaving her to seek companionship with the clearly lesser Harriet Smith.[41] As
Emma admits, after her mistake over Mr. Elton comes to light, "I have been

---

[38] We may even briefly feel we have entered a universe of proto-Dickensian doubles (part of
my story in Chapter 3).

[39] Favret, "Jane Austen at 25," 10.

[40] D. A. Miller, *Jane Austen, or, The Secret of Style* (Princeton: Princeton University Press,
2003), 68.

[41] Aristotle, *Nichomichean Ethics*, in *The Basic Works of Aristotle*, ed. Richard McKeon
(New York: Random House, 1941), 1064 (Bk. 8, Ch. 5). See also Chapters 6 and 14 for
discussions of the need for equality of "station" within friendships.

72   THE NUMBER SENSE

but half a friend to [Harriet]" (*E* 109). Similarly, Emma's position without equals explains her avoidance of marriage; her intention to remain single depends both on her sense that "few married women are half as much mistress of their husband's house as I am of Hartfield" (*E* 68) and on her view, recalling Marianne's fate in *Sense and Sensibility*, that wedlock shouldn't be "entered into" with "half a heart" (*E* 42). Appropriately, her blindness regarding her own deeper desires manifests in (or is perhaps encouraged by) forms of half-awareness: "Emma, alone with her father, had half her attention wanted by him while he lamented that young people would be in such a hurry to marry—and to marry strangers too—and the other half she could give to her own view of the subject" (*E* 139); "But the sight of Mr. Knightley among the most attentive, soon drew away half Emma's mind; and she fell into a train of thinking on the subject of Mrs. Weston's suspicions [of his interest in Jane Fairfax]" (*E* 179). Nevertheless, the novel's reproductive imperative demands more, embodied as it is in Emma, "the complete picture of grown-up health": It demands a form of love that can yield not just a second half but a second-generation copy (*E* 69, 32). (Austen herself, Dear Aunt Jane, gets to realize her heroine's vision by producing *Emma* instead of another little Emma.[42]) So Emma finds herself hoisted on her own petard, as her matchmaking logic of fitting "equals" in bonds of marriage absorbs the heroine into the triple-wedding of the ending.

In fact, Austen's scenarios often make us think, like Goethe's *Elective Affinities* (1809), of atoms jostling in solution until they can finally come to rest in the strongest possible bonds. Take this walking scene in *Persuasion*:

> Everything now marked out Louisa for Captain Wentworth; nothing could be plainer; and where many divisions were necessary, or even where they were not, they walked side by side nearly as much as the other two. In a long strip of meadow land, where there was ample space for all, they were thus divided, forming three distinct parties; and to that party of the three which boasted least animation, and least complaisance, Anne necessarily belonged. She joined Charles and Mary, and was tired enough to be very glad of Charles' other arm.
>
> (*P* 76)

---

[42] See Miller's revelatory account of the cathexis between Austen and her heroine in *Jane Austen, or, The Secret of Style*, 60–8.

The couplings (and third-wheeldom) witnessed here will be disrupted by Louisa's fall, allowing for a very different set of final pairings. But while the novels do settle into their matches, the impression of arbitrariness to the pairings *can* linger: in our sense, already mentioned, that Marianne may have been happier with Willoughby; in our feeling that Henry Crawford might have been reformed by marriage to Fanny, while the love Edmund feels for her can't help but seem a little too Platonic in the more modern sense (if not disturbingly fraternal). That is to say, in notable instances the matches strike us as matters of chance rather than of destiny, as contingent rather than necessary.

Still, something else, something besides the idea of the soulmate *à la* Aristophanes, haunts not only these but also the more satisfying examples of the novels' matchmaking. Contrast Donne's celebration of love in "The Canonization"—"we two being one are it"—and his astonishing escalation of such unruly Platonic math in "Sappho to Philaenis," where Sappho invokes her beloved: "thee, my half, my all, my more."[43] Austen's couples invariably inhabit a world greater than their joint selves. Even in *Persuasion*, the most romantic of the books, where Captain Wentworth's proposal letter comes close to ringing Plato's spiritual note— "You pierce my soul," he exclaims, adding, for good measure, "I am half agony, half hope" (*P* 191)—reunion remains a decidedly terrestrial matter.

Instead, the happiest Austenian matches provide the almost ontological satisfactions of a universe that meets our cognitive, as well as our emotional, demands. It is an experience closer to what Wordsworth gets at in the "Prospectus" to *The Recluse*, when he extolls "*How exquisitely the individual Mind*"

> *to the external World*
> *Is fitted:—and how exquisitely, too—*
> *Theme this but little heard of among men—*
> *The external World is fitted to the Mind.*[44]

Such "fitting" is a half-and-half affair, as we see in "Tintern Abbey," where Wordsworth's "gleams of half-extinguished thought" nevertheless reveal

---

[43] John Donne, *John Donne's Poetry*, ed. Donald R. Dickson (New York: W. W. Norton, 2007), 78, 45.

[44] William Wordsworth, "Prospectus" to *The Recluse*, in "Preface" *to The Excursion, being a portion of The Recluse, a Poem* (London, 1814), xii–xiii (original italics).

74   THE NUMBER SENSE

how his own "eye and ear" participate in that world's formation: it is "both what they half create, / And what perceive."[45] These moments match Emma's musings at the doorway of Ford's when (between what she imagines and what she actually sees; the passage describes both) she finds herself "amused enough; quite enough": "A mind lively and at ease can do with seeing nothing, and can see nothing that does not answer" (*E* 183). For all the almost Shakespearean focus on "nothing," the chiasmus indicates that this is once again a version of thinking by halves.

William Deresiewicz, who has remarked on the Wordsworthian aspects of imagination in *Emma*, also divides Austen's career into two phases, with the Chawton novels' exhibiting a "greater syntactic freedom" that indicates Austen's debt to the Romantic poet. Deresiewicz describes Anne Elliot's first flustered, dash-laden reunion with Wentworth, in which "Her eye half met Captain Wentworth's" (*P* 52), as characteristic:

> For even as we see the late characters' feelings develop moment by moment, so, very often, do we see their thoughts simultaneously doing likewise, evolving in snatches of half-formed and provisional formulations as their feelings search for expression. Nothing could be more like the poetic practice of Wordsworth ...
>
> The early novels know no half-formed thoughts, no feelings groping to understand themselves.[46]

Often (as here), though, the syntactic fragmentation records the maneuvers required by modesty and decorum, consistent concerns for Austen throughout the oeuvre. Her protagonists always negotiate the complex private and social fictions demanded by the suppression of female sexual awareness, whether internally or externally.[47] Later in *Persuasion*, following their conversation in the assembly room in Bath, the "half averted eyes and more than half expressive glance" bestowed on Anne by Wentworth, which allow her to interpret his love, have been dictated not by a dearth of self-knowledge—in either participant—but by the need to cloak it. In fact, while Deresiewicz

---

[45] William Wordsworth, "Lines Written a Few Miles above Tintern Abbey," in *Lyrical Ballads, with Pastoral and Other Poems*, 3rd ed., 2 vols. (London: Longman & Rees, 1802), I.194, I.196–7.

[46] William Deresiewicz, *Austen and the Romantic Poets* (New York: Columbia University Press, 2004), 48–9.

[47] See Ruth Bernard Yeazell's account of such negotiation in *Fictions of Modesty: Women and Courtship in the English Novel* (Chicago: University of Chicago Press, 1991).

may laud the provisional knowledge of the late works, Anne herself (unlike Elizabeth or Emma or Wentworth) wholly knows her feelings from the start.

Instead, we learn during the scene in the assembly room that Anne has been "thinking only of the last half hour," of her conversation with Wentworth, in order to come to a conclusion about *his* emotional state: "He must love her" (*P* 150). I mentioned earlier that many of Austen's numbers are chronological. Surprisingly regularly, these incorporate halves. Frequently, Austen appends the qualifier to short periods to indicate a momentariness that enables the barest recognition (a version of Deresiewicz's "half-formed thoughts"). Thus, when Fanny learns at Portsmouth that despite Tom's illness there is still no plan to bring her back to Mansfield, she "was within half a minute of starting the idea that Sir Thomas was quite unkind" (*MP* 333). Or in *Emma*, we witness the "rapidity of half a moment's thought" that can bring our glass-half-full heroine from mortified gloom back to happy anticipation (*E* 148). *Persuasion*, which takes place over a half year, offers "half a minute" as the time required for Charles Musgrove to hand his sister-in-law over to Wentworth after they run into him following his epistolary proposal, leaving the lovers together and alone in the busy street (*P* 193).

Still, one form of temporal half stands out: Austen's characters tend to work through things in half-hour stretches. So, upon initial receipt of that proposal, we hear that "Half an hour's solitude and reflection might have tranquillized [Anne]; but the ten minutes only" which she is granted can't possibly suffice (*P* 191). In *Sanditon*, when Charlotte experiences a "half-hour's fever" of admiration for Sir Edward (the single symptom of either love or illness, mental or physical, this resolutely healthy heroine displays in a novel generally given over to the romance of hypochondria), she is as soon "cured" as that timeframe indicates (*NA* 320). The half-hours at stake needn't be particularly emotionally charged, though. When Charles Bingley "was tempted by an accidental recommendation to look at Netherfield House," we learn something of both his amiable nature and his amenability to influence from the way that "He did look at it, and into it for half-an-hour—was pleased with the situation and the principal rooms, satisfied with what the owner said in its praise, and took it immediately" (*PP* 11). Thirty minutes is the perfect duration of an Austenian pop quiz of character (a proper test may take longer). When Mrs. Bennet means to put down Mr. Darcy during her gossip with her daughters and Charlotte Lucas about the previous evening's ball, she relates, "Mrs. Long told me last night that [Darcy] sat close to her for half-an-hour without once opening his lips" (*PP* 13). She sounds a bit like Emma, who complains to Frank of Jane

76   THE NUMBER SENSE

Fairfax's reticence: "We shall know more about them all, in half an hour, from you, than Miss Fairfax would have vouchsafed in half a year" (*E* 158). The everydayness of these half hours displays itself in the narrator's celebration of that "half an hour's uninterrupted communication of all those little matters on which the daily happiness of private life depends" (*E* 93).

In fact, Austen's novels draw a link between the half-hour's thought required to process a "revolution" of mind like Anne's on seeing Wentworth's proposal letter (*P* 190) and those that merely absorb or produce the latest social gossip. Another Wordsworthian resonance suggests a reason for the connection. *Persuasion* describes how Mary Musgrove habitually visits her in-laws, an activity in which Anne reluctantly joins: "To the Great House accordingly they went, to sit the full half hour in the old-fashioned square parlour" (*P* 37). The phrase "full half hour," while it seems a bit of a throwaway here, might nevertheless catch our attention for its paradoxical nature: what kind of half hour can be full? But it is equally striking for being the measure Wordsworth uses to describe his lingering at the graveside of the boy of Winander, the child of nature whose tale, originally appearing in the 1800 *Lyrical Ballads*, would later be translated into Book V of *The Prelude*. The ballad relates a twice-doubled parable of call and response between human and nature. The first section begins by describing the boy's "mimic hootings to the silent owls," to which the birds "shout / Across the wat'ry vale and shout again / Responsive to his call." This easy back-and-forth is, however, challenged on other occasions, when "pauses of deep silence mock'd his skill." Yet such silence nevertheless reveals Nature's answer, allowing the boy to hear "the voice / Of mountain torrents" and see how "the bosom of the steady lake" "receive'd" "the visible scene." Once more, we experience a world that is half-created and half-per(re)ceived, that is fitted and fitting. But the silence also prepares the ground for the poem's second section, in which the speaker stands in the churchyard and contemplates a more permanent kind of quiet: "near his grave / A full half-hour together I have stood, / Mute—for he died when he was ten years old."[48] The lyrical ballad thus concludes by wondering whether such final stillness might also be bridged: whether the speaker's muteness comprehends the poem itself, or whether the silent words on the page can nevertheless be received into the bosoms of their readers.[49]

---

[48] Wordsworth, "There was a Boy," *Lyrical Ballads* (1802), II.14–15.

[49] For a classic reading of the poem, see Geoffrey H. Hartman, "Reading and Representation: Wordsworth's 'Boy of Winander,'" *European Romantic Review* 5.1 (1994): 90–100. Hartman appears to use the 1815 text, in which the "full half-hour" becomes a "long half-hour"

JANE AUSTEN, BY HALF 77

What might these two very different "full half hours" have in common? And how did the odd expression arise in the first place? The context in *Persuasion* suggests a basis in social convention, and while I have not been able to locate the source of the idiom or fix its usage, it enjoyed some general circulation.[50] In Austen's day, a proper "morning visit" (itself a paradox, since it did not take place in the morning) was not meant to exceed fifteen minutes, so a "full half hour" might have been a common measure for a double-visit, perhaps one fit for close acquaintances.[51] Hence Emma's embarrassment at allowing Harriet only a quarter hour for calling on the Martins: She understands perfectly the insult the timeframe implies (*E* 146). So when Austen regularly gives her characters a half hour to become acquainted with their own thoughts, she also registers a certain fit between social conventions and our deeper cognitive requirements. Similarly, while both the boy and the speaker in Wordsworth's poem may appear to be alone, at least insofar as it comes to human company, surely his standing a "full half-hour *together*" in the final section implies a kind of company in nature, and even among the living and the dead (just remember that other numbery poem, "We Are Seven"). The half hour in these works is indeed full: It registers the plenitude of a well-matched universe, one suited to our diverse needs, one in which half (to alter the terms of Emma's doorway reflections) can be "enough."

But then again, as *Emma* also proves, sometimes it can't. Which brings us back to where I started: to the ballroom, with its unforgiving numbers game.[52] As it happens, the temporal frame here is also composed by

---

(since he also has the boy dying at age ten, as in earlier versions, rather than at twelve, as in 1815 and subsequently, the edition is hard to fix). Still, the phrase remains surprising enough to merit comment in two footnotes, the first recognizing in it "a near-absurdist tension of its own between various temporalities" (96, n. 2), the second remarking on the "pseudo-specific measurements" in order to ponder how the ballad "heightens our sense of the discontinuity and precariousness of human time compared to nature's more permanent presences" (98, n. 11).

[50] A Google Ngram search shows a sharp rise in usage starting 1815 to a peak in 1835 (https://books.google.com/ngrams/graph?content=full±half±hour&year_start=1800&yea r_end=2000&corpus=15&smoothing=3&share=&direct_url=t1%3B%2Cfull%20half%20ho ur%3B%2Cc0). Accessed January 2, 2019.

[51] See "Calling Cards and Calls," in Daniel Pool, *What Jane Austen Ate and Charles Dickens Knew: From Fox Hunting to Whist—the Facts of Daily Life in 19th-Century England* (New York: Touchstone, 1994), 66–9.

[52] Of which *Emma* offers yet another instance at the Westons' ball—until she is rescued by Mr. Knightley—when Mr. Elton refuses to pair off with Harriet:

The two last dances before supper were begun, and Harriet had no partner;—the only young lady sitting down;—and so equal had been hitherto the number of dancers, that how there could be any one disengaged was the wonder!—But Emma's

78   THE NUMBER SENSE

half-hour stretches. Mrs. Bennet narrates the events in the assembly room by describing Jane's introduction to Bingley, reducing Austenian story-telling to its most basic building blocks: "So he inquired who she was, and got introduced, and asked her for the two next. Then the two third he danced with Miss King, and the two fourth with Maria Lucas, and the two fifth with Jane again, and the two sixth with Lizzy, and the Boulanger—" (*PP* 8). Each "two" would have taken roughly a "full half-hour," as we know from Catherine Morland's retort to Henry Tilney's analogy between marriage and dancing: "People that marry can never part, but must go and keep house together. People that dance only stand opposite each other in a long room for half an hour" (*NA* 54). But in an Austen novel, the one leads into the other, even as the half-hour dances, morning visits, and solitary scenes of meditation link up in a narrative arc that reaches right to the wedding. Halves thus become wholes in more senses than one.

Such thinking by halves yields tremendous satisfactions. It can also feel like constraint. When William Blake first encountered Wordsworth's "Prospectus" to *The Recluse*, he reacted with horror: "You shall not bring me to believe such fitting & fitted."[53] I'm struck by how similar his tone is to that used by the famously anti-Janeite Charlotte Brontë in objecting to Austen's "carefully-fenced, highly cultivated garden with neat borders and delicate flowers."[54] Both revolt against the geometrical precision. But so, occasionally, did Austen herself—obliquely in the novels (as in the painful assertion that "Marianne could never love by halves"), and far more openly in her comparatively *half*-poor juvenile works. In fact, the juvenilia abounds with jokes that find ways to get around the unforgiving math of fitting and fitted, of matching halves. Think of the scene in "Love and Freindship" where Philander and Gustavus discuss how their small travelling troupe manages to put on theatrical productions despite "the Scarcity"—there's that term again—"of Plays which, for want of People to fill the Characters, we could perform": "We did not mind trifles, however.—One of our most admired Performances was *Macbeth*, in which we were truly great. The Manager always played *Banquo* himself, his Wife my *Lady Macbeth*. I did the

> wonder lessened soon afterwards, on seeing Mr. Elton sauntering about. He would not ask Harriet to dance if it were possible to be avoided ...
>
> (E 256)

[53] William Blake, "Marginalia," in *Blake's Poetry and Designs*, 445.
[54] "C. Bell" [Charlotte Brontë] to G. H. Lewes, January 12, 1848, in *Selected Letters of Charlotte Brontë*, ed. Margaret Smith (Oxford: Oxford University Press, 2007), 99.

Three Witches and Philander acted *all the rest.*" Austen's own early dramatic fragment "The Visit" hilariously introduces this logic diegetically, when Miss Fitzgerald must apologize to her guests, two of whom must sit in the laps of their hosts because, while "there ought to be 8 chairs," "there are but 6." "I am really shocked at crouding you in such a manner," she announces, "but my Grandmother (who bought all the furniture of this room) as she had never a very large Party, did not think it necessary to buy more Chairs than were sufficient for her own family and two of her particular friends."[55]

Such humor can make it into the mature novels; "two" is one more friend than Mrs. Norris desires to accommodate in *Mansfield Park* when she insists on moving into a house that has only "a spare room for a friend," so as to ensure that Fanny must remain at the Park (*MP* 22). Austen's later novel also echoes Philander and Gustavus' theatrical predicament when translating it into the amorous maneuverings surrounding the casting of *Lovers' Vows*. But the tone has changed. A scarcity of players has become an excess of leading ladies, and such fitting and being fitted must now be measured in the context of the one-to-one constraints of courtship. The adulterous energies that break out show the resulting squeeze.[56] One can't help but yearn for a space more like the library at Godmersham Park, which the thirty-seven-year-old Jane Austen, by now securely single, describes as a veritable paradise of superfluousness ("O, reason not the need") to Cassandra, whom she trusts to understand her pleasure: "At this present time I have five Tables, Eight & twenty Chairs & two fires all to myself" (*Letters* 249). And even at balls, the older Austen can escape the mathematical compulsion of matched halves, as she relates in 1808: "The room was tolerably full, & there were, perhaps, thirty couple of Dancers; the melancholy part was to see so many dozen young Women standing by without partners, and each of them with two ugly naked shoulders!—It was the same room in which we danced 15 years ago!—I thought it all over—& in spite of the shame of being so much older, felt with thankfulness that I was quite as happy now as then.—We paid an

---

[55] Austen, *Catharine and other Writings*, 104, 49–50.

[56] Contrast the generous expansion when Frank Churchill first imagines holding a dance at Randalls, only to find the space too small to fit everyone Mr. Weston's sociable imagination would like to convene: "Somebody said that *Miss* Gilbert was expected at her brother's, and must be invited with the rest. Somebody else believed *Mrs.* Gilbert would have danced the other evening, if she had been asked. A word was put in for a second young Cox; and at last, Mr. Weston naming one family of cousins who must be included, and another of very old acquaintance who could not be left out, it became a certainty that the five couple would be at least ten, and a very interesting speculation in what possible manner they could be disposed of" (*E* 194–5). Here, of course, a larger space solves the problem when the dance is moved to the Crown.

80 THE NUMBER SENSE

additional shilling for our Tea, which we took as we chose in an adjoining and very comfortable room" (*Letters* 156–7). Enough, indeed.

2.3 Reserve, in lieu of a Coda: *The Odd Women*

When George Gissing returns to the subject of courtship plot math in his 1893 novel *The Odd Women*, he presents a fresh challenge to this vision. As the reflections of his heroine Rhoda Nunn on the term that generates his title suggest (her surname indicates her views of marriage, if not her feelings about religion), we are again dealing with halves—missing ones. "So many *odd* women—no making a pair with them"; that is to say, as with the paucity of chairs in Austen's juvenile play, it's a matching problem.[57]

The pairing of sitters to seats used by Austen in "The Visit" actually serves as a paradigm example of matching, which is, as I have mentioned, the first step on the road to counting and an important part of the process of abstraction that gave us the concept of number.[58] While in Austen's novels such moments tend to evoke financial insecurity only obliquely (as the consequence of a shortage of male suitors, for example), other writers employ very similar scenes to express more blatant poverty or the absence of political room at the table. *The Princess Casamassima* (1886), Henry James's novel about a network of revolutionaries in the 1880s, serves as a kind of waystation on the road between Austen and Gissing. It also, appropriately, includes a running gag about the growing shortage of seats available to the increasing number of visitors to the apartment that the working-class radical figure Paul Muniment shares with his invalid sister, Rosy.[59] Such scarcity is in turn contrasted with the abundance of empty rooms at Inglefield, the country house belonging to the family of Lady Aurora, the philanthropic spinster who visits Rosy. But as one of "thirteen at home"—including eight sisters—Lady Aurora has her own experience of feeling "crowded"—one already familiar to us from Austen's novels.[60] Describing how society has responded to her

---

[57] George Gissing, *The Odd Women*, ed. Margaret Cardwell (Oxford: Oxford University Press, 2008), 44 (original emphasis). Hereafter *OW*, internally documented by page number.

[58] As Dantzig explains, "We enter a hall. Before us are two collections: the seats of the auditorium, and the audience. Without counting, we can ascertain whether the two collections are equal and, if not equal, which is the greater" (*Number*, 6–7).

[59] See Henry James, *The Princess Casamassima*, ed. Derek Brewer (London: Penguin, 1987), 134, 224, 410.

[60] James, *The Princess Casamassima*, 134. James's previous novel *The Bostonians* focuses like *The Odd Women* on the politics surrounding woman's place in society. Wendy Lesser has

decision to pursue charitable work and thus remove herself, effectively, from the marriage market, Lady Aurora admits: "but of course they consider me very *odd*, in every way, as there's no doubt I am." There's that term again. Still, she has her reasons: "My father isn't rich, and there is only one of us married, and we are not at all handsome, and—oh, there are all kinds of things."[61]

While the "odd women" whose lives Gissing chronicles might count Lady Aurora as one of their number, their poverty is more in line with that of the Muniments. Gissing's novel begins in the mode of Austen's opening salvos, in which she lays out a familial dilemma as starkly as a mathematical problem: one vulnerable patriarch, so many dependent women, so many pounds per year. In *The Odd Women*, we initially encounter Doctor Madden in what appears to be a relatively stable state:

> for twenty years he had practised medicine at Clevedon, but with such trifling emolument that the needs of his large family left him scarce a margin over expenditure; now, at the age of forty-nine—it was 1872—he looked forward with a larger hope. Might he not reasonably count on ten or fifteen more years of activity?

That large family becomes a more distinct vision when his eldest child— "Alice Madden, aged nineteen"—is introduced, and we discover that "Mrs. Madden, having given birth to six daughters, had fulfilled her function in this wonderful world; for two years she had been resting in the old churchyard that looks upon the Severn sea." Perhaps, given these circumstances, it should not surprise us that, despite his cheery outlook, the Doctor decides to insure his life "for a thousand pounds" (*OW* 1). All this on the first page of the novel. But in a manner owing more to Thomas Hardy than to Austen, he dies by the end of the opening chapter—too soon to put his plan into action—when his old horse stumbles as the doctor is en route to see a patient.

Chapter 2, "Adrift," proceeds to chart the perilous descent of the Madden sisters into semi-genteel poverty, a tale that is told largely through a series of cruel numbers: we learn the present year ("the spring of '88"

---

written compellingly about the similarities and differences between the two novels in "Even-Handed Oddness: George Gissing's *The Odd Women*" (*The Hudson Review* 37.2 [Summer, 1984]: 209–20).

[61] *The Princess Casamassima*, 221 (emphasis added). This time, the count has changed by one: "We are twelve at home, and eight of us are girls." Presumably, a brother has left the nest in the interim.

82   THE NUMBER SENSE

[*OW* 12]); we are also reminded how "It was now sixteen years since the death of Dr. Madden" (*OW* 14). Similarly, although we could have calculated some of these ourselves, Gissing states the daughters' ages on reintroduction: "The elder [Alice] (now five-and-thirty)" (*OW* 13); "Virginia (about thirty-three)" (*OW* 14). And relentlessly, we hear of their changing pecuniary positions. Gissing sets the contemporary scene by carefully recording their London rent: first for Virginia alone ("five and sixpence" [*OW* 12]), and then, when Alice's ill-health forces her to join her younger sister, for the two eldest sisters together ("seven shillings" [*OW* 13]). The chapter's final episode describes Virginia's walk through the London streets ("Five miles, at least, measured by pavement" [*OW* 22]) to a shop where she buys a copy of Keble's calendrical (and thus numbery) poem *The Christian Year* as a gift for Monica's twenty-first birthday before entering a public house to purchase "refreshment" (brandy). The perambulation is charted with such cartographic precision that it alone justifies the presence of the map that serves as frontispiece to the Oxford Worlds Classics edition of the book (*OW* xxxii). Just before this journey, however, we take an even closer look at the budget. As Alice calculates:

> "Let us see. Put it in another form. We have both to live together on seventeen pounds. That is—" she made a computation on a piece of paper—"that is two pounds, sixteen shillings and eightpence a month—let us suppose this month at an end. That represents fourteen shillings and twopence a week. Yes, we *can* do it!"
>
> She laid down her pencil with an air of triumph. Her dull eyes brightened as though she had discovered a new source of income.
>
> "We cannot, dear," urged Virginia in a subdued voice. "Seven shillings rent; that leaves only seven and twopence a week for everything—everything."
>
> "We *could* do it, dear," persisted the other. "If it came to the very worst, our food need not cost more than sixpence a day—three and sixpence a week. I do really believe, Virgie, we could support life on less—say, on fourpence. Yes, we could dear!"

When Virginia wonders, "Is such a life worthy of the name?" Alice offers the comfort—indeed the "thrill"—of a word that resonates throughout this book, one standing as an alternative to the titular term *odd*: "We shan't be driven to that. Oh, we certainly shall not. But it helps one to know

JANE AUSTEN, BY *HALF* 83

that, strictly speaking, we are *independent* for another six months" (*OW* 19; original emphases).

Recall Emma Woodhouse's invocation of this label in setting her own fate apart from that of Miss Bates: "If I know myself, Harriet, mine is an active, busy mind, with a great many *independent* resources; and I do not perceive why I should be more in want of employment at forty or fifty than one-and-twenty," she tells Harriet, imagining her position not as an "old maid" but as quite another type of woman (*E* 69; emphasis added). But if Emma's resources here refer to her mental plenitude, to what the novelist describes (in the crucial scene in the doorway of Ford's shop) as her facility as an "Imaginist," Austen far more frequently uses *independent* to signal a more purely financial situation. Mr. Weston inherits "a small independence" (*E* 12); Mr. Martin was "not born to an independence" (*E* 24); Mr. Elton "was known to have some independent property" (*E* 28). Austen thus suggests the degree to which Emma's "independent resources" depend upon her monetary ones.

Gissing's work's resemblance to *Emma* is striking; his plot even includes the gift of a piano—a moment so gratuitous that it feels rather like an "Easter egg," a present to the knowing reader.[62] The later novelist was an admirer of the earlier one; Gissing had advised his sister Margaret to read Austen's books in June of 1880, calling them "very healthy."[63] Perhaps no Austen novel so fits this description as *Emma*, whose heroine is described (as I have already mentioned) as "the picture of grown-up health" (*E* 32)—a health that also depends upon those "independent resources," as we are led to understand through the contrast with Jane Fairfax's illness. Notably, Jane recovers almost immediately on achieving the security offered by marriage to Frank

---

[62] The piano is presented as a wedding gift from the novel's hero to Fanny (*OW* 139), the bride-to-be of his old friend Micklethwaite (a mathematician by profession, no less!), who had waited for "seventeen years" to marry while his own financial situation improved and his fiancée supported herself as a teacher (*OW* 105). This marriage serves as a kind of old-fashioned, Platonic ideal against which we are invited to measure the more modern courtships. As Micklethwaite describes it: "But I have never thought of Fanny as a separate person. Upon my word, now I think of it, I never have. Fanny and I have been one for ages" (*OW* 139).

Rather surprisingly, I have been unable to locate any critical discussion of the resemblance between Austen and Gissing—much less these two novels—with the one exception of Melville B. Anderson's comments in "A Chat About George Gissing": "At risk of being thought whimsical, I suggest ... that George Gissing as an artist is own brother to Jane Austen. ... Gissing appears ... [t]o be no more in love with Rhoda Nunn than is Miss Austen with Elizabeth Bennet. The two kindred artists portray their women with feminine detachment, with sympathy excluding sexual passion" (*The Dial* 61 [June 22, 1916], 6).

[63] Gissing, *Letters of George Gissing to Members of his Family* (New York: Haskell House, 1970), 76.

84 THE NUMBER SENSE

Churchill. The links between the novels emphasize how what Alice and Virginia envision when they describe their independence is a far cry from Miss Bates's socially embedded life of reduced circumstances in *Emma*—not to mention from the fully realized existence of Victorian Liberal individualism signaled by the term. It seems nearer, in fact, to Giorgio Agamben's *bare life*.

Bare life rests precariously on the edge of death. The balance could tip either way, at any moment. In the middle of the novel's second chapter, before calculating their present position, Gissing turns back in time to tell the tale of how the sisters got here, again largely through numbers. First, we learn that "When the doctor's affairs were set in order, it was found that the patrimony of his six girls amounted, as nearly as possible, to eight hundred pounds" (*OW* 14). Not enough to live on, that is; the girls must seek employment: "Alice obtained a situation as nursery-governess at sixteen pounds a year. Virginia was fortunate enough to be accepted as companion by a gentlewoman at Weston-super-Mare; her payment, twelve pounds. Gertrude, fourteen years old, also went to Weston, where she was offered employment in a fancy-goods shop,—her payment nothing at all, but lodging, board, and dress assured to her" (*OW* 15). But things get worse:

> Ten years went by, and saw many changes.
> Gertrude and Martha were dead; the former of consumption, the other drowned by the over-turning of a pleasure boat.
>
> (*OW* 15)

And still worse: "Isabel was soon worked into illness. Brain trouble came on, resulting in melancholia. A charitable institution ultimately received her, and there, at two-and-twenty, the poor hard-featured girl drowned herself in a bath" (*OW* 16).[64] Gissing then calculates the current balance of his scenario:

---

[64] This suicide, like the murder-suicide of Father Time and his siblings in Thomas Hardy's *Jude the Obscure* (1895) ("because we are too menny"), can be read not only as an expression of late Victorian Malthusian fears about population growth but also as a reflection on the special place of suicide in statistical thought in the nineteenth century (*Jude the Obscure*, ed. C. H. Sisson [London: Penguin, 1985], 410). Ian Hacking has argued that, in the work of people like Thomas Henry Buckle and Emile Durkheim, suicide involved "a mythology of causation" that made statistical law "safe for determinism"; the constant rate of suicides becomes "proof" of what Hacking calls "statistical determinism" or "statistical fatalism" (*The Taming of Chance*, 71, 126). See also Steinlight, *Populating the Novel*, Chapter 5 ("Because We Are Too Menny"), which considers both *The Odd Women* (briefly) and *Jude* to view "the collapse of the marriage plot" in late Victorian fiction in relation to the period's self-diagnosed "Suicidal Mania" (167). I will return to these issues and to Hardy's attitude toward fate in my Conclusion.

Their numbers had thus been reduced by half. Up to now, the income of their eight hundred pounds had served, impartially, the ends now of this, now of that one, doing a little good to all, saving them from many an hour of bitterness which must else have been added to their lot. By a new arrangement, the capital was at length made over to Alice and Virginia jointly, the youngest sister having a claim upon them to the extent of an annual nine pounds. A trifle, but it would buy her clothing,—and then Monica was sure to marry. Thank Heaven she was sure to marry!

(*OW* 16)

Their numbers had thus been reduced by half. Here we are again, facing a problem of halving.

And, via marriage, a proposed solution: matching (i.e., doubling). Once more, we enter the terrain of courtship plot math. Monica's role as "by far the best looking, as well as the sprightliest, of the family" predicates her fate: "She must marry; of course she must marry!" (*OW* 16). The passage echoes, in a rather more desperate register, George Eliot's declaration of Dorothea Brooke's place in the grand scheme of things: "And how should Dorothea not marry?—a girl so handsome and with such prospects?"[65] But the resemblance also reminds us how Gissing is revealing the financial precarity, which Eliot herself obscured, underlying Austen's assertion "that a single man in possession of a good fortune, must be in want of a wife" (*PP* 3); in other words, a single woman not in possession of a good fortune must be in want of a husband.

Or—recall Jane Fairfax's proposal to take a position as governess—a job. *The Odd Women* participates in the period's debates about what were called "professions for women," one of many follow-ups to W. R. Greg's infamous 1862 article, "Why Are Women Redundant?" In this essay, Greg reviews the implications of the statistical imbalance between the sexes. As he puts it:

There are hundreds and thousands of women—scattered through all ranks, but proportionally most numerous in the middle and upper classes,—who have to earn their own living, instead of spending and husbanding the earnings of men; who, not having the natural duties and labours of wives and mothers, have to carve out artificial and painfully-sought occupations for themselves; who, in place of completing, sweetening, and embellishing the

---

[65] Eliot, *Middlemarch*, 9.

86   THE NUMBER SENSE

existence of others, are compelled to lead an independent and incomplete existence of their own.[66]

Notice how, for Greg, female *incompleteness* is the logical adjunct of *independence*; without a man, a woman will always be half, never whole. Hence his own "solution" to the dilemma: Women should emigrate to countries where the imbalance (of the white population, that is) lies the other way, where there are too many men.[67] Although an uncoupled man may be more positively *independent* (rather than *odd*), he will still enjoy the added comforts of a wife.

When the titular phrase comes up in Gissing's novel, it does so squarely in the context of female employment. Monica has been summoned by Rhoda, who is an old acquaintance of the family (she was present at tea in the opening chapter, when Dr. Madden received the ill-omened summons). Rhoda has been assisting her friend Mary Barfoot in running a school that teaches women secretarial skills to prepare them for office work. The title of the chapter containing the discussion pointedly designates Rhoda as "An Independent Woman"—that *beau ideal* dreamed of by Alice and Virginia—and the conversation about "odd women" helps explain why:

> "But—" [Monica] hesitated—"don't you approve of any one marrying?"
>
> "Oh, I'm not so severe! But do you know that there are half a million more women than men in this happy country of ours?"
>
> "Half a million!" echoed Monica.
>
> Her naive alarm again excited Rhoda to laughter.
>
> "Something like that, they say. So many *odd* women—no making a pair with them. The pessimists call them useless, lost, futile lives. I, naturally—being one of them myself—take another view. I look upon them as a great reserve. When one woman vanishes in matrimony, the reserve offers a substitute for the world's work. True, they are not all trained yet—far from it. I want to help in that—to train the reserve."
>
> (*OW* 44)

---

[66] [W. R. Greg], "Why are Women Redundant?" *National Review* 28 (1862): 434–60; 436. The essay includes many tabulated figures compiled from various censuses.

[67] Austen was already thinking through the implications of emigration as a solution for "redundant" women in her apprentice-piece, "Catharine, or, The Bower," when she imagines how Catharine's friend, the eldest Miss Wynne, is shipped out to India to "gain[] a husband" (Austen, *Catharine and Other Writings*, 188). She was no doubt made sensitive to the subject through her Aunt Philadelphia's experience. See also O'Brien, who posits that Malthus's *Essay* shaped Austen's sense of "what it means to be a redundant female" ("The Cultural and Literary Significance," 560).

I can't help but be struck by the surplus figure—yet another *half*—in this case signaling what Rhoda rather positively terms the "great reserve" of odd women. It seems suited to the matching dilemma addressed by the novel.

All these numbers operate, then, by way of set-up: They are there to fix our initial plot points, allowing us to chart how matters progress once the figures are set in motion by the entrance of (wait for it!) male suitors. And while the novel continues to turn to numbers throughout, they become less prominent after the men arrive. In effect, the work takes shape around two marriage plots. One follows Monica, as she is courted—or, perhaps more accurately, stalked—by Mr. Edmund Widdowson, a middle-aged man who has recently come into what Austen would call "independent" means (Gissing, however, reserves this term for his female characters) when his brother, who had been a successful businessman, leaves him "about six hundred a year" (*OW* 53). Realizing her untenable position (as Rhoda describes it, "Her guardians dealt with her absurdly; they made her half a lady and half a shop-girl" [*OW* 121]), Monica accepts his proposal of marriage, only to find herself oppressed by his jealousy. Widdowson, for his part, discovers that "Monica's independence of thought is a perpetual irritation" to him (*OW* 265). She embarks on an affair but pulls up at the last moment when she realizes the shallowness of her potential paramour; Widdowson unearths her intentions without recognizing their real object and mistakenly assumes she has been unfaithful. The two separate, and Monica dies in childbirth some months afterwards, cared for by her sisters in a house that Widdowson has provided.

The second plot involves the temptation of Rhoda Nunn to abandon her mission, and perhaps also her independence, for the love of a man. Rhoda has little faith in romantic love; as she observes, naturally turning to probabilistic numbers to explain her position, "In real life, how many men and women *fall in love*? Not one in every ten thousand, I am convinced. Not one married pair in ten thousand have felt for each other as two or three couples do in every novel" (*OW* 67–8; original emphasis). But then she meets Everard Barfoot, the free-thinking cousin (and former flame) of her business partner, Mary. Everard is something of a Henry Crawford figure; well into his attempt to win Rhoda over, "he was still only half serious in his desire to take her for a wife, wishing rather to amuse and flatter himself by merely inspiring her with passion" (*OW* 198). But if Henry is attracted by Fanny Price's moral purity, Everard somewhat paradoxically finds himself falling for Rhoda's independence. "He enjoyed her air of equality," we learn (*OW* 114). And he, too, gauges his feelings via statistics: "there are

88   THE NUMBER SENSE

perhaps not half-a-dozen women living with whom I could talk as I have talked with you. It isn't likely that I shall ever meet one. Am I to make my bow, and abandon in resignation the one chance of perfecting my life?" (*OW* 205). So, as in *Mansfield Park*, what began as something of game becomes earnest.

Money facilitates this shift. Everard, having lived alone on his modest fortune of "four hundred and fifty" pounds a year (*OW* 109), comes, like Widdowson, into an inheritance on his brother's death, one that grants him the means to support a wife and retain his own independence. We learn how he "persevered" with Rhoda, "though the world of women was now open to him,—for, on a moderate computation, any man with Barfoot's personal advantages, and armed with fifteen hundred a year, may choose among fifty possible maidens" (another, even more cynical, take on the famous opening sentence of *Pride and Prejudice*, translating its universalizing philosophical tone into more modern statistical terms, albeit delivered through a mock epic idiom) (*OW* 237). Still, Everard's deepest desire is to prove Rhoda as remarkable as he finds her by having her accept a "free union" (*OW* 147). Rhoda, for her part, decides that she can both test his love and her own resolve by pressuring him to ask her to marry him.

The two arrange to "run into each other" on Rhoda's annual walking holiday, taken this year in the Lake District. And they do have one blissful day hiking the hills beyond Seascale and imagining a future together. Everard fantasizes about prolonging this bliss:

> A week—a month, even—with weather such as this. Nay, with a storm for variety; clouds from the top of Scawfell falling thick about us; a fierce wind shrieking across the tarn; sheets and torrents and floods of rain beating upon our roof; and you and I by the peat-fire. With a good supply of books, old and new, I can picture it for three months, for half a year!

But when Rhoda cautions him to recall his own nature, he acknowledges that such happiness can't last. Still, he thinks he has a plan:

> "There is a vast difference between six months and all one's life.—When the half-year was over we would leave England."
>
> "By the Orient Express?"
>
> They laughed together, Rhoda colouring, for the words that had escaped her meant too much for mere jest.

JANE AUSTEN, BY HALF   89

"By the Orient Express. We would have a house by the Bosphorus for the next half year, and contrast our emotions with those we had known by Burmoor Tarn. Think what a rich year of life that would make!"

(*OW* 288)

The "Oriental" vision highlights, though, how romance has taken over from the novel's dominant realistic mode. As Patricia Ingham observes, "in a novel thick with financial calculations," the "practicalities" that would attend on Barfoot's union with Rhoda "are never disclosed" (*OW* xxii); a "free union" is as much of a fantasy as the proverbial "free lunch." Still, Everard's imagined temporal mode is as striking to me as the impracticality of the vision, which, after all, rests on the secure foundation of his "fifteen hundred a year." If Jane Austen's ideal rhythm, for life and for narrative, operates in half-hour blocks, Gissing suggests that half years would suit his protagonists.

That very evening, though, the dream dissolves in a clash of wills. Everard proposes—first a free union, then, when Rhoda applies pressure, conventional marriage. Rhoda accepts the latter, but both parties are disappointed; the charm has broken. Returning to her room, Rhoda hears (a false rumor) that Monica has been discovered in an adulterous affair with Everard. Although Everard denies it, Rhoda will neither credit his denial nor try to unearth the truth from Monica. Everard departs England, and the courtship plot fizzles out (he ends the novel married to a more conventionally progressive woman from his own social circle). It's hard to know whether we should be relieved or disappointed by this failed ending.[68] And Rhoda admits as much, recalling the day months later, after the confusions surrounding Monica's affair have been dispelled. When Everard blames her for "put[ting] the obstacle there," Rhoda objects, "No. An unlucky chance did that.—Or a lucky one. Who knows?" (*OW* 359). (Readers of Austen might recall Anne Elliot's awareness of contingency: "It was, perhaps, one of those cases in which advice is good or bad only as the event decides" [*P* 198].[69])

To clinch her point with Everard, Rhoda resorts to Jane Austen's key figure. She explains that, like Marianne Dashwood, she cannot love—or be loved—by halves. Describing their time together at Seascale (the very place name suggests a delicate tipping point in the relationship), she hedges: "After

[68] Lesser points out the contrast here with the conclusion to *The Bostonians*, which, while it ends more conventionally in marriage, leaves most readers with a decidedly bitter aftertaste ("Even-Handed Oddness," 216).
[69] In *Victorian Contingencies,* Tina Young Choi considers how novelistic narratives were affected by new ideas of contingency that developed in the wake of statistical innovations.

90 THE NUMBER SENSE

all, the perfection of our day was half make-believe. You never loved me with entire sincerity. And you will never love any woman—even as well as you loved me" (*OW* 361). In fact, as my quotations from the novel hint, the prevalence of *half* in *The Odd Women* is very high: .00087278 (*Mansfield Park*, Austen's most *half*-rich novel, clocks in below it, at .00086506). The coincidence suggests once more how the number accords with a set of concerns that form around problems of pairing. So if I have indulged here in plot summary, it has been to stress how the prolix use of a certain figure can identify a group of recognizable themes within a genre—can even help to identify a literary category. *Half* serves, as one might put it, as a generic marker of a particularly rational branch of marriage plot romances.

While the *The Odd Women* often presents like a mathematical problem, its solution is less than clear. The novel may end without a man in sight, but the destination has yet to be reached; the process recalls once more the operations of Zeno's paradox. Given that Monica is dead, and Virginia appears to be half-way there (she is "staying with friends" [370]—presumably to dry out?), one could almost say that the Madden sisters' numbers have again been reduced by half. But this time, there's also a remainder—or perhaps rather "reserve": Monica's baby, another girl, who is being cared for by Alice. Alice, we are told, "had found her vocation; she looked better than at any time since Rhoda had known her." And while she still hopes to open a school when her sister returns, Alice's observation that "here is one pupil growing for us!" suggests a more realistic horizon of expectations. Rhoda expresses optimism, as well: her "work," she tells Alice, "flourish[es]," and she and Mary are launching a publication to spread the word (*OW* 370). "The world is moving!" she declares (*OW* 371). Still, the novel's final paragraph somewhat undermines this vision of female solidarity and vocation, of a community of independent (rather than odd) women:

> Whilst Miss Madden went into the house to prepare hospitalities, Rhoda, still nursing, sat down on a garden bench. She gazed intently at those diminutive features, which were quite placid and relaxing in soft drowsiness. The dark, bright eye was Monica's. And as the baby sank into sleep, Rhoda's vision grew dim; a sigh made her lips quiver, and once more she murmured, "Poor little child!"
>
> (*OW* 371)

Will it ever be enough?

3

Figuring Character in Dickens

3.1 Counting the Leaves

Figure—even, at times, *character*: the very words we use to designate fictional persons can also refer to numerical symbols. Numbers in novels connect with issues of character in a variety of ways, some obvious, some more subtle. In the spirit of my inquiry, we might distinguish three basic categories of interaction. First, and most fundamentally, there's the matter of labeling. Is a character identified by a name or by a number, as in "one woman," "the first man," or even "One Hundred and Five, North Tower"? That last designation is how we initially encounter Dr. Manette in the novel over which I will linger longest here, Charles Dickens's *A Tale of Two Cities* (1859). "My number is 174,517," says Primo Levi towards the beginning of *Survival in Auschwitz* when he tells how he is "baptized" into camp life.[1] The simple statement encodes a history of violence in the relationship between numbers and identity.

Second, there's the detailing: How are numbers used to define the traits of a character, like age (the focus of my next chapter), or height, or net worth (something over which Jane Austen obsessed, as we have seen), or even daily routine? And relatedly, if more abstractly: How do these traits "add up" to produce a sense of character, whether "round" or "flat"? How do units of characterization (often, as I suggest, including numbers) produce—plot, even, like so many points in a portrait by Chuck Close—a three-dimensional individual? In the novel's opening scene at a dinner party, the notably unnamed protagonist of H. G. Wells's *The Time Machine* (1895) uses numerical operations to describe his take on portraiture by outlining a "geometry of Four dimensions" assembled by stacking up likenesses of the same man taken at different ages (it's a moment to which I will return in Chapter 4): "All these are evidently sections, as it were, Three-Dimensional representations of his Four-Dimensioned being, which is a fixed and unalterable

---

[1] Primo Levi, *Survival in Auschwitz: The Nazi Assault on Humanity*, trans. Stuart Wolf (New York: Simon & Schuster, 1996), 27.

The Number Sense of Nineteenth-Century British Literature. Stefanie Markovits, Oxford University Press.
© Stefanie Markovits (2025). DOI: 10.1093/9780198937821.003.0004

92   THE NUMBER SENSE

thing."[2] Wells's addition of a chronological measure to the standard ones of height, depth, and breadth raises the question of just how many variables we need to fix to capture a person.

At roughly the same moment Wells was conjuring forth his Time Traveller, Alphonse Bertillon had decided that the magic number was sixteen (Bertillon's *Identification anthropométrique*, demonstrating the measurements needed for his system of recognition, was published in 1893). The precise figure strikes us now as both dangerous and risible, yet it has been replaced by the singular symbolic configuration of a genetic code. Bertillon's metrics belong to the nineteenth-century culture of statistical research. Discussing how the methods of this culture intersect with ideas of characterization, John Allen Paulos observes, "Even to those we don't know well we can attach a dozen adjectives, a few adverbs, and a couple of anecdotes. Contrast this abundance of personal particulars with most scientific studies where, while there may be a very large number of people (or other data), the people surveyed are flat, having only one or two dimensions—who they will vote for, whether they smoke, or what brand of soft drink or laxative they prefer." Paulos concludes, "Stories and statistics offer us the complementary choices of knowing a lot about a few people or knowing a little about many people."[3] Yet numbers play a significant role in forming both kinds of knowledge.[4]

I'm interested in all these permutations of the numberiness of character. They are in fact connected to one another, and all come with political implications. But I want to begin here with a third, and still more abstract, category of contact between these concepts. Paulos points toward it when identifying a conflict between what he calls the *few* and the *many*; scholars of literature will likely think rather in terms of Alex Woloch's account of the tussle for character space between his *one* and *many*, the protagonist of a work of fiction and the myriad lesser surrounding figures. The implicit

---

[2] H. G. Wells, *The Time Machine* (Floating Press, 2009), 8.

[3] John Allen Paulos, *Once Upon a Number*, 25–6.

[4] Advances in computing and AI are only now beginning to shift our understanding of *data* away from an inherently numerical conception. As the editors of the recent edition of *New Literary History* devoted to "Culture, Theory, Data" point out, "The word still tends to imply that the information it describes is numeric or can be turned into numbers. But these days, what can't be turned into numbers?" Ted Underwood, Laura McGrath, Richard Jean So, and Chad Wellmon, "Culture, Theory, Data: An Introduction," *New Literary History* 53.4–54.1 (2022–3), 520. See also Chris Wiggins and Matthew L. Jones, *How Data Happened: A History from the Age of Reason to the Age of Algorithms* (New York: Norton, 2023).

FIGURING CHARACTER IN DICKENS   93

numberiness of this struggle surfaces memorably in a scene toward the start of *Our Mutual Friend* (1865), when Dickens introduces one of the novel's minor characters as "an innocent"—if rather confused—"piece of dinner furniture" in the home of the Veneerings:

> The name of this article was Twemlow. Being first cousin to Lord Snigsworth, he was in frequent requisition, and at many houses might be said to represent the dining-table in its normal state. Mr. and Mrs. Veneering, for example, arranging a dinner, habitually started with Twemlow, and then put leaves in him, or added guests to him. Sometimes, the table consisted of Twemlow and half-a-dozen leaves; sometimes, of Twemlow and a dozen leaves; sometimes, Twemlow was pulled out to his utmost extent of twenty leaves. Mr. and Mrs. Veneering on occasions of ceremony faced each other in the centre of the board, and thus the parallel still held; for, it always happened that the more Twemlow was pulled out, the further he found himself from the center, ...[5]

The metaphor of the extension table demonstrates the functionalism of minor characters: Twemlow's characterological value lies in his utility, itself a product of his relations rather than anything particular to him. That is, it isn't anything we might associate with him as an individual, as the kind of character occupying the center of Victorian Liberalism and of thinking about the Victorian realist novel in the classic paradigm offered by Ian Watt.[6] *Our Mutual Friend* obsesses over *character* (versions of the word appear eighty-three times); many of the novel's personages fight to maintain bodily and psychic integrity against threats of dispersal (recall Silas Wegg's desire to retrieve his leg, for example) or of being cast to the side (see Betty Higdon).[7]

---

[5] Charles Dickens, *Our Mutual Friend*, ed. Michael Cotsell (Oxford: Oxford University Press, 1998), 6. Hereafter, internally referenced as *OMF*.

[6] When, later in the novel, Georgiana Podsnap meets Sophronia Lammle, she asks, "I wonder what you like me for! I am sure I can't think." Sophronia replies: "Dearest Georgiana, for yourself. For your difference from all around you." Individuality is the keynote here. Georgiana confirms her similar appreciation of her new friend with relief. As she says goodbye, Sophronia checks the status of the relationship: "We are real friends, Georgiana dear?" "Real," Georgie agrees (*OMF* 142), suggesting both a ratification of the term *real*, one so often applied to the genre in which she is located, and its connection to characterological particularity.

[7] J. S. Mill's understanding of character is rooted in possessive individualism: "A person whose desires and impulses are his own—are the expression of his own nature, as it has been developed and modified by his own culture—is said to have a character. One whose desires

94   THE NUMBER SENSE

In this way, we might consider the Veneerings as stand-ins for certain novelists who use minor characters to configure their social arrangements, and we might also wonder how Dickens thinks of his own treatment in comparison to theirs.[8] For, as the numbers count the units that fill in the canvas of the Dickensian milieu, their role in the metaphor also shows how the process of adding more minor characters helps to establish their very "minorness." Twemlow finds himself further and further from the center of the Veneerings' action (even as—and this is a point to which I will want to return—the ruminations through which we learn his fate ensure a more prominent position in Dickens's prose at this moment). Indeed, the episode might bring to mind the rather surprising fact that the term *protagonist* has a numbery derivation: it comes not from our advocacy for his or her role, as one might expect from pairing it with what seems a natural antonym, *antagonist*. Rather, the *pro* refers to this person's position in the cast of characters: the protagonist comes *first*—he is the *proto-agonist* of the drama, as opposed to the second, or *deuteragonist*.[9] I still remember my brother's acting debut and swan song as both "First Lord" *and* "Second Lord" in a production of *The Winter's Tale*. The lack of names and presence of numbers suggest how easily the roles could be compounded, turning him into a kind of one-man chorus. At least Twemlow has a moniker, even if it might feel like a portmanteau of his twelfth position and his lowly status.

While the mood here is comic, however, the scene's numbers also remind me, in both their growth and their attunement to such inequalities, of the process of metastasizing by which the Jacquerie expands to storm the Bastille in Dickens's earlier *A Tale of Two Cities*. Before the Bastille scene, the count

---

and impulses are not his own, has no character, no more than a steam-engine has a character" (*On Liberty*, ed. Elizabeth Rapaport [Indianapolis: Hackett, 1978], 59). Note that *On Liberty* (1859) appeared in the same year as *A Tale of Two Cities*, the novel to which I will turn to consider character in more detail.

[8] Andrea K. Henderson has considered this passage and *Our Mutual Friend* more broadly in relation to Victorian theories of combinatorics in "Combinatorial Characters," in *The Palgrave Handbook of Literature and Mathematics*, ed. R. Tubbs et al., 493–512; see 504–5. As she observes, "characters in these novels are not the fundamental units of social meaning that earlier nineteenth-century novelistic protocols would lead us to expect. They are instead like atoms in a compound or letters in a word; they form variable combinations with others, and it's the combinations that matter" (493).

[9] Woloch mentions this derivation (*The One vs. the Many*, 322).

FIGURING CHARACTER IN DICKENS   95

of the brotherhood had extended no farther than "Jacques Five"[10]—a manageable quantity (literally, since there are five digits to a hand, *manibus* in Latin) that had allowed figures to be tied to identifiable individual character traits; Jacques Three, for example, is always the most blood-thirsty. Now, though, the numbers might be said to get out of hand: "Jacques One, Jacques Two, Jacques One Thousand, Jacques Two Thousand, Jacques Five-and-Twenty Thousand" (*TTC* 207). An emblem for minorness—the replacement of a particularizing name with a number (here one linked to a generic name)—has become a political force that's hard to reckon with: the masses.

Such revolutionary implications may seem far from the social satire of the Veneerings, but Dickens's return to Twemlow's counting proves his investment in this kind of numbery process. The context is the marriage of Alfred Lammle and Sophronia Akershem (the only place she is so designated; previously, she had been labeled "the mature young lady") (*OMF* 115).[11] The wedding will take place from the Veneerings' house, and, as "a family affair," Veneering announces that "our first step is to communicate the fact to our family friends." Twemlow's renewed confusion with number and placement stems from this last categorical designation and echoes his earlier befuddlement:

("Oh!" thinks Twemlow, with his eyes on Podsnap, "then there are only two of us, and he's the other.")

"I did hope," Veneering goes on, "to have had Lady Tippins to meet you; but she is always in request, and is unfortunately engaged."

("Oh!" thinks Twemlow, with his eyes wandering, "then there are three of us, and *she's* the other.")

"Mortimer Lightwood," resumes Veneering, "whom you both know, is out of town; but he writes, in his whimsical manner, that as we ask him to be bridegroom's best man when the ceremony takes place, he will not refuse, though he doesn't see what he has to do with it."

("Oh!" thinks Twemlow, with his eyes rolling, "then there are four of us, and *he's* the other.")

---

[10] Charles Dickens, *A Tale of Two Cities*, ed. Andrew Sanders (Oxford: Oxford University Press, 2008), 160. Hereafter, *TTC*, internally referenced.

[11] The running title introducing the scene—"Two dear friends are to be made one"—reminds us of the numbery operations of the marriage plot that we saw in Austen's novels.

96 THE NUMBER SENSE

"Boots and Brewer," observes Veneering, "whom you also know, I have not asked to-day; but I reserve them for the occasion."

("Then," thinks Twemlow, with his eyes shut, "there are si—" But here collapses and does not completely recover until dinner is over and the Analytical has been requested to withdraw.)

(OMF 115–16)

So Twemlow effectively counts off the "leaves" in the table assembled by Mr. Veneering (and one might be tempted to add, those in the book assembled by Dickens). Tellingly, though, he "collapses" after five, seemingly a crucial limit in the Dickensian mathematical imaginary; we again have a kind of sorites paradox at work, where five is a count and six has suddenly become a heap. The effect resembles my daughter's malapropism during her earliest counting efforts: after she comfortably reached ten, eleven became "anotherone."[12]

But the episode also highlights the role names play in the scenario; each number attaches to a specific name, as though Twemlow were taking the census of the Veneerings' friends. In fact, census takers, those so-called "enumerators" at the heart of the nineteenth-century statistical enterprise—recall that the first modern census was executed in 1801—commenced, beginning in 1841, by accumulating lists of names; these were then dispatched to central offices in which they were translated into usable data. Nathan Hensley has argued how that move involves a kind of "violence associated with the departicularizing processes necessary for inclusion into the democratic state's biopolitical model of care. This is the flattening conversion by which names become numbers, what is outside is brought inside, and what were once singularities become examples of a type and in that process made fit for counting."[13] The statistician William Farr had noticed the dehumanizing effect, describing how, in the process of accumulating statistical data to make up mortality tables, persons "appear divested of all colour, form,

---

[12] Dehaene would here remind us of the importance of manual digits in the development of number sense—and of the fact that Chinese numbers, which follow the logic of the decimal system (based on ten digits, and thus essentially my daughter's method), have proven easier for children to master (see *The Number Sense*, 89–91).

[13] Hensley, *Forms of Empire*, 90. See also Henderson, who considers this process in relation to both chemistry and the marketplace: "Just as exchange strips commodities of their sensuous particularity, reducing them to a number value, the networks of late Victorian capitalism, to be maximally flexible and capable of growth, required that their members be reduced to the fact of their numerical 'valence,' their capacity, like chemical elements, to bond" ("Combinatorial Characters," 501. Critics have also read Wordsworth's "We Are Seven" as a reflection on the census, as I mention in Chapter 1.

FIGURING CHARACTER IN DICKENS   97

character, passion, and the infinite individualities of life: by abstraction they are reduced to mere units undergoing changes as purely physical as the setting stars of astronomy or the decomposing atoms of chemistry."[14]

Focusing on the role of names in Wilkie Collins's sensation fiction, Hensley has elaborated how new or revised aesthetic forms arose to mediate the new forms of democracy that emerged in Britain, especially in the wake of the expansions of the franchise in 1832 and 1867. Novelists had to respond to the transformation Thomas Carlyle observed in "Shooting Niagara, and After" (1867): Reform's "logic of equivalence," whereby "Count of Heads [was] to be the Divine Court of Appeal on every question," represented what Hensley calls "a shift in the matrix of social relations toward number."[15] David Womble describes how Trollope's characterization of the titular protagonist of *Phineas Finn* (1867–8) unfolds against this same cultural backdrop. He shows how statistics can reconfigure subjectivity, as Phineas repeatedly compares himself to other members of the various social groups he inhabits—almost as though tallying votes to decide upon his own course of action or opinion. As Womble observes, "Trollope, by 1867, allows us to witness the construction from the ground up of a character through the process of compiling and synthesizing data. If this mode of writing character makes the difference between a novel and a census seem fuzzy, it is because both the novel and the census, as systems of subject construction and population management, lack any metaphysical supplement that makes characters something more than the cultural information of which they are composed."[16] *Phineas Finn* and its pendant text *Phineas Redux* (1873) narrate the tale of the passage of the second Reform Bill; Womble's point is that part of what is being reformed in this period is a conception of novelistic character.[17]

---

[14] Quoted in Edward Higgs, *Life, Death and Statistics: Civil Registration, Censuses and the Work of the General Register Office, 1836–1952* (Hatfield: Local Population Studies, 2004), 63.

[15] Hensley, *Forms of Empire*, 99. The middle citation is from Carlyle, "Shooting Niagara: And After," *Macmillan's Magazine* 16 (April 1867): 64–87. It is worth noting, too, that the table leaves are brought into service again by Veneering when he decides to run for parliament, thus linking their functionality to notions of democratic representation: "Veneering is a 'representative man'" (*OMF* 244), we are told.

[16] David A. P. Womble, "*Phineas Finn*, the Statistics of Character," 22. I will return to the idea of characterological "supplement" later in this chapter.

[17] For Womble, the shift is ironically (given the time of composition and the political subject) away from what we might think of as liberal subjectivity toward something more collectively and statistically oriented: "*Phineas Finn* turns Phineas into something like a statistical instrument as he aggregates his new social circle around an average in relation to which he can plot himself" ("*Phineas Finn*, the Statistics of Character," 30). In contrast, Elaine Hadley has seen

98 THE NUMBER SENSE

As I hope to demonstrate, Dickens's treatment of name, number, and character offers his own rejoinder to the new numberiness of democracy—especially in his most explicitly revolutionary work. His novels have long been recognized as testing grounds for ideas of character, but *A Tale of Two Cities* has proved especially fertile in this regard in recent years.[18] I want to highlight how this fact relates to this novel's own unusual numberiness. What one critic has called "the politics of the character"[19] that unfolds in the novel is always, on some level, a politics of number.

3.2 Name, Number, Character

At the start of *The One vs. the Many*, Alex Woloch draws attention to the interplay between name and number when he observes the distinction between Achilles and the soldiers who compose the assembled armies (it's a passage that I quoted in reference to Byron's naming and rhyming practices in Chapter 4[20]):

in the novel an attempt (albeit one with mixed results) to embody liberal ideas (*Living Liberalism: Practical Citizenship in Mid-Victorian Britain* [Chicago: University of Chicago Press, 2010], 229–89).

[18] Hensley's chapter in *Forms of Empire* focuses on Wilkie Collins, but he does mention *A Tale of Two Cities* as another novel that "would repay consideration insofar as it narrates a tension between opposed regimes of legality ... and routes its investigation through the idiom of names and doubled identities" (104) (Dickens's list of names, used and rejected, serves as the chapter's haunting coda [132–3]). Recent critics who have turned directly to *A Tale of Two Cities* to think through questions of character include Lanya Lamouria, "Democracy, Terror, and Utopia in Dickens's *A Tale of Two Cities*," *Victorian Literature and Culture* 50.2 (2022): 295–324; Jungmin Yoo, "More or Less than One: Reforming Character in *A Tale of Two Cities*," *Dickens Quarterly* 38.3 (Sep. 2021): 257–76; and Daniel Stout, "Nothing Personal: The Decapitation of Character in *A Tale of Two Cities*." *Novel: A Forum on Fiction* 41.1 (Fall 2007): 29–52; I will return to these scholars in what follows. See also Emily Steinlight's account of "Dickens's Supernumeraries" in *Bleak House*: "Attending to the function of supernumeraries reveals that Dickens's fiction performs its most vital work through what might almost be called its third-rate characters: those who are so inseparable from their milieu that they often remain nameless, susceptible to being confused with, substituted for, or merged with others, virtually ceasing to be characters at all." Steinlight, *Populating the Novel: Literary Form and the Politics of Surplus Life* (Ithaca: Cornell University Press, 2018), 107–37; 123.

[19] Jungmin Yoo, "More or Less than One," 259.

[20] The joke of Byron's Russian names also prepared the way for Dickens's practice of "ring[ing] alphabetical changes" to create names, as Mortimer's office boy Blight does when conjuring imaginary clients (*OMF* 87). In *Bleak House* the politicians' interchangeability is encoded the same way: "Then there is my Lord Boodle, of considerable reputation with his party ... He perceives with astonishment that supposing the present government to be overthrown, the limited choice of the Crown, in the formation of a new ministry, would lie between

FIGURING CHARACTER IN DICKENS   99

The distinction between counting and naming occurs precisely at the fault line where an individual ceases to command attention as a qualitatively distinct being and begins to be viewed as a quantitative unit, absorbed into a larger number even as the ordinary soldiers are encompassed by the "lords of the ships" who represent them and do get named.[21]

Woloch points to the same departicularizing violence on which Hensley focuses; the translation from name to number blurs individual distinctions, turning people into fungible "quantitative unit[s]" that serve specific functions, whether to make a wedding socially impressive or to man an army. In contrast, the reverse move, from number to name, often bestows a more rounded or "qualitatively distinct being" on a character. Reflecting on the effects of serial production on Dickens's creation of character networks, Adam Grener and Isabel Parker notice how in the first installment of *Hard Times*, the novelist introduces an apparently minor figure standing on the fringes of the action. Later, though, Dickens lifts "the man of No. 1" (as the working notes designate him) to prominence with a name: James Harthouse.[22] An unnamed extra becomes a character. Such a move from number to name can register a psychological process, as when the prisoner first encountered as One Hundred and Five, North Tower is "recalled to life" as Dr. Manette. So if Twemlow's counting implies the table leaves' interchangeability, thus emphasizing the minorness of the characters they designate, it is worth observing that Dickens affords each the honor of a specifying name. Both Woloch and Hensley have explored how Dickens's great love of naming (the lists of potential names kept in his notebooks— and put to use in the novels at such a vast scale as to create a critical industry focused on their indexing) cannot be separated from his unusual investment in minor characters.[23]

Lord Coodle and Sir Thomas Doodle—supposing it to be impossible for the Duke of Foodle to act with Goodle, which may be assumed to be the case in consequence of the breach arising out of that affair with Hoodle," and so on. Charles Dickens, *Bleak House*, ed. Nicola Bradbury (London: Penguin, 1996), 190. Since alphabetic letters here function as ordinal markers, this process is closely aligned with operations of number. Indeed, as Dantzig points out, early Phoenician, Hebrew, and Greek systems of numeration used their alphabets to represent ordinal numbers (as opposed to the Roman system, with was based on a tally) (*Number*, 24).

[21] Woloch, *The One vs. the Many*, 5.

[22] Adam Grener and Isabel Parker, "Dickens's Anonymous Margins: Names, Network Theory, and the Serial Novel," *Dickens Studies Annual* 50.1 (2019): 20–47. I will turn to another numbery consequence of serialization in the next chapter.

[23] For Woloch, the investment reflects the specialization required by modern industrialized societies, which yields in Dickens's fictions a kind of disaggregation of identity (*The One vs. the*

100 THE NUMBER SENSE

Obviously, as Byron's many Smiths showed long before Dickens's Jacquerie overtly politicized the idea, names don't guarantee individuality. Often, writers make use of common nomenclature to address problems of identity. Think of generational repeats, a staple of the nineteenth-century novel: the two Elizas of *Sense and Sensibility*, the two Catherines of Emily Brontë's *Wuthering Heights* (1847), the two Lucies of *A Tale of Two Cities*, the *four* Alan Armadales of Wilkie Collins's *Armadale* (1866). Or of how Austen recycles names constantly (not only all the Charleses in *Persuasion*, say, but all the Charleses across her oeuvre[24]). Even distinct names can be overwhelming if there are too many. Austen makes fun of this phenomenon in her juvenile work "Edgar and Emma: A Tale" when she announces a family with "Children [who] were too numerous to be particularly described." "Their family being too large to accompany them in every visit, they took nine with them alternately," Austen explains. When asked, during such a visit, about the wellbeing of her clan, the materfamilias proceeds neither to detail nor to number but merely to name (and place): "Our children are all extremely well but at present most of them from home. Amy is with my sister Clayton. Sam at Eton. David with his Uncle John. Jem and Will at Winchester. Kitty at Queen's Square. Ned with his Grandmother. Hetty and Patty in a convent at Brussells. Edgar at college, Peter at Nurse, and all the rest (except the nine here) at home."[25] The inevitable confusion generated by such a list may be a phenomenon of the "long family" (one with more than seven children), but it will be familiar in a different way to anyone who has struggled to recall, say, a particular Count—even one identified by name—within the sprawling cast of characters in *War and Peace*.[26]

Many); Hensley considers the issue in relation to those who are left uncounted by the institutions of the liberal democratic state (*Forms of Empire*). For the critical industry surrounding Dickens's names, see John Bowen, "Counting On: *A Tale of Two Cities*," in *Charles Dickens, A Tale of Two Cities, and the French Revolution*, ed. Colin Jones, Josephine McDonagh, and Jon Mee (London: Palgrave Macmillan, 2009), 107.

[24] See also D. A. Miller's discussion of Austen's proclivity for the name Emma in *Jane Austen, Or the Secret of Style* (60–1).

[25] Jane Austen, "Edgar and Emma: A Tale," *Catharine and other Writings*, 28–9, 30. The locational aspect of the mother's technique anticipates that used by the girl in Wordsworth's "We Are Seven"; as Hollis Robbins has observed when linking the child's methods to those that would soon be used by census enumerators, they too would take their count by matching names with a dwelling place ("'We Are Seven' and the first British Census").

[26] On the "long family," see Lenore Davidoff, *Thicker than Water: Siblings and Their Relations, 1780–1820* (Oxford: Oxford University Press, 2012). The phenomenon has recently drawn attention from Maia McAleavey and Talia Schaffer in relation to their interest in novels that focus on communities rather than individuals. See McAleavey, "Anti-Individualism in the Victorian Family Chronicle," *Novel* 50.2 (2020): 213–34; Schaffer, *Communities of Care: The Social Ethics of Victorian Fiction* (Princeton: Princeton University Press, 2021).

FIGURING CHARACTER IN DICKENS 101

In fact, while Thomas Hobbes may have announced that "a Proper Name bringeth to mind one thing only," Catherine Gallagher—who quotes this line from *Leviathan*—explains that fictional names arose not so much to identify the singularity of individuals as to distil types (and thus to avoid prosecution for libel).[27] *Don Juan* offers a more nuanced version of this method; as I argued in Chapter 4, Byron uses Juan's name to signify something like *severalness*: not exactly the pure type of the Lothario generally associated with the term, nor novelistic typicality that is simultaneously individuality (one standing in for many), but a kind of iterative resonance that is neither a one nor a many, here produced through the verse-form through which he has been brought to life. And fictional names continue to operate along a broad spectrum of particularity. As it happens, Gallagher turns to *Our Mutual Friend* to consider the subtle effects of naming; she observes how for all the smoke and theatrics around the name of the man who is finally "revealed" to be John Harmon, this appellation signifies only partially:

> although the "real" name that finally carries his destiny—"John Harmon"— resonates with multiple associations, we never read it as his summation. Because we are conscious of their fictionality, novelistic names not only help us to sort characters into major and minor, round and flat, serious and comic but also prompt us to begin—or not to begin—the intense imaginative activity of reading character.[28]

Gallagher's list of opposing categories demands our closer attention. She recognizes how names help us to classify characters not only into families but also into aesthetic categories—what might be called genres of character: "major and minor, round and flat, serious and comic." The order in these pairings isn't arbitrary: *major, round,* and *serious* go together; as do *minor, flat,* and *comic.*[29] Twemlow belongs to the latter genre; so does Podsnap, whose name labels him as precisely as any number (he wants Englishmen, and even more, Englishwomen, to be as alike as peas in a pod). Then again, on the subject of "the *flattening* conversion by which names become

---

[27] Catherine Gallagher, "The Rise of Fictionality," in *The Novel, Vol. 1: History, Geography, and Culture,* ed. Franco Moretti (Princeton: Princeton University Press, 2007), 344.

[28] Gallagher, "The Rise of Fictionality," 353.

[29] While I won't say much about the comic here, E. M. Forster also links it to flatness, in a discussion in *Aspects of the Novel* to which I will return. Forster, *Aspects of the Novel* (New York: Harcourt Brace & Co., 1927), 111.

102 THE NUMBER SENSE

numbers" (in Hensley's words), *Veneering* offers an essay on flattening all by itself.[30]

I will come back to the issue of how number, like name, contributes to the association of minorness with flatness of characterization. Still, there's a difference between such names as *Twemlow*—or even *Veneering*—and "Boots and Brewer." Curiously, it is the mention of this pair, whose duality already signals their deindividuation, that arrests Twemlow's count.[31] One would anticipate their occupationally generated names, which seem especially statistical in orientation, to be well suited to counting. How many brewers does the 1861 census list in London? "Boots" even recalls a passage from Henry Mayhew's *London Labour and the London Poor* (a number-saturated text to which I will also return, and a recognized influence on *Our Mutual Friend*[32]), in which Mayhew describes the practice whereby street-sellers come to be known "not by their names or callings, but by the article in which they deal." As Mayhew declares, in a passage that may have struck Dickens, "This is sometimes ludicrous enough: 'Is the man you're asking about a pickled whelk, sir?' was said to me. In answer to another inquiry, I was told, 'Oh, yes, I know him—he's a sweet-stuff.'"[33] Twemlow's collapse at "Boots and Brewer" appears to record his own objection to such treatment: to count such figures among one's "family friends" explodes his comprehension of the category of friendship.[34]

---

[30] Indeed, returning to the dinner party scene with which I began, we might observe that the Veneerings, while retaining their central position regardless of the number of leaves added to the table, fail to rise to the status of "major" in the novel (much less become round). That is to say, Dickens seems to disrupt conventions of major and minor along both axes, as I will discuss at more length in what follows.

[31] As Henderson observes, even greater deindividuation characterizes the four appropriately named "Buffers" present at the original dinner: "When one of the Buffers 'astound[s] the other three, by detaching himself, and asserting individuality,' that individuality is short-lived: 'herein perishes a melancholy example; being regarded by the other three Buffers with a stony stare, and attracting no further attention from any mortal'" ("Combinatorial Characters," 506). She quotes *OMF* 15.

[32] See Harland S. Nelson, "Dickens's *Our Mutual Friend* and Henry Mayhew's *London Labour and the London Poor*," *Nineteenth-Century Fiction* 20.3 (1965): 207–22.

[33] Henry Mayhew, *London Labour and the London Poor: A Selected Edition*, ed. Robert Douglas-Fairhurst (Oxford: Oxford University Press, 2012), 51.

[34] Derrida recognizes the political implications of such a move in *The Politics of Friendship*, which includes his reflections on the paradox of number in democratic societies, to which I will come. Aristotle had already stressed the crucial role of friendship in political life in his *Nicomachean Ethics*: Book VIII focuses on friendship as a miniature political community, one bonded by more than mere justice. Consider also how the idea of the "real" emerges in Georgie's discussion of friendship (see n. 6, above). And how the poignancy of that moment increases as Sophronia herself becomes more real (and round). Notably, when Sophronia enlists Twemlow to "save" Georgiana—the proof of her "real" friendship—it occurs as the two are looking over a set of portraits of "public characters," including one "so like" Mr. Lammle "as to be almost a

FIGURING CHARACTER IN DICKENS   103

In contrast to these blatant occupational labels, many of Dickens's names merely "resonate," as Gallagher comments wryly of *Harmon*. (*Podsnap* certainly comes with its own numbery acoustical measure, the beat of which is counted by the "discreet automaton" who provides the music for Georgiana Podsnap's coming-out dance, where the set comprises "the figures of—1, Getting up at eight and shaving close at a quarter-past—2, Breakfasting at nine—3, Going to the City at ten—4, Coming home at half-past five—5, Dining at seven, and the grand chain" [*OMF* 137–8].) Still, Gallagher insists, John Harmon's name is not his "summation." I'd like to highlight the mathematical term here, which typifies how accounts of rounded character tend to demand something beyond the countable. Dickens himself suggests as much when he describes how Mr. Gradgrind finds himself caught short in his efforts to sum up Sissy Jupe in *Hard Times*:

> Somehow or other, he had become possessed by an idea that there was something in this girl which could hardly be set forth in a tabular form. Her capacity of definition might be easily stated at a very low figure, her mathematical knowledge at nothing; yet he was not sure that if he had been required, for example, to tick her off into columns in a parliamentary return, he would have quite known how to divide her.[35]

He hasn't quite "got her number," as the common parlance has it, but that's in part because she is irreducible to a number.

Still, this very phrase has been attributed to Dickens, who has Inspector Bucket use it in *Bleak House*.[36] And, by way of contrast, when Lady Tippins sums up the "mature young lady" at the wedding, the snub gestures to her minor status and flat presentation: "Bride; five-and-forty if a day, thirty shillings a yard, veil fifteen pound, pocket-handkerchief a present" (*OMF* 119). But Sophronia Lammle is in the process of being lifted, not so much into the dignities of marriage as into the dignities of a name, with its attendant promise of individuation.[37] Indeed, one might cite Roland

---

caricature," according to his wife. The scenario again points to the novel's preoccupation with the concept of "character" (*OMF* 417–18).

[35] Dickens, *Hard Times*, 89.

[36] "Whenever a person proclaims to you 'In worldly matters I'm a child,' you consider that that person is only a-crying off from being held accountable and that you have got that person's number, and it's Number One" (Dickens, *Bleak House*, 875).

[37] When I looked—unsuccessfully—on Wikipedia to find Sophronia Lammle's maiden name, I noticed that while Harmon may top the list of "major characters," both the Lammles were also granted this status in the site's current hierarchy of characters. Poor Twemlow

104   THE NUMBER SENSE

Barthes, for whom names denote precisely an unquantifiable "remainder" that constitutes individuality:

> What gives the illusion that the sum [of attributes] is supplemented by a precious remainder (something like *individuality*, in that, qualitative and ineffable, it may escape the vulgar bookkeeping of compositional characters) is the Proper Name, the difference completed by what is proper to it. The proper name enables the person to exist outside the semes, whose sum nonetheless constitutes it entirely.[38]

So if Gallagher stresses how the name *equals* "less than" the sum of the parts, Barthes highlights how it signifies "greater than." Nevertheless, they are observing the same phenomenon. For that matter, our "illusion" of such significance overlaps with what Gallagher calls "the intense imaginative activity of reading character": fictionality. Notice, though, that in allowing individuality to seem to escape vulgar bookkeeping, Barthes also alerts us to how tied characterization is to such processes: Regardless of our sense of a remainder, the literary "person" is "entirely" constituted by the "sum" of the semes.

Deidre Lynch makes this last point when citing the passage from *S/Z* in *The Economy of Character*:

> [We can] delineate the historical surface on which psychological depth becomes recognizable as a space of commercial transactions—where goods with prices change hands. I am suggesting that the reified aesthetic value that is the *terminus a quo* of the stories of character's progress (stories in which change is invariably described in qualitative terms) should be aligned with exchange value in the marketplace.[39]

(like the Veneerings) was relegated to the "minor" list. Lady Tippins failed to make the list entirely; for all that she has a name, in this case she ranked among Hensley's uncounted and Steinlight's supernumaries. Still, these categories are more open for dispute in Dickens's work than in that of most novelists, in ways and for reasons that will, I hope, become clearer over the course of this chapter. https://en.wikipedia.org/wiki/OurMutualFriend#Characters. Accessed April 13, 2020.

[38] Roland Barthes, *S/Z*, trans. Richard Miller (New York: Hill & Wang, 1974), 191. Contrast David Womble's account of character in *Phineas Finn*, previously quoted, in which he claims Trollope's characters "lack any metaphysical supplement that makes characters something more than the cultural information of which they are composed" (*"Phineas Finn*, the Statistics of Character," 22).

[39] Deidre Lynch, *The Economy of Character: Novels, Market Culture, and the Business of Inner Meaning* (Chicago: University of Chicago Press, 1998), 128.

FIGURING CHARACTER IN DICKENS   105

Once again, qualitative and quantitative processes prove more intertwined than we might anticipate. Nevertheless, some genres of writing put quantitative exchanges on obvious display, as Aeron Hunt has shown. She uses the concept of *transactional character* to think through the ways in which market processes implicated literary depictions of persons in nineteenth-century writing. Hunt remarks, however, that even in the highly transactional genre of the Victorian business biography, while *character* "could imply quantitative reckonings, ... it also invoked a moral register and a human content that was supplemental to the numbers, but essential to evaluation." Citing the example of company information books, in which character judgment is represented in part through "the interest rate they would offer a particular associate," Hunt observes that this figure quantifies trustworthiness, a category one might classify as belonging to deep characterization. Still, in the 1830s, during debates around joint-stock banking, when discussion arose about requiring the publication of balance sheets, some managers objected that these sheets could hardly relay the full story. As Hunt explains:

> The relationship of numbers to different kinds of information ... cannot be treated as a simple matter of exclusion, in which numerical representation cuts out whole areas of signification, since numbers were often charged with different kinds of meaning. But the bank manager's position resists such representations and asserts that the crucial aspect of character lies beyond the reach of numerical form.[40]

Here again, even in the most commercial of contexts, we see both the crucial—and the crucially limited—role numbers play in the process of character description.

A similar ambivalence appears in Henry Mayhew's character sketches in *London Labour and the London Poor*. There, recourse to numbers affects the toggle between representations of individuals and of "types," examples chosen to stand in for a wider "class" in this particular literary bazaar.[41] Are

---

[40] Aeron Hunt, *Personal Business: Character and Commerce in Victorian Literature and Culture* (Charlottesville: University of Virginia Press, 2014), 4, 86–7.

[41] Caroline Levine calls the type "a middle phase between the particular one and the uncountable many," noting how "[t]he realist novel is of course famously invested in types and typicality." Like the early novelistic names in Gallagher's account, the type offers "a strategy for the novel to imply the many through the one" (Levine, "Enormity Effect," 67, 68). Marjorie Levinson has shown that lyric poetry can also use the concept of the type to work through a concern for the relationship between individuals (the lyric "I") and the masses:

106   THE NUMBER SENSE

Mayhew's speakers—notably all unnamed—individualized "one"s or merely "one of many"s ("units," in the highly charged statistical parlance of the day[42])? When it comes to portraiture, Mayhew practices a paint-by-numbers method based both in his own love of statistics and his focus on characters who are all-too-aware of the perilous realities of the marketplace. Not only does his narrator obsess over computations (as in, for example, "calculating" the amount of "refuse tobacco" that is picked off the streets to be resold[43]), his representative specimens share this proclivity. They, too, speak a language of numbers. Take one of Mayhew's examples of a "skilled labourer": "The Doll's-Eye Maker." His craft might remind readers of *Our Mutual Friend* of Mr. Venus or Jenny Wren, but in this case the focus on

---

"These poems"—she's discussing some of Wordsworth's lyrics about spring, most prominently "I wandered lonely as a cloud"—"are all about number—the many and the one—and also, all about type, that is, the many and the one simultaneously" ("Of Being Numerous," 637 n. 12). Audrey Jaffe's "average" man represents the *typical* rather than a *type*: one whose identity has been filtered through statistical methods that yield "individuals" who behave as "harmonious parts of a larger system." As a result, "a character is imagined as having internalized a composite image of the social whole" (Jaffe, *Affective Life of the Average Man*, 13). In *The Historical Novel* (trans. Hannah and Stanley Mitchell [Lincoln: University of Nebraska Press, 1983]), Georg Lukács discusses the rise of the fictional "type" in Walter Scott's work as a response to the development of historical consciousness during the period of the French Revolution. He introduces the "mass experience of history" in his opening chapter, where he also treats Scott's "middling" hero as a "type" rather than an "individual" (25, 33–5). Lukács writes dismissively of *A Tale of Two Cities* as a product of "petty bourgeois humanism and idealism" and the "escape" into "private life," but his analysis suggests why Dickens might have turned to the Revolution to think through issues of number and character (243).

[42] See Farr's comments above and Victor L. Hilts, "William Farr (1807–1883) and the 'Human Unit,'" *Victorian Studies* 14 (December 1970): 143–50. Novelists often used the term *unit* to indicate a statistical register. In Hardy's *Return of the Native*, "Yeobright loved his kind.... He wished to raise the class at the expense of individuals rather than individuals at the expense of the class. What was more, he was ready at once to be the first unit sacrificed" (ed. Simon Gatrell [Oxford: Oxford University Press, 2008], 170). Eliot's narrator in *The Mill on the Floss* tells us "Miss Unit declares she will never visit Mr. and Mrs. Stephen Guest,—such nonsense! pretending to be better than other people" (ed. Gordon Haight [Oxford: Oxford University Press, 2015], 454). In *Middlemarch*, we find Lydgate musing, "Considering that statistics had not yet embraced a calculation as to the number of ignorant or canting doctors which absolutely must exist in the teeth of all changes, it seemed to Lydgate that a change in the units was the most direct mode of changing the numbers. He meant to be a unit who would make a certain amount of difference towards that spreading change which would one day tell appreciably upon the averages, and in the mean time have the pleasure of making an advantageous difference to the viscera of his own patients" (137). In a passage to which I will return in *A Tale of Two Cities*, Charles Darnay reflects on his fate before the Revolutionary Tribunal: "He had fully comprehended that no personal influence could possibly save him, that he was virtually sentenced by the millions, and that units could avail him nothing" (*TTC* 333). Dickens may be echoing Carlyle's repeated use of the term in *The French Revolution*; for example, writing of "the period which they name Reign of Terror," he observes, "it was not the Dumb Millions that suffered here; it was the Speaking Thousands, and Hundreds, and Units; who shrieked and published, and made the world ring with their wail" (III.vii.6). In *Collected Works* II.239.

[43] Henry Mayhew, *London Labour and the London Poor*, 182.

FIGURING CHARACTER IN DICKENS 107

eyes also suggests a form of narratorial omniscience aligned with the ability to count. The episode's uncanny effect owes much to how the statistical focus on numbers seems to wander from the subject to the interviewer. As is generally the case, most of the episode describing his work is relayed in the artisan's voice. But Mayhew breaks into the monologue (he uses square brackets to distinguish the narrative intrusions) with his narrator's weird experience of the shop full of glass eyes: "190 different eyes, and so like nature, that the effect produced upon a person unaccustomed to the sight was most peculiar, and far from pleasant. The whole of the 380 optics all seemed to be staring directly at the spectator, ... as if the eyes, indeed, of a whole lecture-room were crammed into a few square inches, and all turned full upon you." The episode then closes with the eye-maker's own calculations, in a voice remarkably like that of Mayhew's narrator: "I suppose we make from 300 to 400 false eyes every year. ... Of dolls' eyes we make about 6000 dozen pairs of the common ones every year. I take it that there are near upon 24,000 dozen, or more than a quarter of a million, pairs of all sorts of dolls' eyes made annually in London."[44]

If the Doll's-Eye Maker's measures dissolve the barriers between human and inhuman and observed and observer, in other places numbers can be used to secure a sense of personal identity. Consider Mayhew's famous sketch of the Watercress Girl (I quote at length to give a feel for the numerical saturation of this portrait):

"I go about the streets with water-creases, crying, 'Four bunches a penny, water-creases.' I am just eight years old—that's all, and I've a big sister, and a brother and a sister younger than I am. On and off, I've been very near a twelvemonth in the streets. ...

"Sometimes I make a great deal of money. One day I took 1s. 6d., and the creases cost 6d.; but it isn't often I get such luck as that. I oftener makes 3d. or 4d. than 1s.; and then I'm at work, crying, 'Creases, four bunches a penny, creases!' from six in the morning to about ten. ...

"When I gets home, after selling creases, I stops at home. I puts the room to rights: mother don't make me do it, I does it myself. I cleans the chairs, though there's only two to clean. I takes a tub and scrubbing-brush and flannel, and scrubs the floor—that's what I do three or four times a week,
...

---

[44] Henry Mayhew, *London Labour and the London Poor*, 296, 297–8.

108 THE NUMBER SENSE

"Oh, yes; I've got some toys at home. I've a fire-place, and a box of toys, and a knife and fork, and two little chairs. The Jews gave 'em to me where I go to on a Friday, and that's why I said they was very kind to me. I never had no doll; but I misses little sister—she's only two years old. ...

... I know the quantities very well. For a penny I ought to have a full market hand, or as much as I could carry in my arms at one time, without spilling. For 3d. I has a lap full, enough to earn about a shilling; and for 6d. I gets as many as crams my basket. I can't read or write, but I knows how many pennies goes to a shilling, why, twelve, of course, but I don't know how many ha'pence there is, though there's two to a penny. When I've bought 3d. of creases, I ties 'em up into as many little bundles as I can. ... I aint a child, and I shan't be a woman till I'm twenty, but I'm past eight, I am. I don't know nothing about what I earns during the year, I only know how many pennies goes to a shilling, and two ha'pence goes to a penny, and four fardens goes to a penny. I knows, too, how many fardens goes to tuppence—eight. That's as much as I wants to know for the markets.[45]

The sketch's many numbers do "add up" to something more, to a sense of an individual's experience of the world. The girl's age of eight; her count of having been a "twelvemonth" in the street; the floors cleaned three or four times weekly; above all, those twice-mentioned two chairs (it's not the singularity of Wordsworth's "but there's a tree, of many, one," but the emphasis feels distinctive): they all resonate individualistically. If the marketplace works the Watercress Girl shamelessly and ceaselessly, she nevertheless seems to "step to the music which [s]he [herself] hears, however measured."[46] That is to say, we have left the realm of Dickens's Podsnappery, with its strictly supervised "figures of—1, Getting up at eight and shaving close at a quarter past—2, Breakfasting at nine—," and so on. Moreover, despite its numbers, the passage registers a certain resistance to exact quantification. The girl's numberiness grows out of personal experience rather than any strict synchronization to regimes of knowledge or of the state. This fact is emphasized by the limits of her number sense. She knows as much as she "wants" to know to do the work she has to do: "as much as I wants to know for the markets." So while she "knows the quantities very well," these quantities aren't abstract data to her. Rather, her awareness of measure translates numbers into bodily knowledge: a handful equals a penny, a lapful a shilling. It is *personal*, in the

---

[45] Henry Mayhew, *London Labour and the London Poor*, 48–50.
[46] Henry David Thoreau, *Walden* (New York: Thomas Crowell, 1910), 430.

FIGURING CHARACTER IN DICKENS   109

most intimate sense of the word.[47] As a result, while we may be horrified by the system that forces such routines on her, the girl doesn't (in contrast to poor Georgiana Podsnap) appear particularly alienated or automated by the figures and the work they measure. They represent her own useful knowledge, expressed—and this is no small part of the impact—in her own terms and her own voice. Such is frequently the effect of Mayhew's portraits. While not exactly productive of "roundness," the way his representative figures voice numbers contributes significantly to how each speaker is, as Robert Douglas-Fairhurst so neatly puts it, "in both senses, one of a kind": able to affect us simultaneously as an example of a type and as an individual, like many of the greatest novelistic characters.[48]

Mayhew is writing in the middle of the nineteenth century, in a period when most novelists—at least of the genre's most prestigious forms—were committed to depth-characterization. Deidre Lynch argues that the mathematical processes whereby novelists built up the representations of characters had in fact shifted as the novel itself changed course over time. She describes how eighteenth-century "Characteristic writing ... attempted to achieve universality through addition. The transcription of more characteristics or specimens of human nature made (ideally) for more adequate and more valuable representations." Such characterization had little investment in the creation of psychologies of depth, however, the process whereby a character (as Gallagher puts it) becomes more than the sum of its parts. Lynch suggests that depth be aligned, rather, with something like a geometric progression attending later, nineteenth-century modes of characterization: "At the turn of the nineteenth century, ... the writing and reading of a now *literary* character assist the processes of individual and class formation by virtue of a very different relation to enumeration and evaluation. Literature is hyperbolically constituted."[49] As a hyperbola never does quite

---

[47] Hunt's title, *Personal Business*, makes just this point.

[48] Introduction to Henry Mayhew, *London Labour and the London Poor*, xxxvii.

[49] Lynch, *The Economy of Character*, 132. See Marta Figlerowicz's *Flat Protagonists: A Theory of Novel Character* (Oxford: Oxford University Press, 2016) for discussion of a competing strain of the realist novel in the nineteenth century. Hunt also argues that Victorian business biographies show less investment in roundness or realism and continue to make use of stereotype and cliché in a generic mode that verges on romance (*Personal Business*, 78). Levinson has tracked a shift much like that described by Lynch in lyric poetry, one that resonates with my discussion of name and number here: "Putting Wordsworth alongside Gray's quintessential mid-century elegy highlights the singularizing agenda of *She dwelt* and its late-century shift from types to individuals. The shift is from exemplarity—understood as the rationally derived *one*—to singularity, which we *could* call a numerical *one* but only under a concept of number that is non-additive and in that respect (maybe others too) analogous to the proper name." Marjorie

110   THE NUMBER SENSE

reach its asymptote, so depth characterization can be identified by a some-thing extra that can't be stated or defined by a fixed term, for all that Barthes labels it mathematically as a "remainder."

Lynch uses Jane Austen's novels to describe this shift toward depth psychology. Her focus is *Persuasion*, but we might also consider the beginning of *Emma*: "Emma Woodhouse, handsome, clever, and rich, with a comfortable home and happy disposition, seemed to unite some of the best blessings of existence; and had lived nearly twenty-one years in the world with very little to distress or vex her" (*E* 5). Austen starts the novel by telling us that her heroine is "handsome, clever, and rich" (and almost twenty-one: numbers do enter into this account); the accumulating traits seem characteristic of eighteenth-century additive methods.[50] Moreover, the single-sentence presentation might recall E. M. Forster's famous distinction in *Aspects of the Novel* between flat and round characters. Forster's discussion includes a test for flatness: "The really flat character can be expressed in one sentence."[51] So if the summary offered by the opening lines of *Emma* is fashioned to push her forward into the action of the novel (something will have to "vex" her to get the story going), it also appears as a kind of characterological challenge. Will Emma prove to be beyond such easy definition as spoilt little rich girl? The answer here is obvious to any reader: Austen produces a narrative that shows her heroine to be far more than the simple totting up of elements. In fact, Mr. Weston's riddle on Emma's name—that M and A are the "two letters of the alphabet ... that express perfection" (*E* 292)—almost reads as a parody of a quasi-algebraic proof, one created to undermine the very notion of such mathematical tidiness. Despite that fact that the name *Emma* means *whole*, she certainly exceeds the sum of her parts.

As many readers have observed, Emma's expansion beyond the single sentence, her roundness or depth, arises first-and-foremost out of the novel's extraordinary implementation of free indirect discourse (FID), especially as used to reveal the tenor of Emma's thoughts.[52] (Recall that Twemlow's count

---

Levinson, "Notes and Queries on Names and Numbers," §13; https://romantic-circles.org/praxis/numbers/HTML/praxis.2013.levinson. Republished in Levinson's *Thinking Through Poetry: Field Reports on Romantic Lyric* (Oxford: Oxford University Press, 2018).

[50] The line is reminiscent of Byron's description of Julia in *Don Juan* (discussed in Chapter 1), as "married, charming, chaste, and twenty-three" (1.59.8), which I suggested there as an example of the work's overlapping additive and numerical tendencies. Here one might also consider it as typical of eighteenth-century modes of characterization.

[51] Forster, *Aspects*, 104.

[52] Gallagher cites Dorrit Cohn (among others): "Narratorial omniscience, indirect discourse about the mental states of characters, and representations of interior monologues, for example, all portray the 'intimate subjective experiences of ... characters, the here and now of their lives to

FIGURING CHARACTER IN DICKENS   111

of the Veneerings' "friends" takes place in the bracketed and private realm of interior monologue; this aspect of his characterization also seems to nudge him ever-so-slightly from flat towards round, from minor towards major.) Austen is able to apply this tool to perform what Forster describes as the novelist's "function": to "reveal the hidden life at its source, to "expose[]" "[the] inner as well as [the] outer life" of her characters, to bring their "secrets" into the open.[53] But I also want to highlight a certain paradox here, one to which I will return in my reading of *A Tale of Two Cities*: Forster's account of full disclosure militates against the impression of a "precious remainder" (Barthes's phrase) that seems so crucial to analyses of characterological depth. In truth, because Emma is a mystery to herself as much as *Emma* is a mystery to the reader, both FID and the narrative voice hide as much as they reveal in this instance. Moreover, they reveal by hiding. Emma's roundness arises precisely out of the sense of the many levels of partial portrait that emerge from the text: from what happens to Emma in the world of the novel, from what the narrator tells us about Emma directly, from what is shown of Emma's conscious thoughts through FID, from what we can intuit of her subconscious from these thoughts but remains obscure to Emma herself and unstated by her narrator. As with any three-dimensional object, these many perspectives make it impossible to get a full picture all-at-once; rather, we move around Emma, considering her from a variety of angles, testing and refining impressions of her singular presence.

In contrast to Emma, another Austen figure offers one of Forster's paradigmatic examples of flatness: *Mansfield Park*'s Lady Bertram. As Forster observes, "her 'formula' is, 'I am kindly, but must not be fatigued,' and she functions out of it." Yet he sees her response to her daughters' bad behavior in the novel's climax as a kind of popping out: "the disk has suddenly extended and become a little globe."[54] The language here echoes with terms used by Austen's Mrs. Grant: "Lady Bertram seems more of a cipher now than when

---

which no real observer could ever accede in real life' .... These modes of access to the inner life are recognizable signs that an imaginary persona is in the making" ("Fictionality," 356). See also Michael McKeon, ed., *Theory of the Novel: A Historical Approach* (Baltimore: Johns Hopkins University Press, 2000), on FID and depth characterization (485–91), and Frances Ferguson's influential take on FID as the novel's preeminent formal innovation ("Jane Austen, *Emma*, and the Impact of Form," *Modern Language Quarterly* 61.1 [2000]: 157–80). For a counterview that highlights rather the importance of direct speech in the nineteenth-century novel—and does so via computational methods that align with some of my concerns in this book—see Tara Menon, "Keeping Count: Direct Speech in the Nineteenth-Century British Novel," *Narrative* 27.2 (2019): 160–81.

[53] Forster, *Aspects*, 72, 74–5.
[54] Forster, *Aspects*, 112.

112 THE NUMBER SENSE

he [Sir Thomas] is at home," she tells Mary Crawford.[55] That cipher—a zero or "little disc"—pops into significance with the addition of a masculine digit before it.[56] This passage suggests that the momentary impression of depth may owe as much to the configurations of the character network as to the moral crisis at the novel's close; in fact, Austen herself observes Lady Bertram's only unusual act in relation to Crawford's proposal to Fanny, which prompts her to offer Fanny her own lady's maid's help to prepare her for the ball. But Forster uses her example to show that although here, when the book is closed "Lady Bertram goes back to flat," Austen's characters always have the potential for roundness.[57]

If, however, Austen serves as Forster's prime example of a novelist so invested in roundness that even her flat characters can "pop," Dickens serves as his case-study in the value of flat characterization. His defense of Dickens takes place against a notably data-driven idea of character. Forster quotes from the critic Norman Douglas's open letter to D. H. Lawrence, which had somewhat ironically accused Lawrence of using "the novelist's touch" in a biography even while tarring him with the statistician's brush:

> It consists, I should say, in a failure to realize the complexities of the ordinary human mind; it selects for literary purposes two or three facets of a man or woman ..., [the most] useful ingredients of their character, and disregards all the others. ... Such and such are the data: everything incompatible with those data has to go by the board. It follows that ... The facts may be correct as far as they go but there are too few of them ... That is the novelist's touch.

---

[55] Austen, *Mansfield Park*, 127.

[56] Many writers make use of versions of this metaphor, often opposing a feminine cipher with a masculine digit that appears to carry phallic connotations; I have already noted an example in *Don Juan* (9.55–6). In *A Vindication of the Rights of Woman*, Mary Wollstonecraft remarks how "Riches and hereditary honours have made cyphers of women to give consequence to the numerical figure." In Mary Wollstonecraft and J. S. Mill, *A Vindication of the Rights of Woman and The Subjection of Women* (London: Dent, 1992), 28. In *Middlemarch*, Eliot describes the change in Rosamond's feelings for Lydgate after her disappointments as undermining his previous "effect" on her as "of a numeral before ciphers" (604); his entrance no longer brings her to life.

Patricia Cline Cohen points out that one early objection to Arabic numerals (over Roman) is that they could easily be falsified by adding a figure at the end or beginning (*A Calculating People: The Spread of Numeracy in Early America* [New York: Routledge, 1999], 19). In *Jane Eyre*, when Jane wonders whether there might have been some misunderstanding regarding the size of her inheritance through the accidental addition of a zero, St. John corrects her: "It written in letters, not figures,—twenty thousand" (337).

[57] Forster, *Aspects*, 114. Others might find Lady Bertram's "transformation" less convincing as an example of momentary characterological depth.

FIGURING CHARACTER IN DICKENS   113

Forster responds by defending such methods: "a novel that is at all complex often requires flat people as well as round."[58] He then turns to Dickens to make his case.

Introducing his one-sentence test, Mrs. Micawber had already provided the example: "I will never desert Mr. Micawber."[59] That said, as Forster now remarks, "Dickens's people are nearly all flat"—even the major characters. "Pip and David Copperfield"—the novelist's two most autobiographical figures, both first-person narrators of novels of *Bildung* who are thus prime candidates for realistically fleshed-out portrayal—"attempt roundness, but so diffidently that they seem more like bubbles than solids." As with other central figures in Dickens's novels, their appearance of vitality is a "conjuring trick": "at any moment we may look at Mr. Pickwick edgeways and find him no thicker than a gramophone record. But we never get the sideway view."[60] Indeed this characterological effect, the universal flatness of Dickens's figures, can make it hard for us to tell characters at the center of his novels from those at their margins. That is, flatness contributes to another kind of leveling in Dickens's work: his unusual investment in minor characters. Andrea Henderson goes so far as to claim than in Dickens's late novels—*Our Mutual Friend* is her case in point—*all* characters are minor. She argues that in a novel depicting a society composed by functional "middlemen," minorness necessarily becomes "ubiquitous."[61] Her observations align with Alex Woloch's exploration of Dickens's concern for the phenomenon of minorness as a product of the novelist's attempt to describe the effects of market capitalism and the specialization required by the division of labor. Woloch quotes *Hard Times*: "So, Mr. M'Choakumchild began in his best manner. He and some one hundred and forty other schoolmasters, had been lately turned at the same time, in the same factory, on the same principles, like so many pianoforte legs."[62] So many legs, so many leaves in a table. A mere part, a single unit (digit?), is unlikely to have the quality of characterological roundness—for all that (like a gramophone record) it is turned. Its replicability also encourages numberiness, since it is not one but one of many, a type.[63]

---

[58] Forster, *Aspects*, 107–8.
[59] Forster, *Aspects*, 104.
[60] Forster, *Aspects*, 108, 109.
[61] Henderson, "Combinatorial Characters," 507.
[62] Woloch, *The One vs. the Many*, 170; Dickens, *Hard Times*, 12.
[63] Lynch observes that the term *type* references the movable type of the printing press, thus highlighting both the concept's replicability and its papery flatness (which also links it paper money and currencies of exchange) (see *The Economy of Character*, 5–6).

114   THE NUMBER SENSE

Table legs suggest the functionalism of minorness, the way that such members serve as useful but individually disposable, because replaceable, parts of the body politic (in *Our Mutual Friend*, it prompts memories of Silas Wegg's missing leg and his hunt to be restored to completeness).[64] But what about heads, surely the body part most associated with the whole? Which brings me to the subject of decapitation. Alex Woloch has linked Dickens's strange obsession with this motif to his fascination with minor characters. Observing the pervasiveness of Dickens's use of the "violent topos of decapitation," he describes how

> [t]he separation of the head from the body is a graphic enactment of the fragmentation that can result from that narrative subordination [i.e., minorness] which makes characters both visible and invisible, there and not there: it violently registers the disjunction of surface and depth that occurs when a person's "head"—or interior consciousness—becomes estranged from her "body" or her exterior, socially configured position.[65]

Woloch's remarks about the estranged "interior consciousness" of Dickens's minor characters might remind us that our access to such consciousness was precisely the element of Emma that most contributed to her roundness. In contrast to Austen's rich representation of inner life, Dickens rarely offers the thoughts of his minor characters; instead, both their bodies and their repeated speeches externalize whatever specialized characteristic they have come to represent: "I will never desert Mr. Micawber." For this reason, our private access to Twemlow's numbery befuddlement pushes against his minor status, as I suggested earlier. Still, the particular violence of decapitation works in contradictory ways. While it destroys identity, not only by ending life but by cutting off the most personal part of the person, it also aligns with the very act of intrusion represented by narrative omniscience or FID. When you remove the head, you get to see what is inside.

Woloch focuses his discussion of decapitation on how the motif "seems to pervade" *The Pickwick Papers*.[66] But the most obvious text to which we

---

[64] Maia McAleavey ("Anti-Individualism") considers how chronicles diffuse readerly interest in their many protagonists by suggesting their replaceability (as opposed to the irreplaceability of the central figures in more canonical Victorian forms of novel like the *Bildungsroman*, to which I will turn in conclusion).

[65] Woloch, *The One vs. the Many*, 160, 152.

[66] Woloch, *The One vs. the Many*, 153.

FIGURING CHARACTER IN DICKENS   115

might turn to consider the trope is, of course, *A Tale of Two Cities*.[67] And the character to whom we might look is the most furious proponent of the guillotine in that novel: Madame Defarge. When an online discussion of Forster's account of flat characters in *Aspects of the Novel* provoked the film critic Sheila O'Malley to so categorize Madame Defarge, she imagines her revenge, envisioning "Madame Defarge furiously knitting our names into a scarf because we called her 'flat,'" and proclaiming "Off with your head, you philistine."[68] I'd like to turn now to Dickens's novel of the French Revolution to think more about how numbers figure into this vision.

3.3 Counting Heads in *A Tale of Two Cities*

I have been considering the question of numbers and character widely and often with considerable abstraction, sometimes departing in this regard from my stated focus on what happens when actual numbers appear in a text. Strikingly, though, *A Tale of Two Cities* presents the reader with a veritable deluge of numerical figures, from the "Two" of its title page to the "Fifty-Two" that both names the third-to-last chapter and counts the heads that will roll in it, with Sydney Carton's twenty-third among them. John Bowen has drawn attention to "how often we are asked to register countable numbers" in reading this book, ones that "simultaneously structure and destructure" our experience of it.[69] One might even say that when Dr. Manette finds himself "thinking and counting" after emerging from the relapse into shoe-making that follows Charles and Lucie's marriage, he is engaged in precisely the reader's task (*TTC* 192).

Such numberiness reflects the novel's date of publication between the two Reform Acts.[70] The politics of headcounts is everywhere in the 1850s and

---

[67] Lamouria also reads the trope in *A Tale of Two Cities*. She considers it in relation to the novel's engagement with ideas about democratic reform: "Insofar as democracy does away with the monarchy, it decapitates the nation" ("Democracy, Terror, and Utopia," 297). In Dickens's American writings, she argues, one can find "an equation of headlessness and democracy that serves as a heuristic for interpreting the political significance of *A Tale*'s fixation on the Terror and the guillotine" ("Democracy, Terror, and Utopia," 298).

[68] "24 Responses to 'The Books: *Aspects of the Novel*: "People," by E. M. Forster,'" n. pag., www.sheilaomalley.com/?p=98224. Accessed April 15, 2020. Forster's remarks about Lady Bertram are excerpted as the prompt for this exchange.

[69] John Bowen, "Counting On," 110. As Hughes and Lund note, numbered chapters (Chapter 17, "One Night" and Chapter 18, "Nine Days") are at the very center of the book (*The Victorian Serial*, 69).

[70] Lamouria calls the novel "a reform text" ("Democracy, Terror, and Utopia," 297).

116   THE NUMBER SENSE

1860s. As I discussed in my Introduction, the very sentence "Who counts?" shifts meaning when we consider the verb as intransitive (who gets reckoned? who is accounted for?). This usage arose in the nineteenth century, manifesting the kind of thinking about counting behind Bentham's maxim, quoted by Mill in *Utilitarianism*: "Everybody to count for one, nobody for more than one."[71] But (as his opening section's name hints) Dickens's numbers tell a tale spanning both of the book's "periods" of populist politics: they are as much a product of revolution as of reform. When in *The French Revolution* Carlyle pits large figures against units to account for the failure of the National Assembly to forge a successful constitution, he implicates these two processes simultaneously through the play of numbers: "Consider only this, that there are Twelve Hundred miscellaneous individuals: not a unit of which but has his own thinking-apparatus, his own speaking-apparatus!"[72] Political fictions of the times also turn to counts, whether revolutionary or democratic. If Dickens deploys a chapter title to tally heads sacrificed to the guillotine, Trollope uses one to record the workings of democracy in his Palliser series about British reform; "Seventy-two" names the section of *Phineas Redux* that recounts the vote against disestablishment of the church.[73] These political counts are, then, part and parcel of the larger numbery turn during the decades leading from the 1790s through midcentury. Although Ian Hacking cautions that "Only around 1840 did the practice of measurement become fully established," William Blake had observed how "since the French Revolution Englishmen are all Intermeasurable One by Another."[74] Appropriately, when Hacking describes "an avalanche of printed numbers" unleashed over the course of the nineteenth century, he applies a metaphor Carlyle was prone to adopt to portray that Revolution.[75]

John Bowen's powerful investigation of Dickens's obsession with counting in *A Tale of Two Cities* isolates several patterns in the novel's numbering. He comments on the particular recurrence of ones, twos, and threes.[76]

---

[71] Mill, *Utilitarianism*, 91. For the usage of *counts*, see also Bevis, who notes that the *OED* lists Tennyson's *In Memoriam* as the first instance of *count* being used in the intransitive sense of having value, being counted ("The Poetry of Numbers," 42).

[72] Carlyle, *The French Revolution*, I.vi.1. In *Collected Works* I.184.

[73] See also Womble's treatment of this backdrop in *Phineas Finn* ("*Phineas Finn*, the Statistics of Character").

[74] Hacking, *The Taming of Chance*, 5; *William Blake: Complete Poetry and Prose*, ed. Erdman (New York: Anchor, 1988), 783.

[75] Hacking, *The Taming of Chance*, 2. See for example *The French Revolution*, "The Grand Entries" (I.vii.10), in *Collected Works* I.239.

[76] This feature had been discussed before, most influentially by Catherine Gallagher in "The Duplicity of Doubling in *A Tale of Two Cities*," *Dickens Studies Annual* 12 (1983): 125–45. The

FIGURING CHARACTER IN DICKENS   117

He also alerts us to the interpenetration of numbering and naming; citing Woloch, Bowen remarks that "The question of whether something is named or counted is intensely important"—again, think of the Jacquerie, identified by number; or of Dr. Manette's identity as One Hundred and Five, North Tower; or of the crucial discovery of Charles Darnay's real family name, d'Evremonde. Finally, Bowen elaborates how "the novel seems troubled by the relation of quite small numbers to very large ones."[77] We can see the political impact of this last obsession in the reverse significance of the "Greatnesses" and "small creatures" of Chapter 1 and the "millions" that nullify Charles Darnay's rights as a "unit" as he muses in prison in the chapter titled "Fifty-Two" (*TTC* 333). Ultimately, Bowen shows that Dickens employs the novel's numbers to highlight a fundamental problem of liberal democracy: the troubling fact that a system devised to nurture the individual depends on turning all individuals into interchangeable units. He quotes Derrida's formulation of the paradox: How can we make sense of a "countable singularity"?[78]

Bowen ends his essay, though, with the moment on which I wish to focus: the scene providing the climax of Dr. Manette's hidden narrative, retrieved from the walls of his prison cell—ground zero for the novel's plot of revolution. Manette has been summoned to the deathbed of a young woman (Madame Defarge's sister, we will learn), who has been raped by Charles Darnay's uncle. As the doctor records:

> Her eyes were dilated and wild, and she constantly uttered piercing shrieks, and repeated the words, "My husband, my father, and my brother!" and then counted up to twelve, and said, "Hush!" For an instant, and no more, she would pause to listen, and then the piercing shrieks would begin again, and she would repeat the cry, "My husband, my father, and my

---

prevalence of ones, twos, and threes is on some level unsurprising. Dehaene points to the fact that these numbers are generally common: "Believe it or not, the digits 1, 2, and 3 are about twice as likely to appear in print than all other digits combined!" (*The Number Sense*, 97). They are also the only numbers that do not require "counting," since they can reliably be recognized at a glance.

[77] Bowen, "Counting On," 112.

[78] Bowen, "Counting On," 114; Jacques Derrida, *Politics of Friendship*, 22. Lamouria also considers this paradox in the novel's engagement with democracy, although she associates it with competing aspects of the novel's two nations: "Dickens identifies revolutionary France with the risks of a political democracy that enforces sameness (turning the 'many' into 'One'), while England, a nation of class strivers, is aligned with the threat of a social democracy that prizes an 'isolating' individualism" ("Democracy, Terror, and Utopia," 298).

118   THE NUMBER SENSE

brother!" and would count up to twelve, and say, "Hush!" There was no variation in the order, or the manner.

(*TTC* 308)

They were always "My husband, my father, and my brother! One, two, three, four, five, six, seven, eight, nine, ten, eleven, twelve. Hush!"

(*TTC* 313)

The woman is a prime example of the kind of Dickensian character whom Emily Steinlight designates as a supernumerary—unnamed, uncounted— a fact that lends an extra irony to her tallying lament.[79] But what are we to make of such counting? How does this counting head relate to the headcounts with which the novel concludes?

It emerges that the woman is recalling her husband's death sighs, exhaled in time with the chimes of a clock at noon. In some ways, then, her count expresses the recursive aspect of traumatic experience, thereby also minia- turizing the cyclical trauma that is Revolution as depicted by the novel. The temporal numbering connects to counts of people, as well: it is both linked to her list of relations and oddly in excess of them (no matching here). But I want to propose that her count can be considered alongside issues of characterization. Indeed Bowen suggests a characterological read- ing when he calls the moment "paradoxical, and more than paradoxical," "because the intense singularity of the dead woman's suffering is figured nei- ther through the largess of detail and plenitude of speech that is the usual hallmark of Dickens's fictional characterization nor anything like Carton's idealizing self-projection [in the prophecy that concludes the novel], but through the anonymous and relayed voicing of a circular and potentially endless sequence of temporal enumeration."[80]

Yet the source of the "intense singularity"—and its paradoxical relation- ship to counting—does not strike me as exceptional, at least not primarily so. Rather, it registers some key features of Dickens's more common mode of fictionalizing character, ones I have already considered: his "flatness," his propensity to observe surfaces rather than depths, speech rather than

---

[79] Steinlight, *Populating the Novel*, 107–37. See especially, in the context of my argument, her observation of *Bleak House*'s Jo: "in a genre that typically sets a high premium on the interiority of its principal characters, Jo presents a surface that not only resists interiorization (knowing 'nothink') but also compromises the distinctiveness of those that rise to the level of subjectivity" (122).

[80] Bowen, "Counting On," 122–3.

FIGURING CHARACTER IN DICKENS 119

thoughts. Henry James, decrying "the limits of Mr. Dickens's insight" in a review of *Our Mutual Friend*, corrects himself: "Insight is, perhaps, too strong a word; for we are convinced that it is one of the chief conditions of his genius not to see beneath the surface of things. If we might hazard a definition of his literary character, we should, accordingly, call him the greatest of superficial novelists." James continues in terms that resonate numerically, in ways that should by now be familiar: "He has created nothing but figure. He has added nothing to our understanding of human character."[81] Still, maybe one can "add" to the account of human character precisely by focusing on figures, on what they can be used to conceal as much as what they reveal. The girl's listing and numbering, while tragic rather than comic in vein, are in some ways, then, reminiscent of the Dickensian method identified by Forster, whereby flat character is determined by the repetition of a single (at times, numbery) sentence. Compare Micawber's: "Annual income twenty pounds, annual expenditure nineteen nineteen and six, result happiness. Annual income twenty pounds, annual expenditure twenty pounds ought and six, result misery."[82]

We quite rightly consider Charles Dickens to be a novelist averse to an ethos of counting. Witness Twemlow's table leaves. *Hard Times* begins by indicting the definition of a horse as a "Quadruped. ... Forty teeth, namely twenty-four grinders, four eye-teeth, and twelve incisive."[83] This is the kind of sorting measure that Hacking has associated with the statistical bent ("stutterings," in Sissy Jupe's pronunciation[84]) of what Dickens calls "the Period." Hacking uses the phrase "making up people" to describe how "enumeration requires categorization, and ... defining new classes of people for the purposes of statistics has consequences for the ways in which we conceive of others and think of our own possibilities and potentialities." A horse is a quadruped; a human is a biped. As a result of a set of institutions devoted to determining "numerical facts about the citizen," Hacking describes how "a new kind of man" was brought into being: "the man whose

---

[81] Henry James, "The Limitations of Dickens," review of Charles Dickens's *Our Mutual Friend*, *The Nation* (December 21, 1865): 786–7.

[82] Charles Dickens, *David Copperfield*, ed. Nina Burgess (Oxford: Oxford University Press, 2008), 169. In tracking what comes in and goes out, these figures establish a kind of threshold of character. See also James Buzard on *David Copperfield*'s persistent interest in thresholds and the concern for "the delicate balance between income and outlay" it displays in its characterization. "*David Copperfield* and the Thresholds of Modernity," *ELH* 86.1 (Spring 2019): 223–43. This paradigm for character also recalls the many miserly "Characters" portrayed by the books Mr. Boffin collects for Silas Wegg to read to him (*OMF* 479–86).

[83] Dickens, *Hard Times*, 9–10.

[84] Dickens, *Hard Times*, 59.

120 THE NUMBER SENSE

essence was plotted by a thousand numbers."[85] Michael Klotz has argued that such processes could resonate productively for Victorian novelists who were constructing their fictional characters. He shows how in *Great Expectations* (1861), Dickens focuses on moments where characters view their fates in relation to that of an abstract statistical individual—and notes how these moments, like the novel form itself, "facilitate the structured imagining of unknowable others."[86] But the effect of such plotting and sorting can also be alarming.

Take the case of the eugenicist Francis Galton, who later in the century called for the "Measurement of Character." His so-titled *Fortnightly Review* article opens in terms that resonate with my previous discussion of novelistic characterization, indicating the prestige of "depth" identified by Lynch. "I do not plead guilty to taking a shallow view of human nature, when I propose to apply, as it were, a foot-rule to its heights and depth," Galton preemptively announces. And he continues in this defensive posture: "The powers of man are finite, and if finite, they are not too large for measurement. Those persons may justly be accused of shallowness of view, who do not discriminate a wide range of differences, but quickly lose all sense of proportion, and rave about infinite heights and unfathomable depths ..."[87] Regardless, Galton's proposed metrics became engines of disciplinary state power. Courtesy of his and Bertillon's research, criminals were identified across continents via the telegraphic transmission of precise measurements (rather than photographs, which could not be sent over the wires): height, distance between

---

[85] Hacking, *The Taming of Chance*, 6, 34.

[86] Michael Klotz, "Manufacturing Fictional Individuals," 220. See also Jaffe, *The Affective Life of the Average Man.*

[87] Francis Galton, "Measurement of Character," *Fortnightly Review* 36 (1884), 179. For the flavor of Galton's enterprise, consider his proposal of "instrumental investigations" to measure "inclination" (sexual attraction—the scare quotes are his) by attaching a pressure gauge to chairs and then placing the subjects in them; since people who are attracted to each other literally incline toward each other, a gauge on the front legs of their chairs will measure the pressure, and by extension, the level of attraction (184)!

Eugenics play a significant role in Joseph Conrad's *The Secret Agent* (1907), a novel displaying many of the numbery concerns of *A Tale of Two Cities*. Also centered on what the book's closing refrain calls *"an impenetrable mystery,"* Conrad's work contains two numbers—one spatial, one temporal—that provide vital clues to unravelling the text's secret plots: the address label (34 Brett Street) that is retrieved from the fragment of Stevie's coat collar after his tragic death, when the bomb he was carrying to explode the Greenwich Observatory is prematurely denotated; and the date (24th June 1879) that is engraved on the wedding band left behind by his sister, Winnie, prior to her suicide at sea. Still, Conrad's literary methods diverge crucially from Dickens's: while Winnie's mantra may be that "things do not stand much looking into," Conrad pries open the minds of most of the novel's characters. *The Secret Agent*, ed. John Lyon (Oxford: Oxford University Press, 2008), 224–7, 130.

FIGURING CHARACTER IN DICKENS   121

the eyes, head circumference.[88] Such early biometrics would refine Madame Defarge's "portrait," used to register the spy John Barsad through the counted stitches of her knitting:[89] "Age, about forty years; height, about five feet nine; black hair; complexion dark; generally, rather handsome visage; eyes dark, face thin, long, and sallow; nose aquiline, but not straight, having a peculiar inclination towards the left cheek; expression, therefore, sinister" (*TTC* 170).[90]

Yet the raped woman's vocalized count feels like an antidote to such numbers. Her speech weirdly echoes David Copperfield's description of Barkis's confused language after young Davey's success in securing Peggotty's troth: "In his attempts to be particularly lucid, Mr. Barkis was so extremely mysterious, that I might have stood looking in his face for an hour, and most

---

[88] See Hacking, *The Taming of Chance*, 187.

[89] Knitting—or, rather, weaving—has a role also in the history of computing, given its place in early developments in artificial intelligence; Byron's daughter Ada Lovelace compared the "analytical engine's" algebraic patterns to the weavings of a Jacquard loom, which also used a binary system to store information. In *The Difference Engine* (often regarded one of the first examples of neoVictorian steampunk fiction), William Gibson and Bruce Sterling refer repeatedly to this role in imagining their alternative history of a Victorian England in which Charles Babbage's "analytical engine" had been built. Galton features in *The Difference Engine* as a product of the same numbery historical forces. See also Herbert Sussman, "Cyberpunk Meets Charles Babbage," *Victorian Studies* 38.1 (1994), 4.

Lamouria turns to Babbage to describe one of the modes of characterization briefly imagined in *A Tale of Two Cities*: "*A Tale*'s most radical experiment with character, however, resides in its attempts to imagine a strategy for representing the masses that would encompass everyone and preserve rather than assimilate their irreducible particularity. In these moments of utopian fantasy, Dickens builds on Charles Babbage's idiosyncratic theory, explained in *The Ninth Bridgewater Treatise* (1837), that the 'globe' contains an eternal record of every person's 'words and actions'" ("Democracy, Terror, and Utopia," 311). She cites the narrator's musings on the hypothetical actions of "sublimer intelligences": "And as mere human knowledge can split a ray of light and analyse the manner of its composition, so, sublime intelligences may read in the feeble shining of this earth of ours, every thought and act, every vice and virtue, of every responsible creature on it" (*TTC* 169). This passage occurs in a chapter tellingly entitled "Still Knitting"—indeed, we might think (less optimistically than Lamouria) of Keats' lament regarding the unweaving of the rainbow (from *Lamia*) as an intertext joining Madame Defarge's knitting to the work of such "sublimer intelligences."

[90] See also Daniel Stout: "Madame Defarge's knitted registry of the condemned points out just how thin an operative characterization might be. The compilation of details counts as a sketch of the sort police departments use, but it is not likely to count either as a literary character or even as what Forster calls 'caricature'" ("Nothing Personal," 37). I will return to Stout's essay, which overlaps with my own in its concern for the novel's use of flat characterization. For Stout, flatness registers Dickens's effort to describe a society indifferent to individuals because in it (*contra* Woloch's sense of a contest) "every one is, in fact, a many" ("Nothing Personal," 36). My reading here, as I hope will become clear, stresses rather how flatness—like the numbers that help to produce it—can also offer a form of sanctuary to the individual. I do, however, follow some of Stout's implications when considering the Jacquerie as a kind of army of the Revolution in "Making Soldiers Count: Literature and War in the 1850s," which shares the numbery focus of my argument here.

122 THE NUMBER SENSE

assuredly should have got as much information out of it as out of the face of a clock that had stopped."[91] Woloch remarks of Barkis's inarticulacy that it is "a manifestation of [his] inscrutability," of the way in which he both does and does not "have an interiority as actual as the narrator's own."[92] What about the woman? How does her count speak to her interior life, what kind of "face of a clock" does it present? I want to suggest that a numbery attention to the outward, surface details of the objective world can—like the young woman's counting—paradoxically preserve a space for the most private form of inaccessible experience by deflecting our attention from it, keeping it secret.[93]

Thus, in *A Tale of Two Cities*, characters often emerge out of numbers that simultaneously identify *and* conceal or protect them, as with the Jacques (I have mentioned already how Jacques Three is consistently the most vengeful), or One Hundred and Five, North Tower. This double structure— their combination of public and secret significance—makes these numbers resemble the containers D. A. Miller recognizes as implements used by Dickens's characters to display their mysteries in public. Miller observes that "characters in *David Copperfield* are frequently coupled with boxes" (Barkis-the-carrier, who dies with his strong box hidden beneath his bed, is a major case in point);[94] his remark resonates afresh in a book whose central character is called Carton.[95] But in *A Tale of Two Cities*, while characterological containers may hide untold sums, they tend to be labeled by distinguishing numbers: the Jacques, Dr. Manette, ... even Carton, who is branded as a "Double" (*TTC* 79), "Two" to Darnay's "One" in the list of Lucie's "hundreds" of suitors (*TTC* 97, 96).[96]

---

[91] Dickens, *David Copperfield*, 132.

[92] Woloch, *The One vs. the Many*, 173.

[93] Bowen also notes the links in the novel between secrecy and counting ("Counting On," 117).

[94] Miller, *The Novel and the Police* (Berkeley: University of California Press, 1988), 200. Naming-numbers also function similarly to the cryptographic figures that Jesse Rosenthal has written about in relation to *Little Dorrit* as a symptom of a world in which secret information is publicly mediated ("The Untrusted Medium: Open Networks, Secret Writing, and *Little Dorrit*," *Victorian Studies* 59.2 [2017], 300–1).

[95] While the *OED*'s first usage of *carton* as cardboard box comes from 1891, the word's French significance appears to date to the late eighteenth century. Again, there may be a steampunk inheritance of this trait: Sussman notes that "In *Neuromancer* the prototypical cyberpunk hero is named Case" (Sussman, "Cyberpunk," 10). Comparing such figures to the steampunk soldier-heroes of *The Difference Engine*, he sees them as pointing to "a nineteenth-century formation of masculinity in which fusion with the machine provides a hard external shell or carapace to protect against both the repellent softness of the male interior, exemplified in the image of the pulpy bodies of Wells's Martians [from *The Time Machine*] within their metal fighting machines, and against the threat of a feminized softness without," exemplified by the Eloi.

[96] See also Woloch, who observes of "the doppelganger in nineteenth-century fiction" that his "purely *exterior* configuration (are the thoughts of the double ever narratively articulated?)

FIGURING CHARACTER IN DICKENS   123

The name of *Jarvis Lorry* holds a further pair of vessels—indicating not only his function as conveyance for the novel's plot but also his role as what Daniel Stout calls its "official accountant."[97] Lorry is closely associated with the vaults of the bank he represents; when we first meet him in the coach, he is dreaming of "the strong-rooms underground, ... with such of their valuable stores and secrets as were known to the passenger (and it was not a little that he knew about them), opened before him, and he went in among them with the great keys and the feebly-burning candle, and found them safe, and strong, and sound, and still" (*TTC* 18). Such moments, in which someone fantasizes about securing or unearthing hidden secrets, span Dickens's career, suggesting how fundamental the scenario is to his own novelistic enterprise. This one echoes in a less obviously sinister vein the scene in *Little Dorrit* (1857) where Arthur Clennam walks the London streets, imagining their coffered mysteries:

> As he went along, upon a dreary night, the dim streets by which he went seemed all depositories of oppressive secrets. The deserted counting-houses, with their secrets of books and papers locked up in chests and safes; the bankinghouses, with their secrets of strong rooms and wells, the keys of which were in a very few secret pockets and a very few secret breasts; the secrets of all the dispersed grinders in the vast mill, among whom there were doubtless plunderers, forgers, and trust-betrayers of many sorts, ...[98]

Arthur's reflections might in turn recall the famous moment in *Dombey and Son* (1848) where Dickens dreams of "a good spirit who would take the house-tops off, with a more potent and benignant hand than the lame demon

---

forces the protagonist to confront or conceptualize himself as an object rather than a subject ... [A] double nearly always creates a narrative crisis by inscribing the potential minorness *of* the central figure in the storied world" (*The One vs. the Many*, 238; original emphases).

[97] Stout, "Nothing Personal," 33.

[98] Charles Dickens, *Little Dorrit*, ed. John Holloway (London: Penguin, 1985), 596. Cates Baldridge also notes this resonance in "Alternatives to Bourgeois Individualism in *A Tale of Two Cities*," *Studies in English Literature* 30.4 (1990): 633–54. Baldridge, however, reads *A Tale of Two Cities* quite differently from me: "My contention is that Dickens's deep dissatisfaction with the social relations fostered by his own acquisitive and aggressively individualist society leads him at times to explore with sensitivity and even enthusiasm the liberating possibilities offered by an ideology centered elsewhere than upon the autonomous self" (633–4). His anti-individualist reading anticipates Yoo's, for whom "*A Tale* calls into question the conventional assumption that posits the individual as the basic unit of characterological representation and explores creative ways to capture a more diverse range of entities apart from the individual—a single person distinct from many such persons and considered intact especially in Millian liberalism" ("More or Less than One," 257).

124   THE NUMBER SENSE

in the tale, and show a Christian people what dark shapes issue from amidst their homes."[99]

The clear narratorial perspective of this last reverie matches (in a depersonalized fashion) the Night Shadows passage of Chapter 3 of *A Tale of Two Cities*, a *locus classicus* for considering the issue of secrecy in Dickens from a characterological perspective:

> A wonderful fact to reflect upon, that every human creature is constituted to be that profound secret and mystery to every other. A solemn consideration, when I enter a great city by night, that every one of those darkly clustered houses encloses its own secret; that every room in every one of them encloses its own secret; that every beating heart in the hundreds of thousands of breasts there, is, in some of its imaginings, a secret to the heart nearest it! Something of the awfulness, even of Death itself, is referable to this. ... My friend is dead, my neighbour is dead, my love, the darling of my soul, is dead; it is the inexorable consolation and perpetuation of the secret that was always in that individuality, and which I shall carry in mine to my life's end. In any of the burial-places of this city through which I pass, is there a sleeper more inscrutable than its busy inhabitants are, in their innermost personality, to me, or than I am to them?
>
> (*TTC* 16)

In Night Shadows, the first-person speaker breaks into the narrative to imagine a considerably more intrusive act than that envisioned by *Dombey and Son*'s "good spirit": seeing inside not homes but hearts (or, one might say, given the novel's most explicit form of bodily violence, heads). Still, as Catherine Gallagher reads the passage, in comparison with the novel's record of other invasive procedures—public execution, revolutionary spying and surveillance, and grave robbery—the radical transparency of narratorial omniscience comes across as benign. But while I have long admired Gallagher's reading, I am also struck by how at odds it seems with Dickens's characterological techniques, especially in this book. Instead of a "reassurance" that however deeply he probes, some things will remain "private,"[100] I believe that Night Shadows offers a defense of his refusal to probe, a manifesto: that "whereof one cannot speak, thereof one must be silent."

---

[99] Charles Dickens, *Dombey and Son*, ed. Peter Fairclough (London: Penguin, 1985), 738.
[100] Gallagher, "The Duplicity of Doubling," 141.

FIGURING CHARACTER IN DICKENS   125

And one way to refuse to probe—to go only so far and no further—is to turn to numbers, to count. It is striking how often Victorian novelists have characters resort to math to wrest control over the borders of their own fictional identities. Lewis Carroll's Alice finds herself so changed by the growth resulting from consuming the "Eat Me!" cake that she must ask herself, "Who in the world am I?" Her first impulse is to recite her times tables: "I'll try if I know all the things I used to know. Let me see: Four times five is twelve ..."[101] As this equation suggests, her efforts yield little comfort. But Rudyard Kipling's Kim has more success when he "t[akes] refuge in—the multiplication table in English!" to counteract the mind-bending manipulations of the mesmerist secret agent Lurgan Sahib, who is trying to make him see a broken jar as whole: "The jar had been smashed ... into fifty pieces, and twice three was six, and thrice three was nine, and four times three was twelve. He clung desperately to the repetition. The shadow-outline of the jar cleared like a mist after rubbing eyes. There were the broken shards; ...— and thrice twelve was thirty-six!"[102] The numbers trace the contest between one and many, as Kim's personal coherence depends on his recognition of the shattered fragments of the vessel.

If numbers can help reassert identity, they can also be used to resist intrusions—whether from others or from one's own thoughts. These functions are actually related, the crucial factor in both circumstances being the creation of a barrier between outside and inside. When Mr. Lorry wishes Lucy to control her feelings upon learning of her father's reemergence, he exhorts her to do math: "Let us be clear-headed. If you could kindly mention now, for instance, what nine times ninepence are, or how many shillings in twenty guineas, it would be so encouraging. I should be so much more at my ease about your state of mind" (*TTC* 27). When Leopold Bloom counts in the "Ithaca" episode of *Ulysses*, a particularly numbery section of a very numbery novel, he also does so to avoid confronting the unbearable feelings aroused by his awareness of his wife's adulterous tryst. He keeps his thoughts ordered, controlled, focused on things external—numbing by numbering.

Still, this stance contrasts with the general methods of *Ulysses*, which allow us the most probing insight into both Bloom's thoughts and those of Stephen and Molly, full access to their "streams of consciousness." Dickens is rather more parsimonious in granting his reader direct entry into

---

[101] Lewis Carroll, *Alice in Wonderland* and *Through the Looking-Glass*, ed. Peter Hunt (Oxford: Oxford University Press, 2009), 18–19. Hereafter, internally referenced as *AW*.

[102] Rudyard Kipling, *Kim*, ed. Alan Sandison (Oxford: Oxford University Press, 2008), 154.

126 THE NUMBER SENSE

his characters' minds through standard novelistic methods like free indirect style or focalization. In her exploration of another numbery phenomenon, Aeron Hunt explains how "Dickens's novel [*Dombey and Son*] is deeply ambivalent about the expectations placed on character in the culture of mid-Victorian capitalism"—an ambivalence exposed by the ways the novel recognizes "how deep character and the mode of reading that simultaneously plumbed, generated, and reinforced it were implicated in market subjectivity." As she observes, "Flatness, by this light, can signal preservation."[103] The numbers of *A Tale of Two Cities* can similarly offer the safety of two-dimensionality. In fact, Sydney Carton—the novel's only character to be labeled "round," albeit with some reservation, by Sheila O'Malley[104]— arguably represents the only character whose mental box is opened, to whom we are given repeated access.[105] Even with Carton, our insight often takes the form of a conspicuously acknowledged fiction: *if* he had prophesied, we learn in the final pages of the novel, he would have done so thusly. Moreover, I can't help but feel that Dickens's willingness to pry open his Carton is sacrificial, a function of the fact that this head will soon be taken off to preserve the sanctity of those other heads that remain shut to us.

When we return to the raped woman with such attitudes toward narratorial intrusion in mind, we must acknowledge that it has taken a fair amount of breaking barriers and probing depths to bring her tale forth: the Bastille has been stormed, Defarge has felt his way into the crevice of the prison cell in which Manette had hidden his narrative, and that narrative itself had been brought to the surface only after Manette had broken his own skin to draw the literal blood with which it had been scrawled. But we might also see that while these intrusions reveal the novel's secret *plot*, they do little to expose the woman's private *character*, the sense of self emerging from her experience.

---

[103] Hunt, *Personal Business*, 65.

[104] "I'd put Sydney Carton on the 'round' character list. But I'd have to think more about that!" ("24 Responses," n. pag.). For Lamouria, in contrast, "Carton is less a character from the realist tradition than a fictional construct deliberately designed to address the various problematics that the novel describes." For her, this quasi-allegorical role climaxes with his beheading: "When the narrator reports the speech that Carton would have given on the scaffold, quite possibly after his decapitation, the character is envisioned as a speaking but bodiless head—an image that reverses and cancels out the picture of the 'headless body' that Dickens associates with democracy's risks" ("Democracy, Terror, and Utopia," 310, 299).

[105] We get a single glimpse of Darnay—in "The Loadstone Rock"—and other characters choose to reveal secrets in dialogue or writing, but the effect of such modes of revelation differ significantly from FID.

FIGURING CHARACTER IN DICKENS   127

Indeed, in melding temporality and an implied count of people ("My husband, my father, and my brother!"), the young woman's lament in some ways anticipates the suspenseful action of the novel's close—especially as figured by the Tricoteuses. Daniel Stout has argued that this dark chorus's "replacement of character by number" as they count "dropping heads" (*TTC* 179) (alongside stiches, whether "dropped" or not) "provides a particularly succinct version of the [novel's] indifference to individual distinction"— one he views "as a widespread feature" of a work in which the "modes of characterization ... attempt to come to terms with a world whose interest in groups produced its thoroughgoing indifference to individuals."[106] Yet the knitting women stand, like the mythological Fates they resemble, as figures not only for the biopolitical state (keeping count of its citizens) but also for novelistic plot, as they hold onto the thread of the narrative and measure out its allotted span. They remind us that plot depends on a sequential unfolding predicated by the chimes of the clock, the tick of the second hand—in rhythm, perhaps, with the click of their needles. Dickens was especially alert to this fact as a serial novelist, particularly with *A Tale of Two Cities*, where he struggled so with the pacing required by weekly numbers that he released the novel in more capacious monthly parts, as well.[107] "[T]he knitting-women count Twenty-Two ... Twenty-Three" (*TTC* 360), and the novel stresses the importance of such enumeration: we had also kept count as we left the Darnays rushing towards the safety of England. When the checkpoint guards stop the escaping family a final time to confirm the day's headcount is fifty-two (*TTC* 343), we (as the narrative now addresses us in tandem with the passengers in the coach) feel (the tense has shifted to present) the clock ticking. Earlier, when Barsad agreed to the exchange of Carton for Darnay, he had insisted that Carton's head must drop "if the tale of fifty-two is to be right" (*TTC* 338). *Tale* (the titular term) and *tally* are notably equivalent here, highlighting the connection between plotting and counting. Dickens's narrator had even observed that this particular "number" is "as the weeks of the year" (*TTC* 332), emphasizing the temporal flow of the plot of his historical fiction as we reach our destination.

In contrast,the raped woman's listing and counting preserve her confidences in perpetuity. Such time *won't* tell. Ever. So numbers, those tools

---

[106] Stout, "Nothing Personal," 30, 29.
[107] See also Bowen, "Counting On," n. 21. I will consider the numbery elements of plot at greater length in my next chapter.

128   THE NUMBER SENSE

of the disciplinary state, can in places be redirected to protect the privacy of what Stout terms "individual distinction." Yet, like that of Night Shadows, the dying woman's secrecy is both an inalienable right and an inevitable punishment. Just after Dickens's singular (in both senses) first-person intrusion in Chapter 3, Jerry Cruncher's hair is compared to "a strongly spiked wall," making his head a prison—a reading later reinforced when it is described as "an animated bit of the spiked wall at Newgate" (*TTC* 17, 60). And if solitary confinement is a state of mind, it is also a state of number, since (as I hope I've shown) numbers generally serve as barriers in the novel. I am reminded that the word *one* is simultaneously number and pronoun—a pronoun that guards from the revelations of the "I" by considering the first-person singular from its own outside. Appropriately, then, both Dr. Manette and Charles Darnay, like the young woman, count space and time in response to their imprisonment: Manette by imagining the number of lines that fit onto the surface of the moon glimpsed from his window (*TTC* 181), Darnay by pacing out his cell (*TTC* 247); Manette by scoring a calendar onto his prison wall (*TTC* 210), Darnay by counting off the chimes of the hours he will never again experience (*TTC* 334). All these numbers convey the experience of our fundamental imprisonment in the self. They are shared expressions of radical unknowability and individuality. In a work so deeply ambivalent about the comparative morality of suppression and revelation, numbers both imprison and protect, hide and communicate.[108]

Which isn't to say the numbers don't also resonate politically beyond the individual. Let's take a final walk through Night Shadows. Here, too, it emerges that instead of looking inside of heads we must count them from the outside. In the preceding chapter, the narrator had informed us (he's describing the confusions of the novel's opening coach ride) that "Not one of the three [travelers] could have said, from anything he saw, what either of the other two was like; and each was hidden under almost as many wrappers from the eyes of the mind, as from the eyes of the body, of his two companions" (*TTC* 11). In fact, while its first-person delivery makes it seem out of place in the novel, the strange intrusion of the Night Shadows passage has been motivated by that mysterious stagecoach encounter, as the paragraph following it makes clear:

---

[108] The novel is obsessed with the question of whether "suppression" is healthy (*TTC* 93)—like *Little Dorrit*, it wonders if "Do Not Forget" is the way to move forward. Are some memories best left buried?

FIGURING CHARACTER IN DICKENS   129

As to this [i.e., the radical privacy Dickens describes], his natural and not to be alienated inheritance, the messenger on horseback had exactly the same possessions as the King, the first Minister of State, or the richest merchant in London. So with the three passengers shut up in the narrow compass of one lumbering old mail coach; they were mysteries to one another, as complete as if each had been in his own coach and six, or his own coach and sixty, with the breadth of a county between him and the next.

(*TTC* 16)

The politics of counting here produces a democratic "one"—a leveling effect, joining King and messenger, "Greatnesses" and "small creatures" (*TTC* 9)—despite the distinction between our efforts as readers to carefully keep account of the ones, twos, and threes on the coach ride and to reckon with the shifts between singularity and "hundreds of thousands" in Night Shadows.[109]

Viewed in this light, Dickens's Shadows may echo the "Night-thoughts" recorded by Carlyle in *The French Revolution*, where he quotes the voices of three individuals (the section is called "A Trilogy") who escaped from the July Massacres and whose accounts of the experience he has read: "Thus they three, in wondrous trilogy, or triple soliloquy: uttering simultaneously, through the dread night-watches, their Night-thoughts, grown audible to us! They Three are become audible: but the other 'Thousand and Eighty-nine, of whom Two-hundred and two were Priests,' who also had Night-thoughts, remain inaudible; choked forever in black Death."[110] The voices we hear are on some level arbitrary but nevertheless representative. Such narrative expansion-and-retraction also resembles the effects of the echoing steps that reverberate through the novel, first to resolve into the one, two, three suitors who come courting Lucie Manette, and then to multiply again from the Jacques we have met into the thousands storming the Bastille: "Work, comrades all, work! Work, Jacques One, Jacques Two, Jacques One Thousand, Jacques Two Thousand, Jacques Five-and-Twenty Thousand" (*TTC* 207). So while the girl's numbers preserve her singular privacy, they simultaneously reverberate more widely. When we read the list of relations—"my husband, my father, and my brother"—in conjunction with the circling

[109] See also Lamouria: "'Night Shadows' presents this isolating individualism as the great democratic leveler of late eighteenth-century English society" ("Democracy, Terror, and Utopia," 309).

[110] *French Revolution* III.1.v; in *Collected Works* II.7. Bowen quotes these numbery lines but does not consider their relationship to the Night Shadows passage.

130   THE NUMBER SENSE

chimes of the clock, we may be reminded of how in the era of "Fraternité," relations stop nowhere. "Why stop?" as Jacques Three remarks, prompted by Madame Defarge, for whom "extermination" of "the race" is the only conceivable endpoint (*TTC* 325).

In this context, I'm struck by the similarity of the unnamed girl's counting to another set of Dickensian numbers, ones found in the novel written just before *A Tale of Two Cities*: *Little Dorrit*. I'm thinking of Mr. Meagles's injunction to Tattycoram to count to contain her fury—a fury founded in class inequity (recall her very name has been imposed on her). This, too, is a kind of boxing in, but one with rather different political resonance. In the chapter titled "Five-and-Twenty," having been instructed to try counting to control her mounting anger, Tattycorum balks. "Wouldn't count five-and-twenty," Mr. Meagles informs Arthur Clennam, "couldn't be got to do it; stopped at eight, and took herself off." "You don't know that girl's passionate and proud character," Meagles continues, "A team of horses couldn't draw her back now; the bolts and bars of the old Bastille couldn't keep her."[111] By novel's end the prodigal servant has returned, having learned her lesson (*Bildung*?) in self-suppression: "I'll try very hard. I won't stop at five-and-twenty, sir, I'll count five-and-twenty hundred, five-and-twenty thousand!" But rereading Tattycorum's promise through the lens of the counting in *A Tale of Two Cities*, I am reminded of those burst bolts and bars of the Bastille, and of the "five-and-twenty thousand" Jacques who help to shatter them.

3.4 Coda: Or Ouroboros?

From "Five-and-Twenty" (25) to "Fifty-Two" (52): the number of heads that roll on the guillotine's platform on the day of Carton's execution and the title

---

[111] Dickens, *Little Dorrit*, 369. Elaine Hadley has considered the issue of numbers and indefinite pronouns in Dickens's post-Crimean War novels of the 1850s via the rupture between countability (men as statistical units whose agency is aggregate) and accountability (men as responsible liberal agents); she focuses on *Little Dorrit*, but the pronouns of *A Tale of Two Cities* are equally striking for how they allow Dickens—and his characters—to toggle between individuals and groups. Indeed, Hadley includes the work among Dickens's novels of the period that "meditate[] on the central question of accountability, about whether the ethical character of characters (the fictional depiction of humans as intentional, ethical beings) in any way addresses or redresses large-scale injustices." Hadley, "Nobody, Somebody, and Everybody," *Victorian Studies* 59.1 (Autumn 2016), 83. Jungmin Yoo turns to Hadley's idea of *Somebody* to capture a crucially ambiguous and marginal form of Dickensian character in *A Tale* ("More or Less than One," 271). She focuses on the decapitated woman whose request to transcribe her prophetic thoughts prefigures Carton's, arguing that "Although physically nonexistent and narratively truncated, *A Tale* owes her the momentum to conclude the narrative with the prolonged interior reflections of Sydney rather than a mechanical 'Twenty-Three'" (273). I'd note again how these thoughts stand in place of a number.

FIGURING CHARACTER IN DICKENS   131

of the chapter that records this count. As Stanislaus Dehaene reminds us, "Numbers have multiple meanings. Some 'random' numbers such as 3,871 refer only to a single concept, the pure quantity they convey. Many others, however, especially when they are small, evoke a host of other ideas."[112] While acknowledged in the novel "as the weeks of the year" (*TTC* 332), *Fifty-two* is also a full deck of cards. Dickens himself must have recognized the figure as he envisioned the satisfactions of reaching such a "tally," for novelist and revolutionaries alike.[113] But perhaps the number also gestures toward the fact that these heads are unlikely to be very suitable for rolling, flat as they are. *Suit*able, on the other hand, fits the figure perfectly. When Sheila O'Malley imagined Madame Defarge declaiming "Off with your head" in retribution for being charged with flatness, she was channeling one of the most notoriously flat characters—in the literal sense—in all of fiction: Lewis Carroll's Queen of Hearts.

While the Queen may be designated by both suit and title, her gardeners (appropriately, all "spades"), whom we meet ahead of her entrance, are, like the Jacques, named by number. Alice first encounters them squabbling over their labors:

> Five and Seven said nothing, but looked at Two. Two began in a low voice, "Why the fact is, you see, Miss, this here ought to have been a *red* rose-tree, and we put a white one in by mistake; and if the Queen was to find it out, we should all have our heads cut off, you know."
>
> (*AW* 70)

At this moment, the Queen comes in, followed by her retinue:

> First came ten soldiers carrying clubs: these were all shaped like the three gardeners, oblong and flat, with their hands and feet at the corners: next the ten courtiers: these were ornamented all over with diamonds, and walked two and two, as the soldiers did. After these came the royal children: there were ten of them, ...
>
> (*AW* 70)

How easy it is to fit an entire world into the rubric offered by a deck of cards! Carroll, who was of course a mathematician, is clearly enjoying this parlor

---

[112] Dehaene, *Number Sense*, 178.

[113] Recall that in Chapter 8 of Book III, "A Hand at Cards," Sydney Carton uses the metaphor of a card game to lay his plans for the prison break with Barsad the spy.

132 THE NUMBER SENSE

trick, and the *Alice* books, like his other works, are riddled through with mathematical and logical puzzles. It's a kind of numbers game.

But I do think that the special rage exhibited by the Queen of Hearts toward Alice can be viewed as a reflection of her own characterological status: here is a figure who can surely be captured in one of Forster's single sentences ("Off with her head!"). John Tenniel's illustrations highlight the distinction between Alice's round presence and the flatness of the court cards, whose faces often appear in profile to emphasize their two-dimensional nature. The number cards, such as the gardeners and soldiers, are explicitly described by Carroll as "oblong and flat" and therefore capable of hiding their identities completely from the Queen by "thr[owing] themselves flat upon their faces" (because "the pattern on their backs was the same as the rest of the pack") (*AW* 70, 72). Nevertheless, and rather ironically, given their emphatic "minorness," they are comparatively three dimensional in the illustrations: the gardeners are pictured with rounded limbs and heads, almost like the "sandwich men"—the term has been attributed to Dickens—who were part of Mayhew's London streetscape.[114] It is as though their flattening results from the crushing social position they inhabit rather than any inherent lack of depth. The cards' indistinguishable backs might even imply a democratic leveling impulse. In contrast, the court cards' flatness seems fundamental to their nature. So the Queen's furious desire to remove heads appears to express frustration at her own flatness—and its own more violently leveling urge to reduce the three-dimensionality of others. Alice's roundness poses a challenge to her sovereignty.

The Queen's rage also seems inflected by a related desire to inhibit growth. In most novels, but especially in those we call *Bildungsromane*, growth helps to produce a sense of roundness in characters. But Carroll satirizes the concept by literalizing it, rendering it a matter of figures. Consider the climax of the trial:

> "Hold your tongue!" said the Queen, turning purple.
>
> "I wo'n't!" said Alice.
>
> "Off with her head!" the Queen shouted at the top of her voice. Nobody moved.
>
> "Who cares for *you*?" said Alice, (she had grown to her full size by this time). "You're nothing but a pack of cards!"

---

[114] See S. J. Adair Fitz-Gerald, "Dickens and the Sandwich-Man," *Dickensian* 13.10 (1917): 266–7.

FIGURING CHARACTER IN DICKENS   133

At this the whole pack rose up into the air, and came flying down upon her; she gave a little scream, half of fright and half of anger, and tried to beat them off, and found herself lying on the bank, with her head in the lap of her sister, who was gently brushing away some dead leaves that had fluttered down from the trees upon her face.

"Wake up, Alice dear!" said her sister; "Why, what a long sleep you've had!"

(*AW* 109–10)

Alice has been having trouble with her growth throughout the story, as befits a novel that skirts so close in form to a *Bildungsroman*. Yet for all that she gets bigger (as the Queen says, she is "Nearly two miles high" by the time of the trial—and thus in clear breach of "Rule Forty-two: *All persons more than a mile high to leave the court*" [*AW* 105][115])—Alice isn't really "growing up" at all. One has the feeling—a feeling supported by the historical record left of Lewis Dodgson—that Alice's author would prefer her to remain a child.[116] But now, at least for the moment, her stature seems to have righted itself, a fact that appears to precipitate the disenchantment of the cards and their return to true two-dimensionality, as the papery cards morph into so many dead leaves, figments of a literary imagination.

This understanding of the tale as a kind of distorted *Bildungsroman* appears most clearly in its own coda, a second ending that is set off typographically by a break in the text. Carroll closes with another vision, spawned by Alice's elder sister's thoughts "of little Alice and all her wonderful Adventures": "First, she dreamed about little Alice herself: once again the tiny hands were clasped upon her knee, and the bright eager eyes were looking up into hers." After "the whole place around her became alive with the strange creatures of her little sister's dream," however, Alice reappears:

Lastly, she pictured to herself how this same little sister of hers would, in the after-time, be herself a grown woman; and how she would keep, through all her riper years, the simple and loving heart of her childhood; and how she would gather about her other little children, and make *their* eyes bright and eager with many a strange tale, perhaps even with the

---

[115] "'It's the oldest rule in the book,' said the King," to which Alice retorts, asserting the ordinal relationship between time and count: "Then it ought to be Number One" (*AW* 105).

[116] U. C. Knoepflemacher describes a photo of Alice Liddell that is surrounded by infinity-like doodles suggesting how Alice "cannot age" (*Ventures into Childland: Victorians, Fairy Tales, and Femininity* [Chicago: University of Chicago Press, 1998], 68).

134   THE NUMBER SENSE

dream of Wonderland of long ago; and how she would feel with all their simple sorrows, and find a pleasure in all their simple joys, remembering her own child-life, and the happy summer days.

(*AW* 110–1)

The emphasis of this vision rests firmly on stasis rather than development, on Alice's ability to preserve childhood into her "grown" and "riper years," rather than on any progress from innocence to experience.

In some ways, certainly, such an effort at preserving "the splendour in the grass" marks many a *Bildungsroman*.[117] But Carroll's resistance to change must be recognized as extreme. Recall Alice's earlier effort to assert her identity: "Who in the world am I?" she had asked, before trying to find an answer in the multiplication table: "I'll try if I know all the things I used to know. Let me see: four times five is twelve ..." She keeps going with this mathematical pattern: "and four times six is thirteen, and four times seven is—oh dear! I shall never get to twenty at that rate!" (*AW* 18–19). Martin Gardner explains that "the multiplication table traditionally stops with the twelves, so if you continue this nonsense progression ... you end with 4 times 12 (the highest she can go) is 19—just one short of 20."[118] But "I'll never get to twenty" seems right for a character who despite her uncontrollable physical growth is destined to remain in girlhood.[119] And the point is reinforced in *Through the Looking Glass* (1871), in Alice's "indignant" exchange with Humpty Dumpty concerning her age. "[O]ne ca'n't help growing older," she explains. To which Humpty returns, "*One* ca'n't, perhaps, ... but *two* can. With proper assistance, you might have left off at seven."[120] Talk about division of labor!

Ronjaunee Chatterjee has described Alice's possession of a "a feminine singularity scripted through the numerary"; she identifies Alice as "a subject who counts."[121] While she does not cite it, and while her focus on gender differs from mine here, Chatterjee's reading also shows Alice steering clear of the Scylla and Charybdis of Derrida's paradox of "countable singularity" by reforming the very idea of *singularity*: "the only answer to 'who she is' is

---

[117] Especially, at least according to Franco Moretti, British examples of the genre. Moretti claims in *The Way of the World* that such works might "better be called novels of 'preservation'" than ones of "initiation" (182). In the context of my own argument here, it is also worth thinking about his statement that "The classical *Bildungsroman* narrates how the French Revolution could have been avoided" (64).

[118] Martin Gardner, *The Annotated Alice* (New York: Clarkson Potter, 1960), 38.

[119] Recall Mayhew's Watercress Girl: "I shan't be a woman until I'm twenty."

[120] Carroll, *Through the Looking-Glass* (in *AW* 188).

[121] Chatterjee, *Feminine Singularity*, 28, 31.

FIGURING CHARACTER IN DICKENS   135

Alice's singularity: her existence as a 'one' who is available to counting but not to the recognizable contours of identity and identity's adjuncts, categorization, and classification." In "saturat[ing]" (Chatterjee's term) the novel with "the basic mathematical procedure of counting ones and twos ... rather than the register of language and naming,"[122] Carroll has, I believe, configured Alice's identity to resist if not resolve the paradox at the heart of liberal democracy.

Chatterjee's description also resonates with the world of *A Tale of Two Cities*, with its doubles and its confusions of names. Indeed, Humpty Dumpty's last remark—"With proper assistance, you might have left off at seven"—summons up the ghost of Sydney Carton, whose own "leaving off" is what allows Charles Darnay to keep counting the years. And Alice's sister's dream also brings to mind the vision of futurity at the end of *A Tale of Two Cities*:

> "I see that child who lay upon her bosom and who bore my name, a man winning his way up in that path of life which once was mine. ... I see him, foremost of just judges and honoured men, bringing a boy of my name, with a forehead that I know and golden hair, to this place ... and I hear him tell the child my story, with a tender and a faltering voice."
>
> (*TTC* 361)

Even more emphatically than Alice, Carton himself will never grow older, for all that he may be resurrected in the children who bear his name and whose path his vision charts. It's a more benign, diachronic rather than synchronic, reimagining of the multiplying Jacques. Still, while Dickens's novel records resurrections, restorations, and even conversions (think of Jerry Cruncher's), it, too, is strangely unconcerned with the patterns of individual development that are so central to the *Bildungsroman*.

I have been suggesting that in both *A Tale of Two Cities* and *Alice in Wonderland*, this resistance intersects with the novels' forms of flat characterization, ones that are stamped by the play of their proliferating numbers. Victorian novels can certainly attempt to use the structure of individual *Bildung* to tell stories of political change. In Elizabeth Gaskell's *North and South* (1855), for example, Margaret Hale and Mr. Thornton must change and grow before they can come together at the end of the novel in a marriage plot that unites not only one "man" and one "woman" (as they are pointedly designated)

---

[122] Chatterjee, *Feminine Singularity*, 28.

136 THE NUMBER SENSE

but also the two cultures—North and South, city and country, rich and poor—that they have come to represent.[123] But focusing on a set of interlocking motifs—beheading, cards, and numbers—helped both Dickens and Carroll imagine a different model of political-*cum*-novelistic reform, or perhaps revolution: levelling as flattening.

Such a levelling effect also depends on each work's temporality, which, while it may appear to progress, does so only in cyclical fashion. Alice preserves girlhood into "the after-time," but Lucie represents all ages at once. As Darnay tells her father, before promising that Lucie's marriage to him (a crisis point for development in the traditional British *Bildungsroman*) will make no change in their lives (it doesn't), "I know that when she is clinging to you, the hands of baby, girl, and woman, all in one, are round your neck. I know that in loving you she sees and loves her mother at her own age, sees and loves you at my age, loves her mother broken-hearted, loves you through your dreadful trial and in your blessed restoration" (*TTC* 127). Or think of Mr. Lorry's ruminations on old age. "Does your childhood seem far off?" Carton asks him toward the close of the novel, "Do the days when you sat at your mother's knee, seem days of very long ago?" Lorry answers, "Twenty years back, yes; at this time of my life, no. For, as I draw closer and closer to the end, I travel in the circle, nearer and nearer to the beginning" (*TTC* 298). Revolutionary time is, indeed, revolutionary: "There was no pause, no pity, no peace, no interval of relenting rest, no measurement of time. Though days and nights circled as regularly as when time was young, and the evening and morning were the first day, other count of time there was none" (*TTC* 262), we learn. Again, despite the denial of a count, we might think of the raped woman's paradoxically circular temporal tally: "One, two, three, four, five, six, seven, eight, nine, ten, eleven, twelve. Hush!" (*TTC* 313). And repeat.

But Dickens himself also keeps a more progressive measure, as befits a writer composing a serialized novel. A few paragraphs after describing the circling temporality of the Terror, the narrator informs us that "Charles had lain in prison one year and three months" (*TTC* 263); his escape will trigger the suspenseful count of the family's flight from France.[124] Similarly, Carroll's child-protagonist does eventually make it all the way to twenty, and beyond: The real Alice Liddell died in 1934 at the decidedly "riper" age of eighty-two. This last variety of numerical figure brings me to my next chapter.

---

[123] Elizabeth Gaskell, *North and South*, ed. Angus Easson, intro. Sally Shuttleworth (Oxford: Oxford University Press, 1998), 436.

[124] See also Hughes and Lund, *The Victorian Serial*, 59–74.

4

Plotting Age in Trollope

4.1 Counting the Years

My previous chapter considered how a novelist known for his intricate plots used numbers to work through his ideas about character. Here, I want to turn to a self-designated novelist of character to look at how numbers intersect with the form of his plotting. That Anthony Trollope was unusually concerned with numbers will have struck many of his readers. For one thing, there's the famous obsession with productivity (something he shared with Byron, as I discussed in Chapter 1). "I have allotted myself so many pages a week. The average number has been about 40. It has been placed as low as 20, and has risen to 112. And as a page is an ambiguous term, my page has been made to contain 250 words; and as words, if not watched, will have a tendency to straggle, I have had every word counted as I went," he declares in *An Autobiography* (1883); the compulsion finds its apotheosis in the numerical table of production and profits that provides the summation, QED, and virtual full stop to that work.[1] For another, there are those related figures referenced by Mary Hamer in *Writing by Numbers: Trollope's Serial Fiction*, the dimensions of, say, "16 parts at 48 pages, 8 parts at 33 pages or 32 parts at 48 pages" employed by Trollope to organize his novels, even when not composing for serial publications requiring such strict mensuration.[2]

But while these numbers certainly control the flow of Trollope's fiction—and are thus implicated in the remarkable torrents of his *romans-fleuve*—I will proceed, as is my wont, by investigating a set of figures that appear as such within the works: those used to designate his characters' ages. Such numbers—a common component of works of fiction—might seem to belong, rather, to the characterological matter of my previous chapter. And scholars have focused on age by studying Trollope's techniques of

---

[1] Anthony Trollope, *An Autobiography*, ed. Michael Sadleir and Frederick Page (Oxford: Oxford University Press, 1999), 119, 363–4. Hereafter, internally cited as *Autobiography*.

[2] Mary Hamer, *Writing by Numbers: Trollope's Serial Fiction* (Cambridge: Cambridge University Press, 1987), 87.

The Number Sense of Nineteenth-Century British Literature. Stefanie Markovits, Oxford University Press.
© Stefanie Markovits (2025). DOI: 10.1093/9780198937821.003.0005

138 THE NUMBER SENSE

assembling his casts of characters. Karen Chase has written about his "age-conscious prose," noting especially a concern for old age that she analyzes in relation to "legislative imperatives attempting to rationalize treatment of the elderly in England during the last third of the century."[3] Kay Heath has located in Trollope's writing a persistent and similarly atypical attention to the experiences of middle age.[4] And Laurie Langbauer has found in his curious love for the type of young man he designates as *hobbledehoy* a countervailing narrative to the typical novelistic framework of youthful *Bildung*.[5] But I will look at Trollope's treatment of age in a formal way, via his frequent use of integers to fix the years he has ascribed to his characters, in order to argue that this practice is in fact another kind of "writing by numbers"—one related to the versions of serial construction and productivity that have so fascinated Hamer and others. Thinking through the implications of this peculiar habit lets us better understand some features of Trollope's conception of plotting. It also helps illuminate the fundamental relationship of numbers to narrative.

As we shall see, even though narrative generally depends on keeping track of numbers, not all genres of narrative count in the same ways. Though its proto-sci-fi mode seems a long way off from Trollope's realism, H. G. Wells's *The Time Machine* nevertheless offers a useful model for how a focus on age can—even as it indicates a commitment to portraying character—structure a novel's action. Recall how Wells's Time Traveller describes his vision of a "geometry of Four Dimensions" when trying to explain his experiments to the assembled guests in the book's opening scene: "here is a portrait of a man at eight years old, another at fifteen, another at seventeen, another at twenty-three, and so on. All these are evidently sections, as it were, Three-Dimensional representations of his Four-Dimensioned being, which is a fixed and unalterable thing."[6] Trollope's novels realistically plot such a

---

[3] Karen Chase, *The Victorians and Old Age* (Oxford: Oxford University Press, 2009), 106.

[4] Kay Heath, *Ageing by the Book: The Emergence of Midlife in Victorian Britain* (Albany, NY: SUNY, 2009). Heath opens her essay "Trollope and Ageing" with the observation that "Of all Victorian novelists, Anthony Trollope may have been the most attentive to issues of age" (in *The Routledge Research Companion to Anthony Trollope*, ed. Deborah Denenholz Morse, Margaret Markwick, and Mark W. Turner [New York: Routledge, 2017], 295).

[5] Laurie Langbauer, "The Hobbledehoy in Trollope," in *Cambridge Companion to Anthony Trollope*, ed. Carolyn Dever and Lisa Niles (Cambridge: Cambridge University Press, 2010), 113–27.

[6] H. G. Wells, *The Time Machine*, 8. This treatment of time as a fourth dimension is now a standard practice, but it was new in Wells's day—although Joseph Louis Legrange had argued

PLOTTING AGE IN TROLLOPE 139

geometry, bringing the portrait to life by making it travel through time to tell a story. His numbers show how through ageing, he seeks to embody plot in character, faithfully rendering the temporality of lived experience.

But to reach this conclusion, let's start with the basics. The first thing to remark when considering Trollope's practice is how routinely he gives you a character's numerical age—rough or precise—and usually at the point of introduction. To begin with a stand-alone fiction, here are some instances from *The Way We Live Now* (1875):

> Mr. Longestaffe was a tall, heavy man, about fifty, with hair and whiskers carefully dyed ...[7]

> [Mrs. Hurtle] was in truth over thirty—perhaps almost as near thirty-five as thirty. But she was one of those whom years hardly seem to touch.
>
> (*TWWLN* 201)

> [Mr. Broune] was nearer fifty than sixty, was young of his age, could walk his four or five miles pleasantly, could ride his cob in the park with as free an air as any man of forty, and could afterwards work through four or five hours of the night with an easy steadiness which nothing but sound health could produce.
>
> (*TWWLN* 237)

Even minor characters receive the treatment:

> [Squercum] was a mean-looking little man, not yet above forty, who always wore a stiff light-coloured cotton cravat ...
>
> (*TWWLN* 444)

Or, to switch to examples from a novel within a series, consider how we are reintroduced to some familiar figures towards the start of *The Last Chronicle of Barset* (1867):

---

for it in his *Mécanique analytique* (published 1788). The idea of a spatial fourth dimension (and of Euclidean space more generally) was being developed in the middle of the nineteenth century by Ludwig Schläfli and Arthur Cayley, among others. It was popularized in 1880 with the publication of Charles Howard Hinton's essay "What is the Fourth Dimension" (*Dublin University Magazine* xcvi [1880]: 15–34), likely a source for Wells.

[7] Anthony Trollope, *The Way We Live Now*, ed. Frank Kermode (London: Penguin, 1994), 99. Hereafter *TWWLN*, internally documented.

140   THE NUMBER SENSE

[Mr. Crawley] was now, just as he was approaching his fiftieth year, a perpetual curate, with an income of one hundred and thirty pounds per annum,—and a family.[8]

Of the eldest, Grace Crawley, we shall hear much in the coming story. She was at this time nineteen years old, ...

(*TLCB* 11)

... with him was their daughter Jane, a girl now nearly sixteen years of age.

(*TLCB* 30)

Mr. John Eames at the time of our story was a young man, some seven or eight and twenty years of age ...

(*TLCB* 120)

I'll return to the particular phrases surrounding these numbers, but here let me observe one difference between the instances from the novel participating in the *longue durée* of a larger "chronicle" and those from that which stands solo: in the latter, Trollope is more likely to use decades to indicate approximate age; in the former, even when precise age isn't given, the approximation is a matter of ones rather than tens ("some seven or eight and twenty years of age"). The distinction suggests an imperative to keep track of time between installments of the series, a point to which I will also come back.

Yet despite this distinction, Trollope uses figures so frequently throughout his oeuvre that it becomes noticeable when he doesn't bother—as, say, with Violet Effingham (introduced in *Phineas Finn* [1868]), heiress and orphan, who in the absence of specifics must be assumed to be neither too old nor too young for marriage but "just right." Age might be called one of Trollope's fundamental "vital statistics," like wealth and (more peculiarly) height, the latter also commonly offered not only descriptively but via numbers.[9] Recall Ian Hacking's phrase "making up people," employed to describe how "enumeration requires categorization, and ... defining new classes of people for

---

[8] Anthony Trollope, *The Last Chronicle of Barset*, ed. Helen Small (Oxford: Oxford University Press, 2015), 11. Hereafter *TLCB*, internally documented.

[9] In *Phineas Finn*, Lady Laura is described as "about five feet seven in height." Anthony Trollope, *Phineas Finn*, ed. Simon Dentith (Oxford: Oxford University Press, 2011), 31. Hereafter *PF*, internally documented. Phineas's height in excess of six feet even plays a role in his trial in *Phineas Redux* (1873–4).

the purposes of statistics has consequences for the ways in which we conceive of others."[10] As we saw in the previous chapter, such processes affected how novelists fashioned literary characters. And historically, numbers designating age undoubtedly played a major role in this procedure—mortality tables, used for annuities and life insurance, were among the earliest statistical records. After the Registration Act of 1837, systematic gathering of such information allowed for the significant improvements in accuracy to be found in the work of such reformers as Edwin Chadwick and William Farr (in the 1842 Chadwick–Farr report).[11]

This aspect of the general push to enumerate inevitably colored how literature of the period treated age. Take Thomas Hardy's *Far From the Madding Crowd* (1874). Hardy introduces us to his hero Gabriel Oak via an account of his large and rather ineffectual pocket watch, "a small silver clock" that he uses as talisman instead of timepiece; he knows the hour, rather, from his familiarity with the constellations. Following this setup distinguishing between ineffectual (or at least out-of-place) "modern" time and a more natural chronology, Hardy goes into some detail to describe Oak's time of life: "In his face one might notice that many of the hues and curves of youth had tarried on to manhood: there even remained in his remoter crannies some relics of the boy." He devotes the next paragraph to the subject:

> He had just reached the time of life at which "young" is ceasing to be the prefix of "man" in speaking of one. He was at the brightest period of masculine growth, for his intellect and his emotions were clearly separated: he had passed the time during which the influence of youth indiscriminately mingles them in the character of impulse, and he had not yet arrived at the stage wherein they become united again, in the character of prejudice, by the influence of a wife and family.

But while one might expect the description to end there, Hardy hasn't entirely escaped the influences of his own time. He ends the paragraph, like Trollope, in the modern mode of statistics: "In short, he was twenty-eight, and a bachelor."[12]

---

[10] Hacking, *The Taming of Chance*, 6.

[11] See Tina Young Choi, "Writing the Victorian City: Discourses of Risk, Connection, and Inevitability," *Victorian Studies* 43.4 (2001): 561–89.

[12] Thomas Hardy, *Far From the Madding Crowd*, ed. Ronald Blythe (London: Penguin, 1985), 52–3.

142 THE NUMBER SENSE

Certainly, earlier writers had been age-conscious, too—and conscious in ways that reflected their formal choices. The fact that Shakespeare's Juliet is just shy of her fourteenth birthday ("She hath not seen the change of fourteen years") heightens the tragedy of her premature death through an implied comparison to the sonnet form that introduces her love affair with Romeo; she never quite manages to complete her couplet.[13] And most readers sense Jane Austen's ear ceaselessly listening to the ticking biological clocks of her heroines: think of the giddy fifteen-year-old Lydia Bennet (*PP* 33); of Emma Woodhouse, who at her novel's outset "had lived nearly twenty-one years in the world with very little to distress or vex her" (*E* 5); of Anne Elliot, whose belated romance depends on the fact that "at seven-and-twenty, [she] thought very differently from what she had been made to think at nineteen" (*P* 29). (Austen also can't resist a characteristic *half* when jokily "pinpointing"—in her juvenile production "Henry and Eliza"—the Duchess of F.'s maturity at "about 45 and a half" [*C* 32].)

Indeed, the unusual specificity of the historical setting of Austen's *Persuasion* tracks characters' ages carefully against a precise timeline of the Napoleonic Wars in a manner that will be echoed in some ways, as I shall show, by Trollope's dating. The novel's opening, in which we read alongside the age-obsessed Sir Walter Elliot the many, many dates pertaining to his family history in the Baronetage, sets the tone for such precision:

> "Walter Elliot, born March 1, 1760, married, July 15, 1784, Elizabeth, daughter of James Stevenson, Esq. of South Park, in the county of Gloucester, by which lady (who died 1800) he has issue Elizabeth, born June 1, 1785; Anne, born August 9, 1787; a still-born son, November 5, 1789; Mary, born November 20, 1791."

Precisely such had the paragraph originally stood from the printer's hands; but Sir Walter had improved it by adding, for the information of himself and his family, these words, after the date of Mary's birth—"Married, December 16, 1810, Charles, son and heir of Charles Musgrove, Esq. of Uppercross, in the county of Somerset," and by inserting most accurately the day of the month on which he had lost his wife.

(*P* 9)[14]

---

[13] Shakespeare, *Romeo and Juliet*, I.ii.9. A version of this idea is mentioned in the BBC *In Our Time* podcast about the play, hosted by Melvyn Bragg, featuring Helen Hackett, Paul Prescott, and Emma Smith, and first broadcast on February 17, 2022.

[14] For evidence of Sir Walter's obsession with age, take the character-defining tale he relates about the premature ageing caused by a naval career: "'Old fellow!' cried Sir Basil, 'it is Admiral Baldwin. What do you take his age to be?' 'Sixty,' said I, 'or perhaps sixty-two.' 'Forty,' replied

PLOTTING AGE IN TROLLOPE   143

Note the hint of a historical shift from the patriarchal to something new in the names of the three daughters (the three queens of England) and in the date of the stillborn son's death, coinciding ominously with Guy Fawkes Day and the year of the storming of the Bastille. The passage also foreshadows a link between the Baronetage and its textual antithesis in the novel, the Navy List, which has served as Anne's own "book of books" (*P* 12) as she has tracked Wentworth's history through his absence. We might even find here a trace of the epitaphic gravestone, a ghost-meaning shared by both these documents of names and dates.

Anne's older sister Elizabeth participates in *Persuasion*'s general age-consciousness:

> Thirteen years had seen her mistress of Kellynch Hall, presiding and directing with a self-possession and decision which could never have given the idea of her being younger than she was. For thirteen years had she been doing the honours, ... Thirteen winters' revolving frosts had seen her opening every ball of credit which a scanty neighbourhood afforded, and thirteen springs shewn their blossoms, as she travelled up to London with her father, for a few weeks' annual enjoyment of the great world. She had the remembrance of all this, she had the consciousness of being nine-and-twenty to give her some regrets and some apprehensions; she was fully satisfied of being still quite as handsome as ever, but she felt her approach to the years of danger, and would have rejoiced to be certain of being properly solicited by baronet-blood within the next twelvemonth or two.
>
> (*P* 12)

Elizabeth's position seems to anticipate, albeit in a less histrionic vein, Trollope's Georgey Longestaffe and her ruminations about her career on the marriage market:

> Twelve years had been passed by her since first she plunged into the stream—the twelve years of her youth—and she was as far as ever from the bank; nay, farther, if she believed her eyes. ... Even now the waters were closing upon her. The sound of them was in her ears. The ripple of the wave was already round her lips; robbing her of breath. Ah!—might not there be some last great convulsive effort ... !
>
> (*TWWLN* 726)

Sir Basil, 'forty, and no more'" (*P* 22). He is himself introduced as "remarkably handsome in his youth; and, at fifty-four, ... still a very fine man" (*P* 10).

144 THE NUMBER SENSE

Still, as the very metaphor suggests, with its hint of the dangers lying in the temporal river of a *roman-fleuve*, these maneuvers will register distinctively when we encounter them in relation to characters with whom we travel through the years. *Persuasion* unfolds over the span of half a year (as I might have observed in Chapter 2). Lady Alexandrina De Courcy has high marital hopes in *Doctor Thorne* (1858); compromises, "now at thirty," for Crosbie in *The Small House at Allington* (1863);[15] and is dead before the opening of *The Last Chronicle*.

Trollope's numbers also work differently from George Eliot's. Once in a while, Eliot may be comparably blatant: in the very time-conscious *Daniel Deronda* (1874), she introduces the Rev. Mr. Gascoigne, Gwendolen's uncle, with the rather Trollopean observation, "One of his advantages was a fine person, which perhaps was even more impressive at fifty-seven than it had been earlier in life."[16] Yet far more frequently, her figures are either unstated or arise from a relevant context. Such practice characterizes Eliot's realism. Consider the example of the Garth children in *Middlemarch* (1871-2). The notebook Eliot called her *Quarry* carefully records all their ages under the heading "Garth Family":

> Mary 22; Christy, at Glasgow, 19, Alfred, 15
> James 12; Ben, 10, Letty 8[17]

Notably, though, only some of this precise information makes its way into the text. In contrast, when Trollope's narrator refuses to specify a character's exact age, it is as though he were avoiding greater knowledge than would be held by someone present in the scene. When it comes to age, at least, Trollope is comparatively reluctant to be fully omniscient. He knows most of his personages from the outside, what might be called *socially*, but only some of them, and only sometimes, from the inside and in full. Furthermore, unlike Trollope's, Eliot's rarer numbers tend to arise situationally. Think

---

[15] Anthony Trollope, *The Small House at Allington*, intro A. O. J. Cockshut (New York: Knopf, 1997), 197. Hereafter *TSHA*, internally documented.

[16] George Eliot, *Daniel Deronda*, ed. Graham Handley (Oxford: Oxford University Press, 1998), 23.

[17] George Eliot, *Quarry for* Middlemarch, ed. Anna Theresa Kitchel (Berkeley: University of California Press, 1950), 56. The list continues: "Bulstrode 58, Raffles 51, Joshua Rigg 32, His mother 56." Dickens's working notes exhibit similar concerns about tracking ages over his installments. For example, the notes to *Dombey and Son* include a section titled "Florence's age—Mems:" that in its revisions shows the care Dickens took in following his characters' ageing; at one stage, he revises a space of nine months to six to make the numbers work. See Charles Dickens, *Dickens' Working Notes for his Novels*, ed. Harry Stone (Chicago: University of Chicago Press, 1987), 70–3.

of how we first learn from Mrs. Garth that Alfred is "just at the right age" to be apprenticed, to have that age named only later in the chapter, after Fred Vincy admits to losing Mr. Garth's money. As Mrs. Garth stringently remarks then, while it is all very well to say that the money will ultimately be returned, it is needed *now* for Alfred's premium: "But boys cannot well be apprenticed ultimately: they should be apprenticed at fifteen."[18] Similarly, when Eliot records time passing through changes in characters' ages, she tries hard to naturalize the numbers (I use the term much as it is used in gardening, where it also describes a highly artificial process); we learn, for example, that Dorothea, who is nineteen at the novel's start, has come of age by the time Casaubon's will emerges as an issue. Mr. Brooke vindicates himself through this fact: "depend upon it, as an executrix Dorothea would want to act. And she was twenty-one last December, you know. I can hinder nothing."[19]

In following such practice, Eliot subscribes to a "show don't tell" mantra frequently proclaimed by writing guides. In fact, the question of age in literature now most often arises in craft-oriented writers' blogs, which almost always discuss the importance both of knowing your characters' ages and of letting your readers discover this information through subtler means than Trollope's. Thus, for instance, Janice Hardy asks "An Age-Old Question: How Do You Show a Character's Age?" and answers with three recommendations: "1. Just Say (or Think) It [i.e., in dialogue or FID]," "2. Just Suggest It [through clothes or musical preference, say]," and "3. Show the Context [in a high school ...]."[20] A lot of these guides also warn that anyone intending to write a YA series *à la* Harry Potter needs to have special forethought in determining a character's age at the start.

Like Austen's in *Persuasion*, Eliot's particular care with age in *Middlemarch* intersects with the historical demands of her novel: Her characters grow older not only against a fictional backdrop, like a sequence of school years, but also against the actual events surrounding the passage of the First Reform Bill. In this sense, too, their accumulating years are markers of the real. The *Quarry* for the novel containing the list of ages opens with paired lists of dates, one set "political" (i.e., factual), one "private" (i.e., fictional).[21] And the text frequently reminds us of these coincidences:

---

[18] Eliot, *Middlemarch*, 232, 234.

[19] Eliot, *Middlemarch*, 454.

[20] Janice Hardy, "An Age-Old Question: How Do You Show a Character's Age?" n. pag., http://blog.janicehardy.com/2014/02/an-age-old-question-how-do-you-show.html. 2019. Accessed Jan. 12, 2024.

[21] Eliot, *Quarry*, 43, 45.

146   THE NUMBER SENSE

"As to any provincial history in which the agents are all of high moral rank, that must be of a date long posterior to the first Reform Bill, and Peter Featherstone, you perceive, was dead and buried some months before Lord Grey came into office."[22] Note, however, that while the passage of the Reform Bill into law coincides with Dorothea's wedding to Will Ladislaw, no numerical dates are given to mark this fact. Rather, Chapter 84, announcing the engagement to the family, opens by telling us that these events occurred "just after the Lords had thrown out the Reform Bill"—that is, in May of 1832. Given that the wedding is to take place "in three weeks," we are left to calculate for ourselves that it happens very close to the time of the final passage of the Bill and its signing into law in early June.[23]

Regardless, the challenge Eliot faces—to keep track of two orders of time and preserve their alignment—more closely resembles that confronted by Trollope in his Palliser series than in the Barsetshire chronicles, since the later works similarly narrate "political" events, including the passage of the Second Reform Bill, the Hyde Park Riots, and debates around the ballot, Ireland, women, and Disestablishmentarianism. But unlike Eliot's *Middlemarch*, set precisely against the politics of a two-year period forty years in the past, the Palliser novels loosely follow, over a compositional span of roughly two decades, lightly fictionalized versions of contemporary or very recent events. Indeed, we might say that they track "the way we live now"—with the "now" progressing from book to book, as the years go by. Such contemporaneity famously caused confusion when the Reform Bill, which everyone expected to be passed by a Liberal government, was instead put through by Disraeli. The change forced awkward reshuffling of the plot between *Phineas Finn*—published serially in 1867–8, even as events were unfolding, and in which passage of the bill is attributed to the Liberals—and *Phineas Redux* (with a serial run from 1873–4), in which Trollope rewrites Disraeli's coup of the measure as an unsuccessful push by Daubeny to disestablish the Church of England.

Keeping up with the plot of historical progress as marked by calendrical dates in the 1860s and '70s certainly presented a challenge for Trollope as he composed through the years (readers first encountered Glencora and Plantagenet in 1863 in the Barchester novel *The Small House at Allington*, and Trollope left Plantagenet behind at the end of *The Duke's Children*, published in 1880). But what really stretched Trollope's skills, according

[22] Eliot, *Middlemarch*, 320.
[23] Eliot, *Middlemarch*, 763, 768.

to Nicholas Shrimpton, was figuring out how to align political relevance with the competing goals of contemporaneity (according to when each novel was published) and the ages he specifies his characters to be. Here, it turns out, Trollope is hoisted on his own numbery petard. As Shrimpton observes, "though each individual novel is chronologically coherent, the time sequence of the whole is a muddle." So when Plantagenet—whom we meet as a young man of "about five-and-twenty years of age" in 1860–1 (*TSHA* 277), according to Shrimpton's careful deductions—is revealed to be forty-six by Chapter 72 of *The Prime Minister*, Shrimpton perceives that the numbers don't add up: "Twenty-one years seems a reasonable period in which a man might marry, have four children (the eldest now in his mid- or late teens), serve in Parliament in opposition (twice) and government (three times), rise to Cabinet rank, and spend three years as prime minister. Unfortunately, twenty-one years from 1861 takes us to 1882: eight years after the composition of the novel, and six years after publication" (*PF* 570–1).[24] Age and the novels' *now*ness intersect to form the crux of the problem.

4.2 Liberal Time and the Narrative Now

Trollope's temporal flexibility brings to mind that of the postman at Allington. In *The Last Chronicle of Barset*, we are informed how "The ladies at the Small House at Allington breakfasted always at nine,—a liberal nine; and the postman whose duty it was to deliver letters in that village at half-past eight, being also liberal in his ideas as to time, always arrived punctually in the middle of breakfast, so that Mrs. Dale expected her letters, and Lily hers, just before their second cup of tea, as though the letters formed a part of the morning meal" (*TLCB* 188). Like his fellow postman, Trollope wants to allow us to digest his news in comfort, to which end he also has what might be called a "liberal" sense of time—a phrase nicely suited to his political series. Shrimpton, though, who is a little fussier about chronology, tries to resolve the inconsistencies by suggesting that, as in *Othello*, the Palliser series operates along a double time scheme, in one version of which the meeting between Glencora and Plantagenet is pushed back to 1859.[25] While

[24] A similar dilemma occurs when one works through the ages of Palliser's son Silverbridge, who is born at the end of *Can You Forgive Her?* (c. 1862) but appears to have reached marriageable age by *The Duke's Children* (c. 1880). Recall also my discussion in Chapter 1 of N. E. Gayle's efforts to make sense of Juan's age in *Don Juan*.
[25] He provides a tabular account of the series's chronology in both time-schemes (*PF* 574–5).

148   THE NUMBER SENSE

Trollope's sense of time may be more liberal, the fact Shrimpton feels the need to make the numbers add up attests more generally to the importance of age in structuring these novels, to how Trollopean time inheres in the human bodies of his characters.

Of course, Trollope himself remarked at length on this point in his *Autobiography*, where he announces the realistic ageing of his figures as his primary objective:

> In conducting these characters from one story to another I realized the necessity, not only of consistency,—which, had it been maintained by a hard exactitude, would have been untrue to nature,—but also of those changes which time always produces. ... It was my study that these people, as they grew in years, should encounter the changes which come upon us all ...
>
> *(Autobiography 183–4)*

> On the last day of each month recorded, every person in his novel should be a month older than on the first. If the would-be novelist have aptitudes that way, all this will come to him without much struggling;—but if it do not come, I think he can only make novels of wood.
>
> *(Autobiography 233)*

Recognizing the paradox at the heart of human experience, Trollope saw that to bring his figures to life, he needed to document their inevitable marches towards death. He had to show both their gradual growth through adjustments to present circumstances and the wear and tear that daily living exacts on all of us.

Shrimpton's complicated calculations thus reflect a central Trollopean preoccupation with ageing. Indeed, critics more directly focused on this subject (especially as it relates to gender) have similarly fretted over Madame Max Goesler's apparently fluctuating years. As Kay Heath remarks:

> Madame Max is not allowed to age. When she is introduced midway through *Phineas Finn*, Marie is "probably something over thirty years of age" [*PF* 301], several years older than Phineas, but halfway through *Phineas Redux* (1874) she is "hardly yet thirty,"[26] and later she is said to

---

[26] Anthony Trollope, *Phineas Redux*, intro. Gregg A. Hecimovich (London: Penguin, 2003), 241. Hereafter *PR*, internally documented.

PLOTTING AGE IN TROLLOPE 149

be a few months younger than Lady Laura [*PR* 518], who is said to be the same age as Phineas, thirty-two [*PR* 91].[27]

Heath ascribes the inconsistency to Trollope's discomfort with making Madame Max older than her eventual husband, Phineas. Some of the discrepancy may result, however, from voice; while Heath assumes the earlier guesses at Marie's age come from an omniscient narrator, they might reflect either Trollope's resistance to omniscience or, even more likely, Phineas's perceptive lens. In the latter case, it is unsurprising that as the formidable and foreign Madame Max becomes his beloved Marie, Phineas's view of the age gap separating himself from her would also narrow. Support for this reading can be found in parallel shifts in the novel's treatment of Mr. Kennedy's age; on meeting him we are told, in what feels like the narrator's voice, that he "was not perhaps above forty years of age" (*PF* 49). But when, a few chapters later, Lady Laura tells Phineas that "Years have very little to do with the comparative ages of men and women. A woman at forty is quite old, whereas a man at forty is young," we are also informed that "Phineas, remembering that he had put down Mr. Kennedy's age as forty in his own mind, frowned when he heard this" (*PF* 63). That is to say, the *perhaps* attached to the earlier measure had registered Phineas's doubt.[28] Only in Scotland does Kennedy reveals his own age definitively:

> "It is this very spot where we now stand that made me build the house where it is," said Mr. Kennedy, "and I was only eighteen when I stood here and made up my mind. That is just twenty-five years ago." "So he is forty-three," said Phineas to himself, thinking how glorious it was to be only twenty-five.
>
> (*PF* 101)

Note how eagerly Phineas takes up the chance to "do the math" that will solidify uncertainty into the firmer ground of fact. Still, whether or not Trollope exerts authorial "legerdemain" in regard to Madame Max (as Heath and others have suggested), these ruminations on age attest to both his interest in the subject and his concern for how numbers, those most factual

---

[27] Heath, *Ageing by the Book*, 142. See also Elizabeth R. Epperly, "From the Borderlands of Decency: Madame Max Goesler," *Victorians Institute Journal* 15 (1987): 24–35.

[28] Ruth Bernard Yeazell describes what she calls a type of "tell-tale 'perhaps,'" seeing in some instances of the word a modifier that undermines notions of narrative omniscience by directing our attention to who knows what when. Yeazell, "Perspective," in *The Cambridge Companion to Prose*, ed. D. Tyler (Cambridge: Cambridge University Press, 2021), 100.

150 THE NUMBER SENSE

of things, can nevertheless misrepresent the truth: not all forties are created equal—nor all thirty-twos, as Lady Laura learns painfully in *Redux*. We might recall Mark Twain's famous injunction: "Figures often beguile me, particularly when I have the arranging of them myself; in which case the remark attributed to Disraeli would often apply with justice and force: 'There are three kinds of lies: lies, damned lies, and statistics.'"[29]

That being said, although I have also found myself, like Shrimpton and Phineas, going to some lengths to sort through the math here, Trollope seems to have worried more about readers who wouldn't be bothered to keep track. As he muses in *An Autobiography*, "I had no right to expect that novel-readers would remember the characters of a story after an interval of six years, or that any little interest which might have been taken in the career of my hero could then have been renewed" (*Autobiography* 320). This fear suggests how in the series novels, his numbers are intended to jolt the reader's recollections: "[Mr. Crawley] was now ... approaching his fiftieth year," "Grace Crawley ... was at this time nineteen years old," "Jane [was] now nearly sixteen years of age." They alert us to the presence of what Trollope calls "an interval"—reading our introduction to her in *The Last Chronicle*, we might remember that we have met Grace before, even if we don't recall precisely that when we saw her previously, in *Framley Parsonage* (1861), she had been a "precocious" "young lady of nine years old," hard at work on "Horace and the irregular Greek verbs."[30] For that matter, the numbers do more than just alert us: given the world we inhabit, they do seem to prod us towards the kind of calculations Shrimpton and others have made. And while, as in the Palliser novels, we may find some resultant inconsistencies (here six years have passed by in "real"—publication—time, but ten in fictional chronology), it matters more that we have been forced to think about the interval than that the numbers add up perfectly. Even with readers less numerically observant than Shrimpton, Trollope seems to have succeeded in this regard. As the critic for the *Examiner* wrote in a review of *The Prime Minister*, using the same term over which Trollope had fretted, "It is like meeting old friends whom we have not met for

---

[29] Mark Twain, *Chapters from my Autobiography*, Chapter XX, *North American Review* 186 (July 5, 1907), 471. For the facticity of numbers, see Mary Poovey's *A History of the Modern Fact*, in which she describes the process by which "numbers have come to epitomize the modern fact" (xii), and Theodore M. Porter's *Trust in Numbers: The Pursuit of Objectivity in Science and Public Life* (Princeton: Princeton University Press, 1995).

[30] Anthony Trollope, *Framley Parsonage*, 2 vols. (Leipzig: Tauchnitz, 1861), I.323.

PLOTTING AGE IN TROLLOPE   151

some years, and who have made for themselves in the *interval* a story worth telling."[31] The effect resembles that of the ongoing Granada/ ITV *Up* documentary film series, which tracks every seven years the developments in the lives of fourteen British men and women, whom we first met at the age of seven.[32]

Both this comparison and the *Examiner* reviewer suggest how Trollope's numbers contribute, although in a manner distinct from Eliot's, to his own brand of realism in his series novels. But what concerns me more here is how the space between books structures these novels' temporality: in Trollope's fiction, the interval is formed by the gap between adjacent *now*s, most often measured by age. My early examples from *The Last Chronicle* hinted how frequently Trollope appends this word (or an equivalent phrase like "at this time") to his age-related numbers in the opening chapters of his *romans-fleuves*, but curiously the habit extends more broadly, as we can see in comparing these instances from *Can You Forgive Her* (1865) (a Palliser novel) and *Orley Farm* (1862):

> George Vavasor had lived in London since he was twenty, and now, at the time of the beginning of my story, he was a year or two over thirty.[33]

> Lady Monk was a woman now about fifty years of age, who had been a great beauty, and who was still handsome in her advanced age.
>
> (*CYFH* I.342)

---

[31] Unsigned review of *The Prime Minister*, "Mr. Trollope's Prime Minister," *Examiner* (July 22, 1876), 826 (emphasis added).

[32] This film project has a Victorian analog in Jean Ingelow's *Songs of Seven* (1866), a volume of poetry that records the customary phases of a woman's life from the age of seven to forty-nine ("Seven Times Five" is "Widowhood"; "Seven Times Seven"—divided into seven numbered sections—is already "Longing for Home," i.e., death!). The book was clearly intended as a gift for a young girl, who might use it to track the stages of her own experience, as Andrew M. Stauffer observes in a discussion focused on the pressed flowers he discovers in a copy. See *Book Traces: Nineteenth-Century Readers and the Future of the Library* (Philadelphia: University of Pennsylvania Press, 2021), 68–75.

Richard Linklater's 2014 film *Boyhood*, another remarkable experiment in tracking age, produces a filmic effect in some ways closer to the volume's impact than that of *Up*. This movie was shot over the course of more than a decade, from 2002 to 2013, allowing the characters within it to mature and age naturally as the story progressed. In particular, the protagonist Mason, played throughout by the same young actor, starts as a six-year-old and ends the film on the cusp of young adulthood (we see his fifteenth birthday; the action concludes in the following year when he would presumably have been sixteen or seventeen). But at 2:45 running time, the experience of ageing is compressed for the viewer.

[33] Anthony Trollope, *Can You Forgive Her?*, ed. Andrew Swarbrick, 2 vols. (Oxford: Oxford University Press, 1975), I.35. Hereafter *CYFH*, internally documented.

152 THE NUMBER SENSE

[Burgo Fitzgerald] was now thirty, and for some years past had been known to be much worse than penniless; but still he lived on in the same circles, ...

(*CYFH* I.187)

[Lady Mason] was now forty-seven years of age, and had a son who had reached man's estate; and yet perhaps she had more of woman's beauty at this present time than when she stood at the altar with Sir Joseph Mason.[34]

Mr. Furnival was now fifty-five years of age, and was beginning to show in his face some traces of his hard work.

(*OF* I.96)

These are such characteristic moments, evoking crucial elements of Trollope's temporal reach beyond the bounds of a given story—whether those bounds are given in previous installments of a series (as with Burgo, who is mentioned in *The Small House at Allington*), via the summary-flashbacks that often appear at the start of the novels (as in *Orley Farm*), or remain hints of a story never related in full (as with Lady Monk). The habit is so persistent that—as I have already implied in relation to the Palliser novels—it might be said to turn every one of his fictions into a kind of *The Way We Live Now*.

But the structure's connection to the word *now* appears most vividly in a scene in *The Last Chronicle*, in which Johnny Eames considers renewing his proposal to Lily Dale, one she had refused three years earlier in *The Small House at Allington* (here the fictional interval and the publication interval coincided perfectly for original readers):

And then he considered in what manner it would be best and most becoming that he should still prosecute his endeavour and repeat his offer. He thought that he would write to her every year, on the same day of the year, year after year, it might be for the next twenty years. And his letters should be very simple. Sitting there on the gate he planned the wording of his letters;—of his first letter, and of his second, and of his third. They should be very like to each other,—should hardly be more than a repetition of the same words,—"If now you are ready for me, then, Lily, am I, as ever, still

---

[34] Anthony Trollope, *Orley Farm*, ed. David Skilton, 2 vols. (Oxford: Oxford University Press, 2008), I.19. Hereafter *OF*, internally documented.

PLOTTING AGE IN TROLLOPE   153

ready for you." And then "if now" again, and again "if now;—and still if now." When his hair should be grey, and the wrinkles on his cheeks,—ay, though they should be on hers, he would still continue to tell her from year to year that he was ready to take her. Surely some day that "if now" would prevail. And should it never prevail, the merit of his constancy should be its own reward.

(TLCB 301–2)

This passage captures so much that is crucial to Trollope's fiction. It features the principle of repetition exemplifying both his "accretive" style of stringing subtly revised sentences after each other and his plots, in which protagonists frequently return to previous choices (Phineas *redux*, proposing again to Madame Max—and not proposing to Lady Laura; Lady Mason reliving her trial in *Orley Farm*; Alice Vavasor finally accepting John Grey).[35] In each case, the succeeding instances are "very like," but the passage of time between makes for the slight revisions in which inhere the significance of a life.[36] The letter motif—tightly tying the scene to Trollope's two careers in the postal service and as a writer—attests how writing can preserve the experience of each moment. "Such letters as those she would surely keep," Trollope imagines Eames musing in the next paragraph, as he looks "down into the valley of coming years, and fancied her as she might sit reading them in the twilight of some long evening" (*TLCB* 302). Characteristically, Trollope's temporal river rushes forward as much as back. In imagining the future, Trollope is always thinking about age, as is Johnny: "And then as he remembered that he was only twenty-seven and that she was twenty-four, he began to marvel at the feeling of grey old age which had come upon him, and

---

[35] For the accretive style, see Helena Michie, who offers an example of the critical focus on repetition in Trollope in her discussion of his "internal revision." "Rethinking Marriage: Trollope's Internal Revision," in *The Routledge Research Companion to Anthony Trollope*, ed. Deborah Denenholz Morse, Margaret Markwick, and Mark W. Turner (New York: Routledge, 2017), 154. Langbauer ("Hobbledehoy") also considers this feature.

[36] Here, I'd distinguish my argument from that of Langbauer, for whom Johnny Eames is a perpetual hobbledehoy and thus a representative of Trollope's antidevelopmental tendencies: "Trollope uses the term 'hobbledehoy' to assert youth as intrinsic to the specific form of the novel. The temporal paradox of the hobbledehoy—neither boy nor man—extends adolescence beyond a fixed period in human development to figure instead fluid ways of structuring fantasy that persist lifelong, are reiterative rather than end-determined. In closely relating adolescence and the imagination, Trollope emphasizes the kind of persistence and open-endedness necessary to his ideas of the novel (the narrative impulse which also lends his novels so readily to series)" ("Hobbledehoy," 114–15). While, like Langbauer, I am interested in the patterns of repetition and resistance to closure offered by Eames's story, I do think Trollope wants us to feel the slow progression of ageing here. I'll return to the idea of a "fixed period."

154   THE NUMBER SENSE

tried to make himself believe that he would have her yet before the bloom was off her cheek" (*TLCB* 302). Trollope's repeated "and then"s are both the analogues of Johnny's "if now"s and the markers of the simple form of narrative that Hayden White has identified as *chronicle*—a notably Trollopean term.[37] But I am reminded also of another phrase Trollope often invokes when he puts a number to age: "not yet." Mrs. Dobbs Broughton "certainly was not yet thirty-five" (*TLCB* 199), Felix Graham is "not yet thirty" (*OF* 329), Squercum is—with a contortion that feels like it reaches doubly into the future—"not yet *above* forty" (*TWWLN* 444, emphasis added). Against such an age-conscious backdrop, even that earlier reference to twenty years seems pointed: This is a traditional generational interval (and, not coincidentally, the period that passes between the two trials Lady Mason faces in *Orley Farm*, which have taken her son Lucius from baby to man even as she herself considers the fresh start of a second marriage to Sir Peregrine Orme).[38]

Johnny Eames's musings show how the Trollopean *now* should be distinguished from what Bakhtin has characterized as the novel's generic foundation in "maximal contact with the present (with contemporary reality) and all its openendedness," the feature more obviously indicated by the title of *The Way We Live Now*.[39] It is also different from the lyric "now" Jonathan Culler has identified as one of that genre's essential qualities.[40] Instead, it is a paradoxically durational present—a special marker of the *roman-fleuve*, and, insofar as it is one, a reminder of the odd confluence of this form and the kind of Wordsworthian lyricism that flows through the use of the river image in *The Prelude*. In some ways, it resembles the presentism of epistolary fictions, with their dated headers—what Samuel Richardson famously called "writing to the moment." Or even the diaristic mode employed in novels like *Wuthering Heights*, *The Woman in White* (1860), and *Dracula* (1897) (the novel with which I will conclude this chapter). But in Trollope, *now* crucially becomes a pointed marker of age, as well: one dependent upon this particular type of adjacent number for its force. It colors that number and alerts us

---

[37] Hayden V. White, *The Content of the Form: Narrative Discourse and Historical Representation* (Baltimore: Johns Hopkins University Press, 1987), 4.

[38] "Twenty years" serves as a leitmotif in the novel, appearing sixty-one times. "Twenty" is also the number of pounds Crawley is accused of having stolen in *The Last Chronicle*: it seems a favorite figure with Trollope, who like Palliser appreciates a good round decimal.

[39] M. M. Bakhtin, "Epic and Novel," in *The Dialogic Imagination*, ed. Michael Holquist (Austin: University of Texas Press, 1994), 11.

[40] Jonathan Culler, *Theory of the Lyric* (Cambridge, MA: Harvard University Press 2015), 226.

PLOTTING AGE IN TROLLOPE   155

to its relationship with other numbers, as with previous and future selves. Helen Small opens her study of the literature of old age with the observation that for all his acuity in *Being and Time*, Martin Heidegger was oddly blind to this essential feature of our temporal experience. Yet, as she remarks, "We do not simply persist in time: we age, and our perception of being-towards-death is situated and quantified and scrutinized as well as psychologized in the language of ageing (which is not to say that this is all the language of ageing does)."[41]

Trollope forgets neither the process nor the role quantification plays when it comes to "being in time." In the scene that is both the spur to and the opposite side of Eames's musings, Lily Dale tells Johnny that she has abandoned "All those dreams about love, and marriage, and of a house of my own, and children,—and a cross husband, and a wedding-ring grow-ing always tighter as I grow fatter and older" (*TLCB* 299). While such growth may be hard to quantify, the image of the tightening band offers a bodily analog to the countable tree-rings that have long served as a mate-rial marker for measuring the passage of years. And here, as generally, Trollope gives us the information we require for counting: Lily is *now* only twenty-four, Johnny reminds us. Then we might recall how when we first met her, in *The Small House at Allington*, she had been nineteen. And how even at that first meeting, when Lily was one of many "Girls of nineteen [who] do not care for lovers of one-and-twenty," Trollope had himself recalled Johnny's first attempts toward courtship two years prior, before his initial departure for London, when "Lily Dale was ... seventeen" (*TSHA* 43, 42).

Nevertheless, today Lily tells Johnny, "I will go home and I will write in my book, this very day, Lilian Dale, Old Maid. If ever I make that false, do you come and ask me for the page" (*TLCB* 299). I have been suggesting a metatextual element to Johnny's temporal musings about his courtship of Lily. This aspect seems highlighted by the writerly terms of self-assessment both Lily and Johnny use. "He thought that he could look forward with some satisfaction towards the close of his own career, in having been the hero of such a love-story," Johnny reflects; "if such a story were to be his story," he could be satisfied (*TLCB* 302). One can't help but hear Trollope's own sense of accomplishment in this assessment. It goes without saying that this story belongs to Trollope, not only this particular tale, but this this *kind* of tale: one not so much about climax or even closure as about

---

[41] Helen Small, *The Long Life* (Oxford: Oxford University Press 2007), 6.

156   THE NUMBER SENSE

repetitive process. One in which what *happens* is first and foremost that his characters *age*.[42]

4.3 Plotting Age

In so saying, I am suggesting that Trollope's numbers bear heavily on his form of plotting. While counting may be intrinsic to poetic measure—so much so that *numbers* can serve as a synonym for *verse*, as we have seen— lyric poetry simultaneously strives toward a state beyond number. Shelley describes in "A Defence of Poetry" (1817) how "A Poet participates in the eternal, the infinite, and the one; as far as relates to his conceptions, time and place and number are not."[43] But the act of counting time lies at the very heart of the most basic form of narrative: of a series of "and then"s that come first and second and third, a record of chronology. As Aristotle observes, time itself is "a kind of number"—"not movement, but only movement in so far as it admits of enumeration."[44] The link between numbers and narrative appears already in *Don Quixote* (1605) when Sancho, in order to help his master forget his fear of the nighttime noises that will be revealed to be fulling mills, embarks on a tale about a goatherd. Declaring it to be "the best of stories"—if only he can "manage to relate it, and nobody interferes with the telling"—Sancho asks Quixote to follow closely as the goatherd uses a small boat to carry one goat at a time, of a flock of three hundred, across a river. "[L]et your worship keep count of the goats the fisherman is taking across, for if one escapes the memory there will be an end of the story, and it will be impossible to tell another word of it," he warns, before proceeding with his narrative:

> "... the fisherman lost a great deal of time in going and coming; still he returned for another goat, and another, and another."
> "Take it for granted he brought them all across," said Don Quixote, "and don't keep going and coming in this way, or thou wilt not make an end of bringing them over this twelvemonth."

---

[42] See also D. A. Miller's account of Trollopian plot in *The Novel and the Police*, where he describes Trollope's novels as ones in which "nothing happens," in which plot is programmatically subordinated to character, and in which gestures of closure are only "archly conventional" (122–4).

[43] "A Defence of Poetry," in *Shelley's Poetry and Prose*, ed. Donald H. Reiman and Sharon B. Powers (New York: Norton, 1977), 483.

[44] Aristotle, *Physics* Bk. IV, ch. 11, in *The Basic Works of Aristotle*, ed. McKeon, 292.

PLOTTING AGE IN TROLLOPE 157

"How many have gone across so far?" said Sancho.

"How the devil do I know?" replied Don Quixote.

"There it is," said Sancho, "what I told you, that you must keep a good count; well then, by God, there is an end of the story, for there is no going any farther."[45]

Sancho's story offers a parable of (and perhaps satire on) how all narrative depends on keeping track of numbers.

Not all forms of narrative count in the same way, though. It has long been understood that plot-heavy genres, such as detective fictions, make special demands of readers' abilities to follow figures. Consider "The Musgrave Ritual" (1893), the early Arthur Conan Doyle story in which Holmes decodes the mystery of an old family ritual that has been preserved in a riddle by revealing how it maps out the location of a secret chamber in which Charles I's crown had been hidden. For Peter Brooks, this tale literalizes how detective stories ask us to read for plot.[46] Much of that "plotting," I would add, involves the riddle's numbers. These are both spatial ("'How was it stepped?' / 'North by ten and by ten, east by five and by five, south by two and by two, west by one and by one, and so under'") and temporal ("'What was the month?' / 'The sixth from the first'").[47] Such numberiness allows reader and detective to retrace the steps of the past narrative, almost as on a graph, producing a "plot [that is] the active interpretive work of discourse on story," in Brooks's formulation.[48] In the first of a series of articles on detectives in *Household Words*, Charles Dickens describes his real-life policeman Sergeant Witchem (a pseudonym) as having "a reserved and thoughtful air, as if he were engaged in deep arithmetical calculations."[49] This makes sense, given how often numbers structure the mysteries of detection, especially in stories; they offer an on-the-nose approach to D. A. Miller's suggestion that the forms of such fictions are premised on "the hypothesis that *everything might count*."[50] Consider the cipher, comprised of numbers and symbols, that must be decoded by the pseudo-detective of Edgar Allen Poe's tale, "The

---

[45] Miguel de Cervantes, *Don Quixote*, trans. John Ormsby, 4 vols. (New York: Dodd, Mead, & Co, 1887), 1.367 (ch. 20).

[46] Brooks, *Reading for the Plot*, 23–9.

[47] Arthur Conan Doyle, "The Musgrave Ritual," in *The Memoirs of Sherlock Holmes*, ed. Christopher Roden (Oxford: Oxford University Press, 2000), 123–4. The second couplet was actually added between the original publication of the story in the *Strand* and its appearance in book form. Doyle realized it was needed for the plotting to work.

[48] Brooks, *Reading for the Plot*, 27.

[49] Charles Dickens, "A Detective Police Party [i]," *Household Words* 1.18 (July 1850), 410.

[50] Miller, *The Novel and the Police*, 33 (original emphasis).

158   THE NUMBER SENSE

Gold-Bug" (1843) (composed alongside his tales of "ratiocination" featuring Auguste Dupin). Many of the clues of highly plotted fictions reside in less obviously contrived numerical information: tide-tables, train schedules, times—even heights, as Trollope recognized in arranging Phineas Finn's exoneration in the murder-trial plot of *Redux*. The ease with which one can put together a counting primer from their titles hints at numbers' central role in mysteries and detective fiction:

> *Towards Zero*, Agatha Christie (1944)
> *The No. 1 Ladies' Detective Agency*, Alexander McCall Smith (2003)
> *One, Two, Buckle My Shoe*, Agatha Christie (1940)
> *Third Girl*, Agatha Christie (1966)
> *The Sign of the Four*, Sir Arthur Conan Doyle (1890)
> *Five Red Herrings*, Dorothy L. Sayers (1931)
> *Six Against the Yard*, Agatha Christie (1936)
> *The Seven Dials Mystery*, Agatha Christie (1929)
> *The Village of Eight Graves*, Seishi Yokomizo (1971)
> *The Nine Tailors*, Dorothy L. Sayers (1934)
> *Ten Little Indians*, Agatha Christie (1939)[51]

Each place in this list might have been held by other instances; the vast oeuvre produced by Agatha Christie, that purest of detective fiction plotters, would almost have sufficed alone.

Age-related figures play a role here, their usage serving at times as a kind of litmus test, helping to identify the genre of fiction in which we find ourselves immersed. In *Kidnapped* (1886), Robert Louis Stevenson first introduces us to David Balfour's uncle Ebenezer with the remark that "his age might have been anything between fifty and seventy."[52] Resolving this indeterminacy—which a casual reader may barely notice—ends up being important to the adventure's mystery plot: the fact that he turns out to be younger than David's father secures David's right to the inheritance of the House of Shaws.[53] In Wilkie Collins's sensation novel *Armadale*, the two

---

[51] Originally published with an even more offensive title and later also known as *And Then There Were None*.

[52] Robert Louis Stevenson, *Kidnapped*, ed. Ian Duncan (Oxford: Oxford University Press, 2014), 17.

[53] In *Overwhelmed: Literature, Aesthetics, and the Nineteenth-Century Information Revolution* (Princeton: Princeton University Press, 2019), Maurice S. Lee records that DH tools

PLOTTING AGE IN TROLLOPE   159

junior Allan Armadales, on whom the complicated plot hinges, are distinguished at the start by a single year between their ages (when we meet the younger Allan junior, it is under the assumed name, Ozias Midwinter, which both he and Collins stick to throughout the rest of the narrative—a necessary move given that the two Allans junior become friends). The difference in age lets Allan's mother see the solicitor's advertisement that precipitates the action—seeking the addressee of a deathbed letter from one of the senior Armadales to his son—as being targeted at some other youngster of that name (that is, at Midwinter): "Allan, as you know," she tells her son's tutor, "is sixteen years old. If you look back at the advertisement, you will find the missing person described as being only fifteen. Although he bears the same surname and the same Christian name, he is, I thank God, in no way whatever related to my son."[54] Conversely, uncertainty as to the antiheroine Lydia Gwilt's true age allows her to insinuate her way into Armadale's (and later, Midwinter's) affections without being recognized as the maid who had been complicit in her mistress's (Allan's mother's) deceptive marriage; foreseeing the danger this maid poses to his friend, Midwinter had previously carefully calculated her age as thirty-five, but she looks younger.[55] A similar ambiguity functions as the crux of Jean Hanff Korelitz's thriller, *The Plot* (2021). Jacob, a writer, steals the plot of an unpublished novel by a now-deceased student, only to find himself enmeshed in its action (which proves to have been autobiographical) when he unknowingly marries the murderer, Anna (sister to the original author).[56] The fact that Anna's age is indeterminable— her hair seems to be "prematurely" grey—means that she can be mistaken for her own daughter (whom she has killed). Later, it also helps render her immune to the writer-narrator's—and the reader's—suspicion. While its title refers to the object of Jacob's intellectual property theft (which sets the

suggest that nineteenth-century adventure novels are less averse to counting and numbers than are other novels of the period (109). He focuses his argument about the "stirring enunerations" of such fictions on a reading of Stevenson's *Treasure Island* (1874).

[54] Wilkie Collins, *Armadale*, ed. Catherine Peters (Oxford: Oxford University Press, 2008), 64.

[55] "'If this woman ever attempts to find her way to Allan, I must be prepared to stop her. ... This helps me to something positive,' he went on; 'this helps me to a knowledge of her age. She was twelve at the time of Mrs. Armadale's marriage; add a year, and bring her to thirteen; add Allan's age (twenty-two), and we make her a woman of five-and-thirty at the present time. I know her age'" (Collins, *Armadale*, 126). Or later, in a letter "*From Mrs. Oldershaw to Miss Gwilt*": "I say positively you don't look a day over thirty, if as much. If you will follow my advice about dressing, and use one or two of my applications privately, I guarantee to put you back three years more" (Collins, *Armadale*, 191). I will return to this novel in my Conclusion.

[56] Jean Hanff Korelitz, *The Plot* (New York: Celadon, 2021).

160 THE NUMBER SENSE

narrative of this page-turner going), the novel's prominent use of age suggests again how closely tied ideas of plot are to this most basic aspect of time.

Another literary precedent for Korelitz's device appears in *The Picture of Dorian Gray* (1890), where Dorian is initially saved from James Vane's revenge for the murder of his sister Sybil by the fact that though eighteen years have passed, Dorian still looks so young.[57] Here, though, the Gothic pushes out the ratiocinative logic of detective fiction. We might also compare this effect with the way in which in more realist fictions, indeterminacy of age can register as a subtle influx of uncanniness, a kind of generic intrusion. Think of Jane Eyre, whose age Rochester calculates as "eighteen" only by adding her stay of "eight years" at Lowood to the "ten" she had lived before her arrival there. As he observes, "Arithmetic, you see, is useful; without its aid, I should hardly have been able to guess your age."[58] Dickens's Jenny Wren generates a similar impression—"It was difficult to guess the age of this strange creature, for her poor figure furnished no clue to it, and her face was at once so young and so old. Twelve, or at the most thirteen, might be near the mark" (*OMF* 224)—although in this instance it also gives the sense that she has been stunted in her growth by poverty and been forced to an unnatural maturity by the behavior of her drunkard father (who has regressed to childhood). Such grounding in social context allows the question of Jenny's age to teeter precariously between the gritty social realism of the street (in which her childlike father will eventually be run over) and the mystical space of the rooftop to which she escapes ("Come up and be dead!" [*OMF* 282]).

But uncertainty regarding age produces unnervingly real—and realistic— horror in a work of fiction that in other places traffics in magical realism. Colson Whitehead's *The Underground Railroad* (2016), a novel set on the other side of the Atlantic but during Trollope's times, demonstrates the distortion and perversion of chattel slavery early on with the casual remark that "Jockey's birthday came only once or twice a year" (Jockey is the elder statesman of the community of enslaved people on the plantation where the novel opens).[59] It is a sentence the young Jane Austen might have penned to rather

---

[57] See Oscar Wilde, *The Picture of Dorian Gray*, ed. Joseph Bristow (Oxford: Oxford University Press, 2006), 161.

[58] Charlotte Brontë, *Jane Eyre*, 109.

[59] Colson Whitehead, *The Underground Railroad* (New York: Doubleday, 2016), 12.

PLOTTING AGE IN TROLLOPE   161

different effect; here, its illogic sets the stage for the upending of other natural "facts" of reality, almost as though the more magical parts of the novel
(its literal "underground railway," for example) merely express the blasted
reason of such a world. The enslaved, having no rights over their own bodies, also have no records of their own births. The novel's young protagonist
Cora asks Jockey his age:

> She was sure he had claimed a hundred and one years at his last party.
> He was only half that, which meant he was the oldest slave anyone on the
> two Randall plantations had ever met. Once you got that old, you might as
> well be ninety-eight or a hundred and eight. Nothing left for the world to
> show you but the latest incarnations of cruelty.
> Sixteen or seventeen. That's where Cora put her age. One year since Con-
> nelly ordered her to take a husband. Two years since Pot and his friends
> had seasoned her. ... Six years since her mother left.

Still, while numbers may lose their ability to signify over time, a certain
imaginative freedom also comes with being barred from the realms of State-
sanctioned citizenship and the numbery oversight it involves: "One day
Jockey was bound to choose the correct day of his birth. If he lived long
enough. If that was true, then if Cora picked a day for her birthday every
now and then she might hit upon hers as well. In fact, today might be her
birthday." In the end, Cora dismisses this particular loss: "What did you get
for that, for knowing the day you were born into the white man's world? It
didn't seem like the thing to remember. More like to forget."[60] To flee the
plantation, Cora will need herself to be forgotten, to escape the detective
skills of her various pursuers. In this sense, the fewer numbers that can lead
to her, the better.

Trollope intimates the clue-like aura of the many numbers that would
be set within detective fictions in his somewhat waspish remarks on Wilkie
Collins's methods of plotting:

> Wilkie Collins seems so to construct his [novels] that he not only, before
> writing, plans everything on, down to the minutest detail, from the begin-
> ning to the end; but then plots it all back again, to see that there is no piece
> of necessary dove-tailing which does not dove-tail with absolute accuracy.

---

[60] Whitehead, *The Underground Railroad*, 25, 26.

162   THE NUMBER SENSE

The construction is most minute and most wonderful. But I can never lose the taste of the construction. The author seems always to be warning me to remember that something happened at *exactly half-past two o'clock on Tuesday morning*; or that a woman disappeared from the road just *fifteen yards beyond the fourth mile-stone*. One is constrained by mysteries and hemmed in by difficulties, knowing, however, that the mysteries will be made clear, and the difficulties overcome at the end of the third volume. Such work gives me no pleasure.

(*Autobiography* 257, emphasis added)

Such highly charged numbers do regularly punctuate Collins's novels, indicating the genealogical ties between the genres of sensation and detection. Consider how in *The Woman in White*, the proof of the plot to exchange Lady Glyde's identity with that of the (now deceased) Anne Catherick resides in a "a discrepancy between the date of the doctor's [death] certificate and the date of Lady Glyde's journey to London." As Walter Hartright explains to Marian Halcombe, "the owner of the Asylum told you that she [i.e., Laura, Lady Glyde—although, at this point, she is being mistaken for the missing Anne Catherick] was received there on the twenty-seventh of July. ... In that case, she must have started on the twenty-sixth, and must have come to London one day after the date of her own death on the doctor's certificate. If we can prove that date, we prove our case against Sir Percival and the Count."[61] It's all in the numbers. And others took note of Collins's careful plotting. While he's thinking here about its famously dispersed narrative structure (assembled from the different points of view of Collins's cast of characters) rather than about Trollope's exact measurements, E. S. Dallas, in his review of *The Woman in White* in the *Times*, uses the very same term to which Trollope would later turn. Describing the lack of realism behind the careful construction the novel's plot, Dallas asks: "Is it natural to suppose that a number of persons, some of them at daggers drawn, others with a horrible aversion to writing, should conspire together to compose a

---

[61] Collins, *The Woman in White*, 453, 459. The other great "Secret" of the novel—the fact of Sir Percival Glyde's illegitimacy—also has a numbery proof, in the missing record of the marriage (a combination of names and dates) that distinguishes the clerk's copy of the parish register from that found in the vestry of the church at Old Welmingham. There, the false marriage had been squeezed in at the bottom of a page in a gap that had been left because there wasn't room for the next recorded marriage—a double wedding. But the phenomenon of tampering with an official register also recalls the fear of adding digits to numerical records that I mentioned in Chapter 3 (n. 56).

PLOTTING AGE IN TROLLOPE   163

novel, of which the several parts *dovetail* into each other with astonishing precision?"[62]

Dallas's review proves, however, to be more interested in time than in perspective. This focus makes sense: Chronology's crucial role in sensation fiction has been discussed by Nicholas Daly, who has shown how "the sensation novel provides a species of temporal training" by "synchroniz[ing] its readers with industrial modernity," partly through the attention it pays to railway time, the clock of industrial modernity.[63] We may, then, be surprised at how Dallas begins his article by presenting Collins's narrative as a kind of chronological antidote to the more drawn-out story-telling he sees as typical of his day. He distinguishes the reader's experience of *The Woman in White* from a decidedly Trollopian kind of reading:

> *The Woman in White* is a novel of the rare old sort which must be finished at a sitting. No chance of laying it down until the last page of the last volume is turned. We have lately got into the habit—strange for these fast days—of reading our novels very leisurely. They are constructed on the principle of monthly instalments, and we read a chapter on the 1st of every month, quietly sauntering to the end of the story in about a couple of years. ... These works of fiction profess to be natural, and therefore avoid the intricacies of a too elaborate plot. The authors take life as they find it, and spend their strength rather in the elucidation of character than in the unravelling of a subtle intrigue. In doing so, they are apt to underrate the advantage of a good plot, and to despise the talent required for its construction.

Notice how the slow burn of character development contrasts here with the immediate experience of plot (viewed now as a throw-back element, despite our "fast days"). Chronology's crucial role in this dynamic next resurfaces in what might seem an odd reference to the famously confused timespan of *Othello*, employed by Dallas to argue that if Shakespeare can be "unmindful of the plot" in his wholehearted focus on character, why might "lesser men"

---

[62] [E. S. Dallas], review of *The Woman in White*, *The Times* (October 30, 1860), 6 (emphasis added). This review appears on a particularly number-saturated page of the newspaper. Page 6 also includes the tabular "The Weather: Meteorological Reports," with its list of barometric pressures, temperatures, and wind speeds and directions in various British and European locales; the "Arrivals of corn in the port of London from Oct. 22 to 27," another numbery table (weights); and "Current Prices of British Grain and Flour in Mark-lane," yet a third (shillings per quart)!

[63] Nicholas Daly, *Literature, Technology, and Modernity, 1860–2000* (Cambridge: Cambridge University Press, 2004), 37.

164   THE NUMBER SENSE

not follow his lead? Again, Dallas seems at this stage of the review to be intent on explaining the modern predilection for novels of character, like Trollope's, and considering the relative disinterest in plot displayed by such works.

Yet while the entrance of Shakespeare may look like a convenient tribute to the playwright often deemed the inventor of modern literary character, *Othello* serves as the loaded gun on the stage of Dallas's review—and it is waiting to be used against Collins, rather than in defense of novelists like Trollope.[64] The essay is best remembered for the way Dallas points out a specifically chronological error that mars *The Woman in White*'s dovetailing. Like the careful craftsman he himself is, Dallas holds off until the review's third act to deploy his charge:

> The question of a date is the pivot upon which the novel turns. The whole of the third volume is devoted to the ascertaining of this date. Everything depends upon it. But it is lost in the most marvelous obscurity—it is lost even to Mr. Wilkie Collins, who is a whole fortnight out of his reckoning. If we dared trespass upon details after the author's solemn injunction, we could easily show that Lady Glyde could not have left Blackwater-park before the 9th or 10th of August. Anybody who reads the story, and who counts the days from the conclusion of Miss Halcombe's diary, can verify the calculation for himself. He will find that the London physician did not pay his last visit till the 31st of July, that Dawson was not dismissed till the 3rd of August, and that the servants were not dismissed till the following day. The significance of these dates will be clear to all who have read the story. They render the last volume a mockery, a delusion, and a snare; and all the incidents in it are not merely improbable—they are absolutely impossible. Nor is this the only impossibility of the tale; we could point out a dozen scarcely less glaring.

Dallas is correct, as Collins himself quickly recognized. He wrote to his publisher the following day:

> If any fresh impression of *The Woman in White* is likely to be wanted immediately, stop the press till I come back. The critic in the Times is (between ourselves) right about the mistake in time. Shakespear [sic] has

---

[64] Recall Shrimpton's use of *Othello* to describe Trollope's temporal confusions in the Palliser novels.

made worse mistakes—that is one comfort. And readers are not critics, who test an emotional book by the base rules of arithmetic—which is a second consolation.[65]

Dallas had observed in closing the extraordinary talents of a novelist whose work could endure having his own gun turned on him: "What must that novel be which can survive such a blunder?" But the overlaps suggested by the review with Trollope's practice (and malpractice) hint how Trollope's echo of Dallas's *dovetail*ing may show him to be protesting too much. In their shared use and abuse of numbers, the two novelists seem to approach one another, even if the immediate correction of the errors of calculation in *The Woman in White* also distinguishes between Collins's and Trollope's modes of engagement with the "rules of arithmetic."[66]

This snapshot of a pair of novelist's mutual yet distinctive fretting over their figures thus highlights how Trollope's age-related numbers describe, in a quasi-geometric sense, his characteristic type of plotting. In this regard, Trollope's ages remind me of another of Austen's precocious juvenile efforts at mastering the aspects of her craft. Austen begins her remarkable work "Jack and Alice: A Novel" (1793) by inviting her readers to keep count, much like Sancho Panza. Here, though, we are counting the passage of time:

Chapter the First

Mr. Johnson was once upon a time about 53; in a twelve-month afterwards he was 54, which so much delighted him that he was determined to celebrate his next Birth day by giving a Masquerade to his Children and Freinds. Accordingly on the Day he attained his 55th year tickets were dispatched to all his Neighbours to that purpose.[67]

The youthful Austen plays this moment for comedy—and as preparation for her enquiry into the forms of rivalry and sociability allowed by a "neighborhood" setting and its cast of characters. Yet I can't help but feel it carries

[65] See Andrew Gasson "*The Woman in White*: A Chronological Study" (2010), n. pag. https://wilkiecollinssociety.org/the-woman-in-white-a-chronological-study/. Accessed March 30, 2023. Gasson also gives a detailed list of the "dozen" other errors found in the text. Most of these were corrected for the 1861 one-volume edition of the novel and have thus been removed from the passages I quoted above.

[66] My argument here resembles the one I make about the overlapping effects produced by the diamonds of Collins's *The Moonstone* and Trollope's *The Eustace Diamonds* in "Form Things: Looking at Genre through Victorian Diamonds," *Victorian Studies* 52.4 (Summer 2010): 591–619.

[67] In Jane Austen, *Catharine and other Writings*, 11.

166 THE NUMBER SENSE

some of the implicit recognition of her mature works: that the most fundamental form of novelistic plot is the process of ageing itself (as Carolyn Williams has recognized, parody defines genre[68]). Or, to put this observation into terms that Trollope might have used, ageing results when plot is not so much subordinated to as embodied in character.

4.4 Counting Down

Of course, no matter how resistant Trollope may be to the kind of tidy conclusion in which "the mysteries will be made clear, and the difficulties overcome at the end of the third volume," the plot of ageing is predetermined: it always ends with death. Trollope's *Last Chronicle* is *last* in part by virtue of the two deaths that help bring the series to a close: that of Mrs. Proudie and, even more resonantly, that of Mr. Harding. Victorian plots, however, more frequently offer an alternative form of closure to tragic death through comedic marriages (implicitly carrying the promise of new birth). So, while the deaths of Mrs. Proudie and Mr. Harding prove the *series* has ended, these deaths come some way before the *novel's* conclusion, which assumes the rather conventional form of Grace Crawley's marriage to Major Grantley. Still, the fact that Lily Dale continues to refuse Johnny Eames testifies to Trollope's resistance to the idea of such artificial means of concluding a story: Lily and Johnny will just keep getting older. Glencora Palliser's shocking demise in the interval between *The Prime Minister* and *The Duke's Children* seems similarly to militate against conventional endings: it is death as anticlimax, and the story continues with her offspring.[69] Trollope's numbery attention to age reveals a related ambivalence; while he may express distaste at too much fussing over precision, he is simultaneously alert to both the appeal and the payoffs of keeping count. (After all, he knew well that his own pay depended on all the carefully counted words through which he produced his seemingly countless volumes.) His proclivity for counting may thus also explain his curious tendency to use what I will call a *countdown plot* to achieve closure.[70]

[68] See Carolyn Williams, *Gilbert and Sullivan: Gender, Genre, Parody* (New York: Columbia University Press, 2012).

[69] In contrast, the interval deaths of Mary Finn (née Flood Jones) and Lady Alexandrina (Crosbie née De Courcy) seem orchestrated to allow their husbands to escape the closure of the marriages with which previous installments in their respective series had ended.

[70] Although I focus more on the play of numbers in creating the dynamic, my *countdown plot* overlaps in part with what Nicholas Daly has observed, in relation to sensation fiction

PLOTTING AGE IN TROLLOPE   167

One famous version of this narrative structure can be found, as its title suggests, in Jules Verne's *Around the World in Eighty Days* (1872). A generation younger than Trollope, Verne may be the most extraordinarily numbery writer of fiction in the nineteenth century—consider also his *Twenty Thousand Leagues Under the Sea* (1870), in which the title sums up the total distance travelled underwater by the *Nautilus* and Captain Nemo on their journey, and in which characters are constantly pausing to calculate, as the thirteenth chapter heading puts it, "A Few Figures."[71] In *Around the World*, the plot not only reflects but actually follows the directions of the title, even as the narrative keeps careful and numbery track of the time and distance progressed since our hero, Phileas Fogg, has set out on his quest to circumnavigate the world to win a wager he stakes during a game of whist at the Reform Club. Verne also keeps track of the diminishing contents of a bag, containing at the start 20,000 pounds, that might be said to fuel the journey. A Bradshaw's *Continental Railway, Steam Transit and General Guide* is Fogg's bible, its columns and rows of names and figures granting him both a purpose and the means to achieve it. As the narrator ventriloquizes Fogg, "everything would sort itself out mathematically! That was the word he used."[72]

In its purest form, though, the countdown plot has become a recognizable feature of contemporary detective fictions. There, the novelist begins by letting her reader know that a character has only so long to live before he or she will be murdered. Thus, Tana French introduces us to the teenage victim of *The Secret Place* (2014) by announcing:

Chris Harper is all ready for this year, he can't wait; he's got plans.

He has eight months and two weeks left to live.[73]

---

in general and *The Woman in White* in specific, as "a temporal trope that will later become a staple of the suspense plot: what we might call the dramatic time limit, or deadline" (*Literature, Technology, and Modernity*, 49).

[71] In a characteristic moment from that chapter, Nemo invites his guests and the reader to follow along: "These two measurements will allow you to calculate the surface area and volume of the *Nautilus*. Its surface area is 1.011.45 m^2, its volume 1,500 m^3—which is the same as saying that, when completely submerged, it displaces 1,500 m^3 or weighs 1,500 tons." Jules Verne, *Twenty Thousand Leagues Under the Seas*, trans. William Butcher (Oxford: Oxford University Press, 2009), 83. The novel is very much a product of its systematizing and numbery times, leaning heavily also on taxonomies and classification.

[72] Jules Verne, *Around the World in Eighty Days*, trans. William Butcher (Oxford: Oxford University Press, 1999), 81–82.

[73] Tana French, *The Secret Place* (London: Penguin, 2015), 21.

168 THE NUMBER SENSE

As we follow him and his companions through those eight months and two weeks, French repeats the gesture as a refrain: he "has a little over seven months left to live," he has "six months, three weeks and a day left to live," and so on, until the murder.[74] Or consider the first sentence of *The Private Patient* (2008), by P. D. James: "On November the twenty-first, the day of her forty-seventh birthday, and three weeks and two days before she was murdered, Rhoda Gradwyn went to Harley Street to keep a first appointment with her plastic surgeon ..."[75] By beginning on a birthday, James stresses that her novel considers what happens when the natural plot of ageing is curtailed artificially by violence. And while Trollope may be suspicious of many of the numbery devices of plot-oriented fictions, his own obsession with age seems to drive him, twice, to experiment with a kind of murder-mystery style countdown plot: once in relation to marriage, once in relation to death.[76]

The comedic version occupies a subplot of *Orley Farm* in which, prior to the novel's start, the hyper-rational Felix Graham has arranged to have a young girl, Mary Snow, educated to become his wife. But as the novel begins, he meets Madeline Staveley, who disrupts this tidy plan. As Felix muses:

> Mary Snow knew very well what was to be her destiny, and indeed had known it for the last two years. She was now nineteen years old,—and Madeline Staveley was also nineteen; she was nineteen, and at twenty she was to become a wife, as by agreement between Felix Graham and Mr. Snow, the drunken engraver. They knew their destiny ...
>
> (*OF* 332)

Trollope repeatedly draws the reader's attention to how age figures into Felix's scheme of "moulding." Generally, the narrator remarks, "Such a frame of mind comes upon a bachelor, perhaps about his thirty-fifth year, and then he goes to work with a girl of fourteen. The operation takes some ten years,

---

[74] French, *The Secret Place*, 40, 62.

[75] P. D. James, *The Private Patient* (New York: Vintage, 2009), 3.

[76] In Chapter 1, I discussed another kind of countdown plot, one of diminishing population (in the shipwreck episode of *Don Juan* and the war-deaths of the khan's sons). This is of course also a trope of certain kinds of detective fiction (Agatha Christie's *And Then There Were None*, for example) and of many a horror film, to boot. A version of such a plot in *Dracula*—one that is curiously blended with concerns regarding ageing—will help me close out the argument of this chapter.

PLOTTING AGE IN TROLLOPE   169

at the end of which the moulded bride regards her lord as an old man." But Trollope's own "prudent" modern Pygmalion has started the process earlier: "With Felix Graham the matter was somewhat different, seeing that he was not yet thirty, and that the lady destined to be the mistress of his family had already passed through three or four years of her noviciate" (*OF* 329). Nevertheless, Felix learns the error of such Wilkie Collins-style precision plotting: life intervenes, or, in this case, Madeline Stavely intervenes, much as she cuts into Felix's thoughts in the paragraph just quoted. Yet it is worth noticing that one part of his plan proves faultless: the novel concludes with Felix's marriage to a twenty-year old Madeline Staveley, right on time (even the initials match). For present purposes, though, the key point here is that this plot involves a countdown: Felix plots not just the *who* but also the *when* of his marriage. That is to say, the period of the story is fixed, and, as with Alfred Garth's apprenticeship, it is fixed by age.[77]

Which brings me to my own destination, courtesy of what is perhaps Trollope's strangest story: his late, dystopian tale, *The Fixed Period* (1882).[78] It is here that he returns to the countdown plot in its tragic vein, as it leads toward death—although tragedy is the wrong word, since Trollope's protagonist, John Neverbend, hopes to convert a timely death into a consummation devoutly to be wished, and the scenario plays out in an oddly tragicomic satiric tone. The concept is simple, if bizarre: Neverbend, the governor of an imaginary antipodean island that has recently declared independence from Britain (the year is 1980), wishes to secure the wealth and welfare of his citizenry by legislating a gentle form of euthanasia, one enacted with much pomp, circumstance, and honor toward the victim, but enacted at a prescribed age. The narrator relates at some length the Assembly's process of determining that age:

> What should be the "Fixed Period"? That was the first question which demanded an immediate answer. Years were named absurd in their intended leniency;—eighty and even eighty-five! Let us say a hundred, said I aloud, turning upon them all the battery of my ridicule. I suggested sixty;

[77] We might contrast how often Trollope's characters debate over the length of an engagement period and how many resist "fixing" this period: Alice Vavasor, Violet Chiltern, even Lily Dale during her engagement to Crosbie.

[78] Chase considers this text as indicative of Trollope's participation in contemporary legislative debates over the definition of and care for the elderly (*The Victorians and Old Age*, 98–112).

170   THE NUMBER SENSE

but the term was received with silence. I pointed out that the few old men now on the island might be exempted, and that even those above fifty-five might be allowed to drag out their existences ... I think now that sixty was too early an age, and that sixty-five, to which I gracefully yielded, is the proper "Fixed Period" for the human race. ... they demanded that seventy should be the "Fixed Period."

How long we fought over this point need not now be told. But we decided at last to divide the interval. Sixty-seven and a half was named by a majority of the Assembly as the "Fixed Period."[79]

So the law is passed. But as the first citizen not grandfathered out approaches the crucial age, Neverbend discovers it won't be easy to implement. That citizen (who happens to be Neverbend's good friend and his son's intended father-in-law) contests his fate, finding it intolerable to be treated by his loving daughter "as one who was already dead." "[She] feels that my days are numbered unless I will boldly declare myself opposed to your theory," he explains (*FP* 91).[80]

My days are numbered.[81] We usually feel, as we go through our lives, that we are counting up, adding each passing year to our tally as we get older. But from a certain omniscient (or just future) perspective, we are also, inevitably, counting down towards death. Similarly, while Trollope may have obsessed over the daily count of words added to his sum, he also knew as he wrote— often laboring to meet what is appropriately called a *deadline*—that he was reckoning to the end of the installment, to end of the volume, to the end of the novel, even, at times, to the end of the series. And we know this, too, as readers—especially as readers of books instead of serial installments in a magazine. We can see and feel what Jane Austen so memorably describes as the "tell-tale compression of the pages" (*NA* 185). So perhaps it makes sense that we struggle to decide whether this particular novelist's vision of a society in which death can reliably come at the end of a volume of known length— without recourse to violence—is utopian or dystopian. For someone to

---

[79] Anthony Trollope, *The Fixed Period*, ed. R. H. Super (Ann Arbor: University of Michigan Press, 1990), 8–9. Hereafter *FP*, internally documented.

[80] This citizen is saved when the British Navy arrives to reassert control over the former colony and bring Neverbend back to England for prosecution (he composes the narrative en route).

[81] The phrase echoes the Psalms: "So teach us to number our days, that we may apply our hearts unto wisdom" (Psalm 90:12 *KJV*). It is a teaching both hampered and demanded by the vagaries of the count: "The days of our years are threescore years and ten; and if by reason of strength they be fourscore years, yet is their strength labour and sorrow; for it is soon cut off, and we fly away" (Psalm 90:10 *KJV*).

whom ageing and plot are coterminous, wouldn't this system seem to promise perfection? To fix on a form where closure comes without any need for extra manipulation, where the story is guaranteed to end at just the right moment ... As none other than Wilkie Collins recalls in his assessment of *An Autobiography*, when "an intimate friend" called *The Fixed Period* "a grim jest," Trollope "stopped suddenly in his walk, and grasping the speaker's arm in his energetic fashion, exclaimed: 'It's all true—I *mean* every word of it.'"[82] Neverbend, not Neverend. Surely, the first-person voice in which the tale is written—a stark aberration from Trollope's normal practice—suggests also an unusual affinity between Neverbend and his author. And just as surely, Collins himself, he of the dovetail-precision, of the counted minutes and yards and "the difficulties overcome at the end of the third volume," couldn't help but note the fitness of Trollope's own death soon after the publication of this tale, "at an age in singular accordance with his own theory": sixty-seven.[83]

4.5 Afterlife: One More Count(down)

As many contemporary readers agreed, Count Fosco, *The Woman in White*'s arch-plotter, was also Collins's best-realized character; Dallas delighted in the Count, calling him the book's "one interesting character" and comparing him to Milton's Satan.[84] But Fosco's dangerously seductive charm, aristocratic mien, cosmopolitanism, and Italian background—even his proclivity towards fat—combine as well to give him a Byronic cast. And, like Byron, he is an inveterate counter, most markedly resembling the poet in his reassurance to Sir Percival that his wife Laura's prior affections for Hartright are par for the course:

> My dear friend! what is there extraordinary in that? They are all in love with some other man. Who gets the first of a woman's heart? In all my experience I have never yet met with the man who was Number One. Number

---

[82] [Wilkie Collins], "*Autobiography* of Anthony Trollope," *Blackwood's Edinburgh Magazine* 134 (Nov. 1883), 594.

[83] [Collins], "*Autobiography*," 594.

[84] [Dallas], review of *The Woman in White*, 6. Collins himself is said to have thought the Count "his best creation." See "A Novelist on Writing: An Interview with Mr. Wilkie Collins" (1887), quoted in Lauren Goodlad, *The Victorian Geopolitical Aesthetic: Realism, Sovereignty, and Transnational Experience* (Oxford: Oxford University Press, 2015), 115. Other readers may feel that Marian Halcombe is slighted in this ranking.

172   THE NUMBER SENSE

Two, sometimes. Number Three, Four, Five, often. Number One, never! He exists, of course—but I have not met with him.[85]

The Count's many counts serve like a metronome in the narrative, setting its rhythms. Think of how he "exercises" his canaries: "Come out on my little finger, my pret-pret-pretties! ... Come out and hop upstairs! One, two, three—and up! Three, two, one—and down! One, two, three—twit-twit-twit-tweet!"[86] Characteristically, Fosco prepares to write his own "Narrative"—which he will compose to a deadline, in a race with the counted chimes of a clock—by listing a set of numbered inventories: of "questions," of "conditions" to his dealings, of creatures in his menagerie.[87] Hence the irony when he records the doctor's certification of Anne Catherick's death as the "weak place" in his carefully plotted scheme: "no efforts on my part could alter the fatal event of the 25th."[88] Like his author's, Count Fosco's plot is undone by a number. One might say her death date (or, rather, its registration) aborts the Count's count; his own dead body brings Collins's story to a stop.[89]

So Counts who keep count have a history that long precedes *Sesame Street*.[90] Drawing attention to Norman Stiles's puppet creation Count von Count, Maurice S. Lee mentions "the folklore that vampires suffer from arithmomania—compulsive counting." This aside (itself a digression from his reading of *Treasure Island*) arises in the context of observing how Bram Stoker's Dracula masters the measures of the railway schedules Harker finds him poring over early in the novel.[91] In fact, while Fosco's decided sweet-tooth may seem to indicate a very different type from Dracula (whose "peculiarly sharp white teeth" are adapted to facilitate the vampire's thirst for

---

[85] Collins, *Woman in White*, 338.

[86] Collins, *Woman in White*, 271–2.

[87] Collins, *Woman in White*, 609, 628, 605, 611. See also Daly, who notes how the "deadline" to Count Fosco's furious writing is determined by the letter Hartright leaves with Pesca as a kind of detonator (it would reveal Fosco's identity to his enemies), to be set off (by being sent off) if Hartright does not return by 9 a.m. "To extract a date from Fosco, one might say, Hartright uses a time," Daly observes (*Literature, Technology, and Modernity*, 49).

[88] Collins, *Woman in White*, 625.

[89] The novel itself famously ends with a sunnier prospect: of Marian holding up the Hartrights' baby, the future proprietor of the Fairlie family estate.

[90] Collins seems to have liked the title so much that he incorporated it as the name of another constantly calculating character in *No Name* (1862): Madame Lecount.

[91] "Perhaps such informational reading explains why the aptly titled count falls asleep during the workday, though even to attempt a joke of this sort is to ignore the stirring, chilling enumerations that are everywhere in Stoker's novel." As what follows should prove, I agree. Maurice S. Lee, *Overwhelmed*, 139.

PLOTTING AGE IN TROLLOPE   173

blood), readers recognized the hereditary connection between Collins's and Stoker's Counts from the first.[92] Several contemporary reviews of *Dracula* noticed how it shared many structural features with *The Woman in White*, most prominently the narrative assemblage of first-hand experience from diaries, letters, and so on.[93] Recent critics have observed also the overlapping character networks in the two works: Marian and Mina; Laura and Lucy; Hartright and Harker; and, obviously, the two Counts, Fosco and Dracula.[94] Appropriately given my own story in this book, Count Dracula shares Fosco's Byronic lineage: John William Polidori's *The Vampyre* (1819), often deemed the first modern vampire narrative, was initially accredited to Byron and was doubtless inspired by him (Polidori was his physician, and the tale grew out of the same evening of ghost stories that gave birth to Mary Shelley's *Frankenstein* [1818]).

Like that of *The Woman in White*, *Dracula*'s dispersed narrative structure puts a premium on available forms of documentary data storage (registers, death certificates, tombstones, diaries, letters)—and, as Friedrich Kittler has famously argued, their technological mediation (typewriters, telegrams, Edison wax cylinders).[95] Much of this data consists of numbers. So it is logical that numbers proliferate through Stoker's text, which begins with the dates and times recorded in Jonathan Harker's shorthand journal (including those railway schedules): "*3 May. Bistritz.*—Left Munich at 8.35 p.m., on 1st May, arriving at Vienna early next morning; should have arrived at 6.46, but train was an hour late" (*D* 5). Stoker had studied mathematics at Trinity College Dublin; he is at home in numbery discourse. The novel's opening lines indicate that, as in Collins's fiction, chronological figures will be key to

---

[92] Bram Stoker, *Dracula*, ed. Roger Luckhurst (Oxford: Oxford University Press, 2011), 20. Hereafter, internally referenced as *D*. I include this text in a study of *British* literature because of its connections to a network of British texts; I do not mean to deny—or to deny the importance of—Stoker's Irishness, or to subsume Irish literature into the category of the British.

[93] See "Recent Novels," *Review of Politics, Literature, Theology, and Art* 79 (July 31, 1897): 150–1; "Dracula," *The Glasgow Herald* (10 June 1897), 10; "Book Reviews Reviewed," *The Academy: A Weekly Review of Literature, Science, and Art* (July 31, 1897), 98. See also Katrien Bollen and Raphael Ingelbien, "An Intertext that Counts? *Dracula, The Woman in White*, and Victorian Imaginations of the Foreign Other," *English Studies* 90.4 (August 2009): 403–20. In his introduction, Roger Luckhurst calls Collins's novel "Stoker's obvious model" (*D* xiv).

[94] See Mark M. Hennelly, "Twice-Told Tales of Two Counts: *The Woman in White* and *Dracula*," *Wilkie Collins Society Journal* 2 (1982): 15–31; and Alison Case, "The Documentary Novel: Struggles for Narrative Authority in *The Woman in White* and *Dracula*," in *Plotting Women: Gender and Narration in the Eighteenth- and Nineteenth-Century British Novel* (Charlottesville, VA: University of Virginia Press, 1999), 147–86.

[95] See Friedrich Kittler, "Dracula's Legacy," *Stanford Humanities Review* 1 (1989): 143–73; *Discourse Networks 1800/1900*, trans. Michael Metteer, with Chris Cullens (Stanford, CA: Stanford University Press, 1990), 352–6.

174   THE NUMBER SENSE

unravelling the mystery of *Dracula*. Later, before typing out the contents of Dr. Seward's audio diary in order to make it searchable (she hopes its contents will "add to the *sum* of our knowledge of that terrible Being [i.e., the Count]" [*D* 206, emphasis added]), Mina explains how "In this matter dates are everything, and I think that if we get all our material ready, and have every item put in chronological order, we shall have done much" (*D* 208). She types these records up in triplicate, using—this is a term and concept to which I will return—"manifold" paper (*D* 208). But she also employs an old-fashioned verb to describe her activity, one that takes us back to Madame Defarge's record-keeping in *A Tale of Two Cities*: "Mrs. Harker says that they are knitting together in chronological order every scrap of evidence they have," Dr. Seward reports (*D* 209).

Still, the kind of measure on which I have focused in Trollope—that which counts a character's years of life—is surprisingly rare in this novel. While we may have a general sense for the maturity of the members of his band of vampire fighters, Stoker almost never applies numbers to specify age. Lucy Westenra presents an exception. Her case arises in a context that again recalls Dickens's fiction of the Revolution—not least because the heroine's name mirrors Lucie Manette's. Stoker's Lucy is writing in excitement to her friend Mina:

> Here am I, who will be twenty in September, and yet I never had a proposal till to-day, not a real proposal, and to-day I have had three. Just fancy! THREE proposals in one day! Isn't it awful! I feel sorry, really and truly sorry, for two of the poor fellows. ... Well, my dear, number one came just before lunch. I told you of him, Dr. John Seward, the lunatic-asylum man ...[96]
>
> ... [N]umber two came after lunch. He is such a nice fellow, an American from Texas, and he looks so young and so fresh that it seems almost impossible that he has been to so many places and has had such adventures.
>
> ...
>
> P.S.—Oh, about number three—I needn't tell you of number three, need I?
>
> (*D* 55–9)

---

[96] In an earlier letter, Lucy had also designated Seward's age when suggesting how he seems suited to Mina: "We met some time ago a man that would just do for you, if you were not already engaged to Jonathan. He is an excellent *parti*, being handsome, well off, and of good birth. He is a doctor and really clever. Just fancy! He is only nine-and-twenty, and he has an immense lunatic asylum all under his own care" (*D* 54). The only other example I could find appears in Dr. Seward's medical record of Renfield, which opens "R. M. Renfield, aetat. 59" (*D* 60).

PLOTTING AGE IN TROLLOPE   175

These three proposals (from Seward, Quincey Morris, and Arthur Holm-wood, the last of which she accepts) harken back to the three men (Carton, Stryver, and Darnay) pursuing Lucie in *A Tale*, whose multiplication into "hundreds" of suitors (by Miss Pross) would also pave the way for the prolif-erating echoes of the crowds storming the Bastille. But I am almost tempted to say that Lucy's mention of her own age here sounds her death-knell.

Or should I say, her "un-death knell." Because Lucy's experiences sug-gest how precise ages matter less in a novel in which death can be undone. Perhaps more accurately, her almost-twenty is a kind of provocation; recall Alice's cry in Wonderland, "I shall never get to twenty at that rate!" (*AW* 19). *Dracula* is, after all, devoted to the pursuit of the Un-Dead, to destroying a Count whose own years seem to defy the limits of a discrete count. In place of exact measures of years, the term *old* is a favorite descrip-tor, arising 167 times in this rather short book; thus we first meet the Count as "a tall old man, clean-shaven save for a long white moustache, and clad in black from head to foot, without a single speck of colour about him anywhere" (*D* 18). While nowhere near as frequent (it makes fifty-nine appearances), *young* also marks age in the novel; Van Helsing is especially fond of it, using it to contrast his own maturity with the youth of his assem-bled band. But the work's supernaturalism is premised on the instability of the distinctions between such categories—on the idea that time's effects on the body can be stopped, or even reversed. As Jonathan Harker says on first seeing Dracula after his reappearance in London, "I believe it is the Count, but he has grown young. My God, if this be so!" (*D* 161). So Trollopean ageing—a signal of the natural—no longer represents a funda-mental fact of existence. Tellingly, the vampire hunter Professor Van Helsing figures the uncanny reemergence of the ancient that characterizes the novel's brand of modernity by comparison to a more ordinary example of unnatural ageing:

> Ah, it is the fault of our science that it wants to explain all; and if it explain not, then it says there is nothing to explain. But yet we see around us every day the growth of new beliefs, which think themselves new; and which are yet but the old, which pretend to be young—like the fine ladies at the opera.
>
> (*D* 178)

How the reversal of ageing is achieved, though, involves a different set of numbers. Stoker's work revives Dickens's thematics of being "recalled to life" in a rather more sinister vein (I am tempted to say, using this expres-sion literally). We can see the process unfold when Van Helsing leads from

176   THE NUMBER SENSE

his remarks about the interpenetration of ancient and modern into his main topic, which is to explain what has happened to Lucy (she has become Un-Dead). He sets things up by turning to two kinds of count, suggesting thereby a connection between them: "Why was it that Methuselah lived nine hundred years, and 'Old Parr' one hundred and sixty-nine, and yet that poor Lucy, with four men's blood in her poor veins, could not live even one day!" (*D* 179). The "four men's blood" refers to the multiple transfusions that had been given to Lucy—by Seward, Van Helsing, Quincey, and Arthur—to replace the blood that had been sucked out by Dracula. Van Helsing points toward a failure in the process of conversion whereby *four* men might afford through their donation so many more years of life to Lucy. Implicitly, then, we are also dealing, in addition to the kind of accumulated years suggested by *nine hundred* and *one hundred and sixty-nine*, with a different kind of tally: with a proliferated form of identity that in important ways resembles Mina's manifold typescript. Or, for that matter, Dickens's echoing steps, or his Jacquerie; hence the many resonances in this novel of *A Tale of Two Cities*. That is to say, we are back in a world ruled by counts of functionally interchangeable people, rather than the progress inherent in an individual life. Given this math, one might observe that Lucy's accumulated store of the lifeforce of four men doesn't stand a chance against Dracula, whose own strength is repeatedly compared to that of "twenty men" (*D* 189, 220, 232)—a number that ironically echoes the final span of Lucy's years. Again, I am reminded of Carroll's Alice, this time, of her defense of her age in *Through the Looking-Glass*. When she explains to Humpty Dumpty that "One ca'n't help growing older," Humpty returns, "*One* ca'n't, perhaps, ... but *two* can. With proper assistance, you might have left off at seven" (*AW* 188). Once you bring in multiple actors, counts can both leave off *and* continue.

The novel's most extreme version of this process emerges in its climactic countdown plot. This plot concerns the discovery and destruction—via the insertion of communion wafers—of each of the fifty "boxes" of earth that serve as Dracula's unholy sanctuaries on his travels. These migratory "plots of ground" (as we might consider them) seem in some ways to revise the kind of literal "plotting" we saw in Conan Doyle's "Musgrave Ritual." But we can also view the boxes—again, as in Dickens's novels—in relation to character (remember Carton?). They embody the novel's employment of a kind of compound or distributed character as a solution to the problem of ageing. In place of a single life lived for fifty years, we have the fifty boxes that translate into fifty lives. The overall effect resembles that of Voldemort's Horcruxes in

PLOTTING AGE IN TROLLOPE   177

the Harry Potter books; eternal life depends upon something like the fracturing of identity—or, perhaps more accurately, on the assumption of an essentially *manifold* form of identity enabled by Dracula's parasitism.

The fifty boxes also feel very modern, turning the defeat of the Count into a matter of logistics (in the technical sense: the management of the transport of goods). The vampire hunters don't so much seem to be tracking Dracula himself as they seem to be following the tracking on a particularly complicated shipment. Harker records his initial discussion with the Count's solicitor, who explains that his client

> had "taken no chances," and the absolute accuracy with which his instructions were fulfilled, was simply the logical result of his care. I saw the invoice, and took note of it: "Fifty cases of common earth, to be used for experimental purposes." Also the copy of the letter to Carter Paterson, and their reply; of both of these I got copies. This was all the information Mr. Billington could give me, so I went down to the port and saw the coastguards, the Customs officers and the harbour-master. They had all something to say of the strange entry of the ship, which is already taking its place in local tradition; but no one could add to the simple description "Fifty cases of common earth." I then saw the station-master, who kindly put me in communication with the men who had actually received the boxes. Their tally was exact with the list ...
>
> (*D* 211)

For much of the final third of the novel, the reader follows the fate of these fifty boxes—and tallies their count—alongside the band of vampire hunters. As Van Helsing puts it:

> We know ... that from the castle to Whitby came fifty boxes of earth, all of which were delivered at Carfax; we also know that at least some of these boxes have been removed ... [O]ur first step should be to ascertain whether all the rest remain in the house beyond that wall where we look to-day; or whether any more have been removed.
>
> (*D* 224–5)

When the hunters do raid the Count's main London abode "beyond that wall" (Carfax Abbey, conveniently located next to Seward's asylum), Van Helsing observes that "The first thing is to see how many of the boxes are left" (*D* 234). The results are mixed: "There were only twenty-nine left out

178 THE NUMBER SENSE

of the fifty!" (*D* 234). If readers don't want to do the math, they can follow along: "We now know of twenty-one boxes having been removed, and if it be that several were taken in any of these removals we may be able to trace them all" (*D* 237). The twenty-one, it turns out, have in fact been divided into multiple deliveries. Regarding the first twelve, we learn from a man overseeing their transport, "There were ... six in the cartload which he took from Carfax and left at 197, Chicksand Street, Mile End New Town, and another six which he deposited at Jamaica Lane, Bermondsey" (*D* 242). We are down to nine, again in two groups, as Harker discovers on interviewing the porter charged with the task of unloading this shipment: "Yus; there was five in the first load an' four in the second. It was main dry work" (*D* 245). When the vampire hunters arrive at the house, though, "In the dining-room, which lay at the back of the hall, we found eight boxes of earth. Eight boxes only out of the nine, which we sought! Our work was not over, and would never be until we should have found the missing box" (*D* 279). And then there was one. This the hunters track back to Dracula's native ground, where, after its destruction, they are able also to put an end to what it was designed to contain: Dracula himself.

So his ability to tally the goods (or should I say, evils?) allows Van Helsing and his crew to defeat the vampire. But—especially now, in the wake of the Covid-19 pandemic—the hunt for the boxes also conjures up the response to a disease outbreak.[97] In this form it shadows a *locus classicus* of the numbery discourse of the nineteenth century: the process whereby in 1854 John Snow discovered the source of cholera. T. W. Körner's *The Pleasures of Counting*, a popular casebook introduction to mathematics, opens with a discussion of "Unfeeling Statistics" as represented in the example of "Snow on cholera" in which—via both tables and diagrammatic maps replete with figures—he charts Snow's solution to the contagion.[98] The language of "sterilization" used to describe the neutralization of Dracula's boxes highlights the resonance with medical discourse.

Yet the boxes also suggest how, as Stephen Arata has shown, Stoker figures the infection as a fundamentally foreign invasive threat: this is, after all, alien soil we are talking about. Thus, for Arata, Van Helsing's recognition of the imperative that they be *sterilized* (*D* 225, 255, 271, 281)

---

[97] Martin Willis has described how the novel intersects with Victorian disease theory, especially the debate between proponents of germ-theory and miasmatism. See "'The Invisible Giant,' *Dracula*, and Disease," *Studies in the Novel* 39.3 (2007): 301–25.

[98] It is, appropriately, a numbered section: 1.1. See T. W. Körner, *The Pleasures of Counting* (Cambridge: Cambridge University Press, 1996), 3–14.

PLOTTING AGE IN TROLLOPE   179

demonstrates the Count's "virility": his "ability to produce literally endless numbers of offspring."[99] In other words, Arata sees the term operating in the context of post-Malthusian anxieties about population control that had been aggravated by the growing sense of what he calls "reverse colonization"— the influx of racially-other foreigners to the metropole from the colonial periphery. Such large numbers work in a register akin to that of Dickens's exponentially growing Jacquerie, whose revolutionary actions also threaten implicitly to spread from abroad to home. Harker introduces the menace of invasion when he first sees the Count asleep in his coffin (the moment also introduces the reverse-aging, thereby making it seem as much a product of the box as of his feeding on blood):

> The great box was in the same place, ... I raised the lid, and laid it back against the wall; and then I saw something which filled my very soul with horror. There lay the Count, but looking as if his youth had been half-renewed ... He lay like a filthy leech, exhausted with his repletion. ... This was the being I was helping to transfer to London, where, perhaps, for centuries to come, he might, amongst its teeming millions, satiate his lust for blood, and create a new and ever widening circle of semi-demons to batten on the helpless.
>
> (*D* 51)

The passage confirms that the invasive "teeming millions" (as they are once more designated later [*D* 167]) are vectors of the disease. (Such a conflation of alien threats has also resurfaced in the virulent xenophobia attached to the Covid pandemic.)

Nevertheless, the exclusive usage of the concept of *sterilization* in regard to the *boxes* is a little odd, given that both the disease itself and the population of vampires spread, rather, via vampiric feeding, as the novel shows through Lucy's and Mina's infections. So (while Lucy must certainly be tracked down and effectively "sterilized," in gruesome and misogynistic rituals performed in a chapel) the boxes of inert earth seem both to supplant and confine the threat of proliferation; their count forms an arithmetic rather than a geometric series (as would occur if, say, Dracula fed on three women, who in turn fed on three women, and so on). Such sleight of hand, whereby

---

[99] Stephen D. Arata, "The Occidental Tourist: *Dracula* and the Anxiety of Reverse Colonization," *Victorian Studies* 33.4 (1990), 631.

180   THE NUMBER SENSE

the unmanageable becomes manageable through manipulation of the numbers, is something we have seen many times across this study. We might compare it to how Byron encouraged our sympathetic response to the horrors of war by letting us follow the fate of the khan and his five sons, for example. But whereas the logic in that instance was iterative, like a fractal, here something both different and more sinister seems to be happening. It's rather like a game of three-card monte, in which our attention can be diverted by the glamorous lure of these seemingly "factual" numbers—much as a politician can pick and choose among available sets of statistics to make an argument seem plausible. We are distracted from the possibility of the uncontainable and teeming millions, capable of entering through tiny cracks in a window or wall, capable of reproducing themselves by merely feeding off a host. Instead, Stoker invites us to focus on those fifty boxes: tangible, even cumbersome (just ask that thirsty porter!)—literal objects of containment. So the Count can be stopped, the Un-Dead can be "fixed." Period.[100]

---

[100] Such closure is, however, open to some doubt—or at least modification. We seem to end, as with Sydney Carton in *A Tale of Two Cities*, with a more salutary kind of "rebirth" than that offered by the Un-Dead: Jonathan Harker records that his and Mina's son was born on the date on which the child's namesake, Quincey Morris, died slaying the Count (*D* 351). What Harker conveniently represses, though, is the fact that this little Quincey also carries some of Dracula's blood in his veins, inherited through his mother (who had been infected when she was forced to drink from the vampire's wound [*D* 262]). Perhaps this merely inoculates him from the contagion, but the jury is out.

Conclusion

C.1 First Things First: *Three* Redux

One, two, three; beginning, middle, end. Three is a magical number, as I started to show in my Introduction; to round things off, I return to it here in conclusion. The Pythagoreans recognized the special, "noble" status of what they termed *triad*: it is the only number whose sum is that of the digits below it, and the only one whose sum added to those below equals their product multiplied by itself (1+2=3; 1×2×3=1+2+3). In *The Russian Folktale*, in his chapter on "Wonder Tales," Vladimir Propp finds himself digressing in an effort to explain why "everything is triple" in such stories.[1] He seems almost to attribute agency to the integer, stating that it is "at the origin of the most ancient of all genres, namely, the folktale." Propp cites the anthropologist Lucien Lévy-Bruhl, observing his finding that "many languages of primitive peoples do not have numbers higher than 3. Three meant 'many,' as many as it was possible to count." It has always been a threshold figure.

For Propp, part of the power of three lies in the contrast it enables: "The trebling [in folktales] takes the shape of the schema 2+1, and the three links of the tripling are not equal in their rights. One turns out to be decisive—the last one. So, of three brothers only one is the hero of the narration. The other two brothers serve as a contrasting background for him."[2] The mathematician Sarah Hart explains a more fundamental version of this phenomenon, noting how three is the smallest number that allows for repetition (the most basic form of pattern) and difference (breaking the pattern).[3] But in the two works I will consider here—Wilkie Collins's *Armadale* and Thomas Hardy's first published novel, *Desperate Remedies* (1871), an early effort that tried to mine the vein of Collins's success—the third time is not so much a charm (or a prince charming) as the ultimate proof of a pattern. Twice may be coincidence; thrice seems more like fate. As we shall see through these

---

[1] Propp, *Russian Folktale*, 175–7.
[2] Propp, *Russian Folktale*, 177.
[3] See Hart, *Once Upon a Prime*, 116.

The Number Sense of Nineteenth-Century British Literature. Stefanie Markovits, Oxford University Press.
© Stefanie Markovits (2025). DOI: 10.1093/9780198937821.003.0006

182   THE NUMBER SENSE

novels, the number three thus mediates sensation fiction's obsession with the relationships among agency, accident, and destiny. It also lets me exercise my number sense one last time to show how numerical figures can shift in significance against the backdrop of the numbery nineteenth century.

Ian Hacking has described how, in the wake of the rise of statistics, various false doctrines arose alongside the century's gradual "erosion of determinism." Although the general historical trend was to "clear" "a space" for the notion of chance, the ground prepared in the process produced some surprisingly fast-growing weeds.[4] One of the most curious of these may have been "statistical fatalism" (also called "statistical determinism"), the idea that "if a statistical law applied to a group of people, then the freedom of individuals in that group was constrained."[5] To cite perhaps the most famous example of this principle, the historian Thomas Henry Buckle argued influentially that "In a given state of society, a certain number of persons must put an end to their own life" over a given stretch of time.[6] His model made suicide, seemingly the most personal of choices, appear to involve what Hacking calls "a mythology of causation"; the constant rate of suicides becomes "proof" of statistical fatalism. This new twist in the old determinism/free will debate arose as population-wide regularities in behavior became apparent through the routine and large-scale collection of statistical numbers. Adolphe Quetelet, among others, was impressed by the consequences: "Society prepares the crimes and the guilty person is only the instrument," he observed excitedly; as Hacking explains, given such a worldview, "The issue that was hidden was not the power of the soul to choose, but the power of the state to control what kind of person one is."[7] Hacking cites Tom Gradgrind's defense of his crime (a bank robbery) to his father toward the end of *Hard Times*: "So many people are employed in situations of trust; so many people, out of so many, will be dishonest. I have heard you talk, a hundred times, of its being a law. How can I help laws?"[8]

The numbers involved in statistical fatalism were vast, as I have said. But what I want to propose here is that a much smaller measure—three—participated in similar dynamics. This is of course mathematical nonsense;

---

[4] Hacking, *The Taming of Chance*, 3, 1.

[5] Hacking, *The Taming of Chance*, 116, 121. In contrast, after 1926 the uncertainties of quantum mechanics opened up room for ideas of freedom.

[6] Thomas Henry Buckle, *The History of Civilization in England*, Vol. 1 (London: John Parker & Son, 1857), 20.

[7] Hacking, *The Taming of Chance*, 71, 126, 116 (quoting Quetelet), 121.

[8] Dickens, *Hard Times*, 262; see Hacking, *The Taming of Chance*, 118.

CONCLUSION   183

the Law of Large Numbers requires, as its name suggests, large numbers to hold true. Nevertheless, when we read the suicide of Father Time in Thomas Hardy's last novel, *Jude the Obscure* (1895)—"Done because we are too menny"—against the backdrop not only of Malthus but also of statistical theories of suicide like Buckle's, we are picking up on the wider resonances of that "menny."[9] And we might recall that the current count of Jude and Sue's children was but three (Father Time has two younger siblings, whom he also murders). This confluence of *many* and *three* hints at the strange doubleness of the number's effect in the period, as the "many" for which it stood among Lévy-Bruhl's "primitive peoples" is not only overwritten by mythical significance but also tinged with an oddly statistical cast. Hence the weird effect of Father Time's expression, which describes what is an immense loss when it comes to the emotional calculus of the novel but a mere blip in statistical terms. Moreover, in the context of the "long families" of Victorian fiction—and Victorian reality—three does seem rather few.[10] Compare Dickens's narrator's reflections on the problem faced by both him and poor Mr. Wilfer in *Our Mutual Friend*:

> Not to encumber this page by telling off the Wilfers in detail and casting them up in the gross, it is enough for the present that the rest were what is called "out in the world," in various ways, and that they were Many. So many, that when one of his dutiful children called in to see him, R. Wilfer generally seemed to say to himself, after a little mental arithmetic, "Oh! here's another of 'em!" before adding aloud, "How de do, John," or Susan, as the case might be.
>
> (*OMF* 34)

While we never learn the precise number in the case of this "Many," it is certainly more than three.

---

[9] Hardy, *Jude the Obscure*, 410.

[10] As indeed are four, if we add the expected child (who precipitates Father Time's deed and is miscarried in its wake). On the prevalence of the "long family," see Davidoff, *Thicker than Water*. That said, Kelly Hager and Karen Bourrier have tallied sibling groups in fifty frequently read Victorian novels to show how rarely their "long families" are comprised of fully-individuated siblings, and how surprisingly common "short families" prove to be: "in a data set of 50 novels, the average family size was 2.8; the median, or middle value, was two; and the mode, or most frequently occurring number, was one." Nevertheless, the historical average of just under six live births casts a shadow over Father Time's definition of three as "too menny." Hager and Bourrier, "How Many Siblings Had Philip Pirrip?: Counting Brothers and Sisters in the Victorian Novel," *ELH* 89.1 (2022): 159–84; 159; 181, n. 8.

184 THE NUMBER SENSE

Yet the theories circulating around the act of suicide mean that while three was already a crowd in the bleak prospect offered by Hardy's novel, Emily Steinlight is right to see more at stake in the dynamic than a fear of the implied Malthusian millions. Rather, as she explains, varieties of "causal explanation" also hover in the balance. Steinlight quotes from Jude's own citation of medical expertise: "It was in his nature to do it. The Doctor says there are such boys springing up amongst us—boys of a sort unknown in the last generation—the outcome of new views of life. ... He says it is the beginning of the coming universal wish not to live."[11] "Menny" in this case seems, then, as much to reflect on what is being "done" (the suicidal deed) as it does on the number of people to whom it is done (a Malthusian population). As Steinlight observes, "In *Jude the Obscure* ... hereditary biology and sociology"—including ideas of statistical fatalism—"often vie for explanatory authority."[12] The struggle contributes to how Hardy's novels work by "constitut[ing] a statistically registered counter-norm that challenges the universality of the laws they charge themselves with breaking."[13] Steinlight concludes that "by producing an excess of causal explanation for both [hereditary and sociological] models of errancy and showing how such explanation relies on figurative language to link otherwise contrary claims about failed development, these novels work as an immanent counterargument to the double bind" of such paradigms of action.[14] My own focus here will be on how one example of "figurative language"—the number three—can crystallize the "excess of causal explanation."

In sensation fiction, modern hereditary and sociological conceptions of causality coexist with other modes: not only contemporary liberal ideas of cause and effect channeled through the choices of protagonists (as in the traditional *Bildungsroman*) but also ancient supernatural forms of agency. And in the two novels to which I will turn now, threes appear at the crux of them all. (It is surely no coincidence that in each, the antagonist also exits the narrative through suicide.) The way the threes of these novels are being made to do work often unsuited to the figure's scale thus shows how numbers

---

[11] Hardy, *Jude the Obscure*, 410–11. See Emily Steinlight, *Populating the Novel*, 203 (she ultimately links this view to Freud's death drive).

[12] Steinlight, *Populating the Novel*, 170.

[13] Steinlight, *Populating the Novel*, 170. For Steinlight, such confused attitudes toward causation contribute to late-century naturalism's tendency to "empty" "the conventions [of the *Bildungsroman*] of their purpose," to "sap" the form's "vital energy" (168). Once again, the *Bildungsroman*, the period's preeminent vessel of singularity, is reformed by concerns over larger numbers.

[14] Steinlight, *Populating the Novel*, 170.

CONCLUSION 185

can operate in this period at the weird convergence (a Hardyesque term, as it happens!) of old and new, emotional and rational, and scientific and aesthetic methods of signification.

C.2 Two Threes in *Armadale*

While it directs us to the work's central preoccupation, the query posed by the title to Book II, Chapter 9 of Wilkie Collins's *Armadale*—"Fate or Chance?"—oversimplifies the myriad structures of causation considered by this novel. *Armadale* tells a tale of inherited guilt and of the efforts people can make to avoid repeating the past.[15] It has with justice been called "One of the most overplotted novels in English literature"—so much so that I will refrain here from any attempt to provide a total overview of the action.[16] Instead, we might point to its central symbolic emblem: the elaborate clock, complete with mechanical sentries who are meant to march at noon, over which Major Milroy (father of the novel's ingénue, Neelie) labors obsessively and fruitlessly. As readers have long recognized, Collins uses the clock to "parod[y] the notion of 'the clockwork universe'" in the context of a story that is "deeply concerned with the working-out of lives in time and with the issues of determinism, free will, providence, and chance"; it also serves to draw attention to Collins's own elaborate and sometimes faulty plot mechanics.[17] Still, the titular question "Fate or Chance?" points even more explicitly to the centrality of models of causation in the novel, suggesting why Daniel Martin views the book as "Collins's most deliberate exploration of fate and accident in the universe."[18] As Martin and others have observed, such exploration occurs against the backdrop of Hacking's increasingly statistical culture, one in which "the quantification of modern

---

[15] Suggestively, this summary of the novel could also apply to *A Tale of Two Cities*, another numbery work in which concerns regarding agency are mediated through processes of doubling.

[16] Some plot summary appears in Chapter 4, where I discuss age in the novel. Winifred Hughes, *The Maniac in the Cellar: Sensation Novels of the 1860s* (Princeton: Princeton University Press, 1981), 155. The novel's intricate plot necessitates and is necessitated by its interrogation of causal structures.

[17] Lisa M. Zeitz and Peter Thoms, "Collins's Use of the Strasbourg Clock in *Armadale*," *Nineteenth-Century Literature* 45.4 (1991), 502, 498. See also Daly, who calls the clock "a *mis-en-abîme* of the novel's action" and views its mechanics as implicated in how Collins's characters can seem like "automata" (*Literature, Technology, and Modernity*, 50). Hensley, too, points to the metafiction in *Forms of Empire* (121).

[18] Daniel Martin, "Wilkie Collins and Risk," in *A Companion to Sensation Fiction*, ed. Pamela K. Gilbert (London: Blackwell, 2011), 192.

186   THE NUMBER SENSE

risks of all kinds" demanded assessment of the possibilities of imaginable outcomes—especially negative ones.[19]

So it makes sense that here, as in Collins's works more generally, characters often approach branches in the plot by turning to numbers: "choices" can seem like the roll of the dice. Collins's previous novel, *No Name*, includes a particularly complex version of such a game of chance. Not coincidentally, it occurs in relation to a possible suicide. Magdalen Vanstone looks out at the sea and deliberates whether to end her life: "For one half-hour to come she determined to wait there and count the vessels as they went by. If in that time an even number passed her, the sign given should be a sign to live. If the uneven number prevailed, the end should be Death." We watch her waiting and count alongside, both minutes and ships, until in the final seconds she "saw the EIGHTH ship": "'Providence?' she whispered faintly to herself. 'Or chance?'"[20] In *Armadale*, though, more often than not the choices are three; in one remarkably on-the-nose scene, in a chapter titled "The March of Events," Ozias Midwinter (the name assumed by the slightly younger of the two eponymous heroes) even finds himself lost at a literal crossroads described as "a point at which three roads met."[21]

Such questions concerning categories of causation converge in the novel's most prominent three: the Three Dreams, also called Visions, experienced by Allan Armadale (that is, the older Allan junior, current lord of the manor of Thorpe Ambrose, and the son of the man who had—unbeknownst to him—been murdered by Midwinter's father). The Visions come to Allan as he sleeps aboard the wreck of the portentously christened *La Grace de Dieu*, the same vessel on which the original murder had been committed and upon which Allan and Midwinter, who are friends, have been stranded

---

[19] Martin, "Wilkie Collins and Risk," 189. Christopher Kent also considers the novel's engagement with statistical determinism. See Kent, "Probability, Reality and Sensation in the Novels of Wilkie Collins," *Dickens Studies Annual* 20 (1991): 259–80. One might compare Sandra Macpherson's account of the eighteenth-century realist novel's attention to accident and injury in the context of strict liability law, a source of its "tragic form"; Collins's works (and Hardy's) seem similarly influenced by the (now even more numbery) modes and methods of insurance law. See Sandra Macpherson, *Harm's Way: Tragic Responsibility and the Novel Form* (Baltimore: Johns Hopkins University Press, 2010). See also Tina Young Choi, *Victorian Contingencies*, for further thinking on the narrative implications of both probability and contingency for novel form. Choi begins her study by considering how Babbage's work on actuarial tables allowed him to think about "the expressive potential of numbers." As she observes, "The numerical sequence was no longer, in its ideal form, a reflection of reliability and predictability, but came instead to approximate narrative, in which contingency was at once a sign of authorial intention and a reflection of the complexity of the natural and social worlds" (19).

[20] Collins, *No Name*, ed. Virginia Blain (Oxford: Oxford University Press, 1998), 499–500.

[21] Collins, *Armadale*, 244. Hereafter, internally referenced as *A*.

for the night. Subsequently recorded by Allan and printed in the novel as "Allan Armadale's Dream," in a list comprised of no fewer than seventeen numbered entries that trace their details step by step, the visions culminate in Allan's apparent death by poisoning at the hands of a shadowy couple (*A* 170–2). This list seems an effort to translate Allan's disconnected "visions" into something more like "the fast-lengthening chain of events" that has long been recognized as a central feature of sensation fiction plotting (*A* 244).[22] That is to say, the *three* might even be read as a simplified *seventeen* here, compressing, in the manner of some triptych paintings, the story into its essential narrative elements of beginning, middle, and end.

Appearing at the close of the novel's first book (of five), in a chapter titled "The Shadow of the Future," the trio of visions does in fact offer a preview of the novel, as both readers and characters wait with bated breath to see whether—and increasingly how and when—the dreams will be realized.[23] But we are also encouraged to assess the causal forces at work in their realization. Right after listing Allan's visions, they are subjected to scientific scrutiny by a local doctor (the borrowing of whose sailboat had occasioned the incident). Notably, this man of science tries to undermine any supernatural significance to the dream's tripartite nature (*third time's a charm*) by giving it a valence derived from experimental psychology: He traces back aspects of the first two dreams to Allan's recent interactions with others, and then suggests that these are melded and corrected in his mind's third effort at making sense of things. As he explains, "After having tried to introduce the waking impression of the doctor and the landlady separately, in connection with the wrong set of circumstances, *the dreaming mind comes right at the third trial,* and introduces the doctor and the landlady together, in connection with the right set of circumstances" (*A* 181, emphasis added). "What a thing science is!" a delighted Allan declares, giving his own vote to an explanatory model rooted in objective methods, albeit ones that can be hard to put one's finger on; the scenario seems to owe as much to Goldilocks and the Three Bears as to science. As Lauren Goodlad observes, "Collins plays with his readers' expectation of a 'natural explanation' while prolonging their fascination with fatalism."[24] And Midwinter, who believes he is

---

[22] See Walter M. Kendrick, "The Sensationalism of *The Woman in White*," *Nineteenth-Century Fiction* 32 (1977): 18–35.

[23] One might compare the three visions Marian has of Walter Hartright's Central American adventures in *The Woman in White* (278–9).

[24] Lauren Goodlad, *The Victorian Geopolitical Aesthetic*, 144.

188 THE NUMBER SENSE

fated to be implicated in his friend's death—even as his father had murdered his friend's father—remains unconvinced.

Indeed, he remains throughout the story the novel's strongest proponent of fatalism. It is a role to which Midwinter has, with tragic irony, been triply fated by his birth: first by his racial inheritance from his enslaved Black mother, itself a doubled chain of supposedly racially based superstition and historical bondage; and then by his inheritance of his father's crimes. The largely repressed specter of slavery also stands behind the novel's explorations of the "chain" of events as bondage to fate. Goodlad (who explores this feature of the novel in some detail) explains:

> Ozias's "superstitious nature" [A 165, 223] is figured, on the one hand, as a racialized attribute of African descent and, on the other, as the expression of a complicated transatlantic past. Hence, while the "hot Creole blood" [A 479] of his Trinidadian mother is tied to a variety of un-English characteristics, Ozias's "hereditary superstition" [A 124] is explicitly the legacy of his guilty white father.[25]

For Christopher Kent, "the deciding factor in the outcome is left unclear in such a way as to justify referring it to chance. This is a distinctly 'modern' way of settling the dilemma of free will versus determinism that vexed discussions of probability in Collins's time."[26] Still, the complexity here yields further causal uncertainty; very little is *settled*. The lack of clarity seeps into Midwinter's attitudes. If in places he seems to echo Tennyson's May Queen (discussed in my Introduction)—"if it come three times, I thought, I take it for a sign"—it takes a lot longer for the third vision to appear in a novel of over eight hundred pages than in a lyric of sixty lines.[27] Midwinter thus has plenty of time and opportunity to doubt his fatalistic nature, repeatedly testing the validity of the dreams against the evidence with which he is presented and entertaining other, more realistic, explanatory structures. For example, after another rational explanation has been given to him, he muses, "If the Dream was proved to be no longer a warning from the other world, it followed inevitably that accident and not fate had led the way to the night on the Wreck, and that all the events which had happened since ... were events in themselves harmless, which his superstition had distorted from their proper

---

[25] Goodlad, *The Victorian Geopolitical Aesthetic*, 116.
[26] Kent, "Probability, Reality and Sensation," 259–60.
[27] In *Tennyson*, ed. Ricks, 422.

shape" (*A* 338–9). Hence also the punctuation of that chapter title, "Fate or Chance?"

Given the three Dreams' central role in structuring the novel's approach to the question posed by this title, it is appropriate that this chapter sees the first of the visions realized, when a woman—revealed to be the novel's antiheroine, Lydia Gwilt (the disguised former maid of Allan Armadale's mother, currently entering the scene as governess to Allan's love interest Neelie)—appears at the edge of a dark pool. But Lydia, whose entry jolts the reader awake as much as it does Midwinter, will also introduce a competing causal structure through which the second half of *Armadale's* plot unfolds. In place of three Visions, she offers the apparently more agential option of a scheme by which she aims to inherit Armadale's wealth.[28] The plan arises after she discovers Midwinter's true name and status as the legal heir of Thorpe Ambrose. Naturally, it too comes in three parts. As Lydia reflects in her diary:

> The whole series of events ... have been, one and all—though I was too stupid to see it—events in my favor; events paving the way smoothly and more smoothly straight to the end.
>
> In three bold steps—only three!—that end might be reached. Let Midwinter marry me privately, under his real name—step the first! Let Armadale leave Thorpe Ambrose a single man, and die in some distant place among strangers—step the second!
>
> Why am I hesitating? Why not go on to step the third, and last?
>
> I will go on. Step the third, and last, is my appearance, after the announcement of Armadale's death has reached this neighborhood, in the character of Armadale's widow.
>
> (*A* 538)

Still, if such plotting agency ("bold steps") and her ability as an actress align Lydia with other sensational antiheroines, these steps are from the first embedded within the fateful "series" or, more ominously, chain "of events" that binds the novel's characters.[29] Lydia's repeated *lets* here highlight her

---

[28] Nathan Hensley calls her "the representative of an epoch of free agents" (*Forms of Empire*, 122).

[29] See E. S. Dallas: "When women are thus put forward to lead the action of a plot, they must be urged into a false position ... This is what is called sensation. It is not wrong to make a sensation; but if the novelist depends for his sensation upon the action of a woman, the chances are that he will attain his end by unnatural means." Dallas, *The Gay Science*, 2 vols. (New York: Johnson Reprint Corporation, 1969), II.296–7. This book was first published in 1866.

190 THE NUMBER SENSE

passive orientation toward enabling circumstance. Earlier, having learned Midwinter's real identity, she even seems to channel his superstition in her first response to the revelation: "And there are two Allan Armadales—two Allan Armadales—two Allan Armadales. There! three is a lucky number. Haunt me again, after that, if you can!" she proclaims, as if the triple-repetition will prevent a curse attendant on her knowledge (*A* 511).

If, however, she hedges her bets as to whether she is contending with fate or chance, she nevertheless focuses her own decision-making through a very modern concept associated with the latter category: risk. After embarking on her plan ("It is done. The first of the three steps that lead me to the end is a step taken"), Lydia admits the risk involved: "I am going blindfold, then—so far as Midwinter is concerned—into this frightful risk? Yes; blindfold" (*A* 546). As Hacking explains, chance was "tamed" when risks could be calculated through the careful assessment of probabilities produced by the large-scale collection of statistical data. These cultural dynamics, Daniel Martin observes, underlie why "To 'run a risk' in a Collins novel is normal behavior."[30] From her introduction, though, Lydia Gwilt seems unusually aware of her position, caught up in the race and running with a handicap (or might her "blindfold" function rather like the blinders that help a skittish horse run straight?). Collins associates her with the term *risk* throughout the novel. Penning an anonymous note as "naturally" as "if I had been a professed novelist" (she is pretending it is from a servant), she glories in the idea: "here I am, running headlong into a frightful risk—and I never was in better spirits in my life!" (*A* 559). Other early choices seem equally happy: "I risk nothing by marrying Midwinter in my maiden instead of my widow's name," she declares (*A* 593); her plot holds tight.

But, as the novel progresses, she will come to see her alignment with the novelist for the fiction it is: she can't entirely control the action.[31] At the same time, the category of risk comes to highlight how her "three steps" enmesh the actor in a chain of increasingly burdensome consequences, partly because she herself has changed along the way. Having fallen in love with Midwinter, she begins to reframe her attitude toward the three steps,

---

[30] Martin, "Wilkie Collins and Risk," 184.

[31] See Hannah Arendt's observation that "although everybody started his life by inserting himself into the human world through action and speech, nobody is the author or producer of his own life story. In other words, the stories, the results of action and speech, reveal an agent, but this agent is not author or producer." Hannah Arendt, *The Human Condition* (Chicago: University of Chicago Press, 1958), 185.

CONCLUSION 191

aka the "Grand Risk," in a conditional tense that registers the uncertainty of all enterprise in such an uncertain universe:

> Supposing I was not the altered woman I am—I only say, supposing—how would the Grand Risk that I once thought of running look now? I have married Midwinter... I have taken the first of those three steps which were once to lead me, through Armadale's life, to the fortune and the station of Armadale's widow. ... Well, having taken the first step, then, whether I would or no, how—supposing I meant to take the second step, which I don't—how would present circumstances stand toward me? Would they warn me to draw back, I wonder? or would they encourage me to go on? It will interest me to calculate the chances ...
>
> (*A* 663)

Lydia does continue to calculate her chances as she takes each of the three bold steps, but she also increasingly shares Midwinter's sense, expressed on seeing the third of the Visions realized, that "there is a fatality in our footsteps" (*A* 683). A motif that entered the novel promising agency departs it trailing the burdensome chains of a form of fatalism that the focus on risk colors as statistical, even as its tripartite structure suggests older conceptions of fate.

Things come to a crux in a remarkably ornate scene of attempted murder, in a "sanitorium" to which Allan has been lured by the promise of a meeting with Neelie. Notably, it is Lydia's third attempt at killing him: two earlier efforts have failed (*A* 728). And just as notably, Collins orchestrates the scene though numbers. The murder weapon is an air-borne poison that is to be dispensed into a specially designed room (room "Number Four") through a mechanism in the wall. The drops of poison must be deployed in succession, with "six separate Pourings" (*A* 801) being required for death to be assured; thus the scenario depends upon a slow sequential process that both compresses and doubles the three bold steps of the larger plot. But Midwinter, who suspects mischief is afoot, swaps bed chambers, putting Allan into room Number Three; he himself takes Number Four. Lydia discovers the switch only after "the fourth Pouring," when, her suspicions having been raised, she looks into Number Three to discover not Midwinter's sleeping form but Allan's: "There lay the man whose life she had attempted for the third time, peacefully sleeping in the room that had been given to her husband, and in the air that could harm nobody!" (*A* 804). Recognizing the "inevitable conclusion," Lydia nevertheless has the strength of will to save

192   THE NUMBER SENSE

her husband, who has passed out in the tainted atmosphere of the other room; she manages to open the door—of course, only on the "third time"— and pull Midwinter into fresh air (*A* 804). And then, in place of the third bold step, she administers the third round of Pourings (the Fifth and Sixth) and shuts the door of Number Four on herself.

Readers of the novel baulked at the preposterousness of this plot— especially as regarded the Three Visions—from the start. Collins was prepared for the objection. He meets it head-on, as when he makes Lydia declare herself "completely staggered by this extraordinary coincidence" after learning of Allan's Dreams and of her own role in fulfilling them (*A* 682). "How unnatural all this would be if it was written in a book!" she proclaims, in one of many such moments where her self-acknowledged artifice suggests alignment with her author (*A* 684). Collins also tried to preempt the charge in his Appendix, where he invites his audience to choose freely among possible interpretations of the Visions:

> NOTE—My readers will perceive that I have purposely left them, with reference to the Dream in this story, in the position which they would occupy in the case of a dream in real life: they are free to interpret it by the natural or the supernatural theory, as the bent of their own minds may incline them.
>
> (*A* 817)

Regardless, many remained unconvinced. The critic for the *Saturday Review* objected that "the story of *Armadale* hinges almost entirely on miraculous combinations, the arithmetical chances against which are simply infinite." Moreover, the review points to the speciousness of Collins's offer to choose freely, given the novelist's silence regarding the real causal structure behind the narrative: "As for the dream in the story, Mr. Wilkie Collins's readers, unless they are singularly simple-minded, will not be long in puzzling themselves between natural and supernatural. Being an invention of the author's fancy, it is much more simply accounted for on the theory that it has pleased Mr. Collins to invent it."[32] Still, when this critic observes that Collins makes "the wonders of science do duty side by side with the marvels of the supernatural world" and notes how "a hundred agencies are brought to play" in

---

[32] Unsigned review of *Armadale*, *Saturday Review* 21 (June 16, 1866), 727.

CONCLUSION   193

this process, I am struck rather by how often those agencies are simplified and channeled through threes.[33]

C.3 Third and Last: *Desperate Remedies*

In the wake of his failure to publish *The Poor Man and the Lady*, Thomas Hardy needed to change course. He listened to George Meredith's advice urging him to produce something "with a more complicated plot"—that is, something more in the mode of Wilkie Collins, with a greater leavening of sensation.[34] *Desperate Remedies* fulfills this charge by telling what happens when the recently orphaned Cytherea Gray comes to work as a lady's companion to the woman she later discovers to be both her namesake and her father's first love, Cytherea Aldclyffe. Miss Aldclyffe (as she has remained) maneuvers matters to force the younger Cytherea to break off her engagement with her beloved Edward Springrove and accept instead the hand of Aeneas Manston, Miss Aldclyffe's estate manager and unacknowledged illegitimate son. But when the death of Manston's previous wife—purportedly in a fire—becomes subject to doubt, Cytherea's brand-new marriage does, too. The latter parts of the novel shift into a mystery plot, as Springrove and others (including a professional "detective") try to follow an assortment of "clue[s]" to find out the truth behind the first Mrs. Manston's fate, even as Manston, who (it finally emerges) had in fact killed her, tries to hide it.[35] After his arrest, Manston commits suicide in jail, leaving Cytherea free to marry Edward. The novel's complexities combine many of the standard elements of sensation fiction. As Walter Kendrick observes, "By 1871 the genre was well defined and perhaps already dying. ... Indeed, the most striking feature of *Desperate Remedies* is its extreme orthodoxy, verging on the parodic."[36]

---

[33] Unsigned review of *Armadale*, 726.

[34] Quoted in Lawrence O. Jones, "*Desperate Remedies* and the Victorian Sensation Novel," *Nineteenth-Century Fiction* 20.1 (June 1965), 35.

[35] Thomas Hardy, *Desperate Remedies*, ed. Patricia Ingham (Oxford: Oxford University Press, 2009), 354. Hereafter, *DR*, internally documented. Critics have observed the generic shift in the latter parts of *Desperate Remedies*. For example, Jones distinguishes between its first half, which he views as properly tragic in the mode of Hardy's later works, and its sensational second half, in which "the chance events, which had had some significance as examples of the arbitrary workings of Natural Law, become mere authorial manipulations" ("*Desperate Remedies* and the Victorian Sensation Novel," 49).

[36] Walter M. Kendrick, "The Sensationalism of Thomas Hardy," *Texas Studies in Literature and Language* 22.4 (1980), 490.

194   THE NUMBER SENSE

In the context of my argument here, however, I'd like to emphasize how the parodic impulse yields an extraordinarily numbery novel. One might point to the central role played by railway timetables; recall Nicholas Daly's observation that "The sensation novel ... provides a species of temporal training" by "synchroniz[ing] its readers with industrial modernity" through the attention it pays to railway time.[37] In a scene that epitomizes this tendency, Manston misses the arrival of his first wife Eunice when he too "hurriedly cast his eyes down the column of *Bradshaw* which showed the details and duration of the selected train's journey" and thus mistakes the time at which he should meet her at the station:

> He did not perceive, branching from the column down which his finger ran, a small twist, called a shunting-line, inserted at a particular place, to imply that at that point the train was divided into two. By this oversight he understood that the arrival of his wife at Carriford-Road Station would not be till late in the evening: by the second half of the train, containing the third-class passengers, and passing two hours and three-quarters later than the previous one, by which the lady, as a second-class passenger, would really be brought.
>
> (*DR* 161)

The branching of the line here also represents a branching in the plot: Manston's failure to meet his wife angers her and initiates the cascade of events that ends in her murder.[38] Hardy even highlights the episode's crucial nature, introducing it as the first in "a day of singular and great events, influencing the present and future of nearly all the personages whose actions in a complex drama form the subject of this record" (*DR* 161).

Desperate Remedies's numbery tendency—and this tendency's foundation in chronologically ordered "events"—appears already in the Table of Contents, in which each of the twenty-one listed chapters that comprise the novel's three volumes takes the form of "The Events of X," with X being a given period, ranging in duration from "Thirty Years" (Volume I, Chapter I) to "Three Hours" (Volume III, Chapter VII). Moreover, these chapters are themselves divided chronologically into numbered sections, which are

---

[37] Daly, *Literature, Technology, and Modernity*, 37.

[38] In *The Taming of Chance* Hacking quotes the Victorian mathematician James Clerk Maxwell, who describes the "singular points" that constitute free will and agency in a deterministic universe as making us like the pointsman on the railway, who does nothing most of the time but can "direct the train on one of two divergent lines at certain junctions" (156).

CONCLUSION 195

in turn time-stamped to indicate the period covered in each part (thus, §2 of Volume I, Chapter VI, "The Events of Twelve Hours," is labeled *Two to five, a.m.*"; while §1 of Volume I, Chapter I, "The Events of Thirty Years," is labeled *"December and January, 1835–36"*). As Kendrick has calculated, "Counting the unnumbered 'Sequel,' there are an even hundred of these subdivisions, and taken in order they make, with one exception, a continuous sequence of time from December 1835 to Midsummer Night 1867."[39] We have returned to the mental landscape of Dante's Divine Comedy, with its perfectly rounded hundred Cantos.

But we are also back in the world of Dante's threes—or, should I say, Collins's? That's because, as in *Armadale*, the threes of *Desperate Remedies* are deeply implicated in the novel's investigation of the relationship between fate and chance. Hardy's interest in the dynamics of causality has long been recognized, and it helps make sense of why a later master of a mode of realistic naturalism would have been willing to try his hand at sensation early in his career.[40] Patricia Ingham describes how the patterns of Hardy's plots—the "string of coincidences" that so often constitute them—instantiate a "paradox" in that "they are represented as the result of chance and at the same time as predetermined" (*DR* xxiii). One senses again the cultural backdrop of statistical fatalism (in which such forces also overlap) that lay behind *Armadale's* central question, "Fate, or Chance?" Not coincidentally, games of chance feature prominently in Hardy's novels, but their conclusions generally feel destined. Consider the central and pivotal dice game in *The Return of the Native*, in which Wildeve wins and loses the fifty guineas Mrs. Yeobright had intended as a peace offering to her son Clym (it is another remarkably numbery episode). The ultimate winner, Diggory Venn, wants to use the jackpot to help smooth the relationship between mother and son, yet he ends up furthering the familial divide when he misdirects the entire gift to Mrs. Yeobright's niece Thomasin. In *Desperate Remedies*, as Ingham observes, the pattern of coincidences-that-raise-issues-of-causality climaxes in the scene in which the construction of a bonfire coincides with

---

[39] Kendrick, "The Sensationalism of Thomas Hardy," 492.

[40] See Gillian Beer's influential reading of Hardy's concern for causality in *Darwin's Plots: Evolutionary Narrative in Darwin, George Eliot and Nineteenth-Century Fiction* (London: Ark, 1985). Laura Faulkner observes that while "[k]nown as a realist, Hardy tries readers' patience with plots that test the limits of the probable." As she also notes, "Excessive use of coincidence in nineteenth-century fiction is usually associated with sensation fiction," a mode most would distinguish from Hardy's usual naturalism. Faulkner, "'That's convenient, not to say odd': Coincidence, Causality, and Hardy's Inconsistent Inconsistency," *Victorian Review* 37.1 (2011), 92.

196 THE NUMBER SENSE

Eunice Manston's arrival on the scene (via the aforementioned train). This moment leads to the conflagration that offers Aeneas Manston a smoke-screen for his act of murder (it is long assumed that Eunice dies in the flames when the inn where she is staying burns to the ground). And it is another moment grounded in the number three.

Specifically, the fire erupts because Farmer Springrove—Edward's father and the owner of the inn—makes what Daniel Williams identifies as an error based in the "too-rapid induction of counted instances."[41] Williams's fascinating reading of *Desperate Remedies* takes its cue from Hardy's plausible familiarity with the work of the logician John Venn—Diggory's likely namesake—especially his ideas about probability, frequency, and set theory. While these developments are distinct from the statistical advances I have been discussing, they rely similarly on the difference between large and small numbers, and they share a concern for risk.[42] Indeed, Venn had quoted Buckle's observations on the constancy of suicide in *The Logic of Chance* (1866), calling them both "absurd" and increasingly "prevalent," given "the spread of statistical information and study."[43] That being said, as Ian Hacking notes with some irony: "Venn had a diagnosis of the attractions of statistical fatalism, but someone bitten by statistical fatalism would not be cured by Dr. Venn."[44]

Hardy sets the scene: following ploughing and harrowing, "The couch-grass extracted from the soil had been left to wither in the sun; afterwards it was raked together, lighted in the customary way, and now lay smouldering in a large heap in the middle of the plot." This "middle of the plot"— suspiciously, rendered both literal and literary here—had been "kindled," we are told, "three days previous to Mrs. Manston's arrival." (Recall how the plot of the novel, as the first chapter title had recorded, was kindled "Thirty Years" ago.) "One or two villagers," we learn, "had suggested that the fire was almost too near the back of the house for its continuance to be unattended with risk" (*DR* 165)—and there's that statistical term again.[45] But Farmer

---

[41] Williams, "Slow Fire: Serial Thinking and Hardy's Genres of Induction," 25.

[42] Williams, who observes the role played by the character Diggory Venn in *The Return of the Native* ("Slow Fire," 23), is interested in the implications of Venn's work on series for the concepts of "class" and genre.

[43] John Venn, *The Logic of Chance* (London: Macmillan, 1866), 355. Quoted in Hacking, *The Taming of Chance*, 126.

[44] Hacking, *The Taming of Chance*, 126.

[45] In a further indication of the statistical backdrop of the novel, Hardy discusses how Farmer Springrove had been forced to drop his fire insurance for the inn after the insurance company decided that "the uncertainty and greatness of the risk of thatch"—with which the inn is roofed—was prohibitive (*DR* 179). This fact leads to the dissolution of Edward and Cytherea's

CONCLUSION   197

Springrove, being of "sanguine temperament" and anxious to get the grass burnt before the rain returns, decides merely to keep watch on the fire. The "first evening after the heap was lit," he "takes survey" "two or three times." The next day, he looks again, twice, "but less carefully than on the first night." When the third day comes:

> The morning and the whole of the third day still saw the heap in its old smouldering condition; indeed, the smoke was less, and there seemed a probability that it might have to be re-kindled on the morrow. ...
>   The farmer glanced at the heap casually and indifferently in passing; two nights of safety seemed to ensure the third ...
>
> (*DR* 166)

And yet, it doesn't: a breeze kicks up, the fire catches, and, with that, the inn burns down to the ground. As Williams points out, "The fire happens because Farmer Springrove refers to a series that is brief and discrete—one, two, three—to make a prediction about a continuous process in a world where the weathering of long-run series should have compelled a more cautious approach."[46]

I would say, though, that his confusion arises in no small part through the discrete charms of the number three. Williams points to the novel's competing epistemologies: on the one hand, *Desperate Remedies* references the logical mode of what he calls "serial thinking," "an approach to representation and cognition that emphasizes repetition, enumeration, and aggregation," one that is influenced by recent developments in nineteenth-century mathematics concerning "whether and how series can be used to make inferences and how the problem of establishing appropriate boundaries to series can engender faulty inferences and thwart prediction"; on the other hand, Hardy's novel expresses "the constant lure of a rival epistemology— of chance and coincidence, of intuition that proceeds preternaturally, not by logic."[47] But more than any other number, three speaks to both of these modes: it can import some of the magical thinking of myth and fairy tale into a world of inductive logic.

---

engagement when Miss Aldclyffe, who is Farmer Springrove's landlord and can thus hold him liable for the costs of rebuilding the inn, manipulates Edward's sense of filial duty to compel him to forsake Cytherea in return for the cancellation of his father's debt (she wants Cytherea free for her son, Manston).

[46] Williams, "Slow Fire," 22.

[47] Williams, "Slow Fire," 19, 28–9, 25. See also Gillian Beer, "The Reader's Wager: Lots, Sorts, and Futures," *Essays in Criticism* 40.2 (1990): 99–123.

198 THE NUMBER SENSE

This fact appears in an earlier scene that prefigures—again literally, through their shared use of the number three—the burning down of the inn. It is Cytherea's first night at Miss Aldclyffe's, during a three-hour stretch of time running from "*Two to five, a.m.*," to be precise (as the section title informs us). Unable to sleep because of her excitement at her new job and the unfamiliarity of her surroundings, Cytherea lies listening to the sounds of the night. She hears—and places—a first sound: the nearby waterfall. Then, a "second" arises, "quite different from the first." This she deciphers to be the waterwheel by the old manor house on the property. The two initially mysterious sounds are nevertheless enough to establish an eerie pattern in Cytherea's mind: "there could be nothing else left to be heard or to imagine ... Yet just for an instant before going to sleep she would think this— suppose another sound should come—just suppose it should!" And "Before the thought had well passed through her brain, a third sound came": a "soft gurgle or rattle." Its "accidental" arrival "upon the heels of her supposition" makes her jump out of bed: "One logical thought alone was able to enter her flurried brain. The little dog that began the whining must have heard the other two sounds even better than herself. He had taken no notice of them, but he had taken notice of the third. The third, then, was an unusual sound" (*DR* 86–7). Recall Sarah Hart's observation: three is a special number because it is the smallest to allow recognition of both a pattern of repetition and a break from that pattern. As John Bayley has remarked, this sequence "parodies the elimination and deduction technique of a detective mystery," presenting us with "the idea of *sequence as form*, which makes the book."[48] At stake, though, is not mere *sequence* but also the nature of the connecting tissue between the sequential events: *cause*. And while it may seem indebted to a logical mode, part of the parody lies in how it also echoes more mystical thoughts like those of Tennyson's May Queen. Here, as in that poem, the third noise augurs death: it proves to be Miss Aldclyffe's father's belabored final breaths, occurring shortly before "A clock on the landing struck three" (*DR* 88).

Hardy ensures our recognition of the importance of this motif of triple recurrence by making his heroine address it directly, in a discussion with her brother following the noises-in-the-night sequence and shortly before the fire at the inn. Having detected a series of heretofore unknown links between herself and Miss Aldclyffe, she again induces a meaningful pattern:

---

[48] John Bayley, *An Essay on Hardy* (Cambridge: Cambridge University Press, 1978), 134. He also recognizes the scene's echo in the later conflagration.

CONCLUSION 199

"Do you believe in such odd coincidences?" said Cytherea.

"How do you mean, believe in them? They occur sometimes."

"Yes, one will occur often enough—that is, two disconnected events will fall strangely together by chance, and people scarcely notice the fact beyond saying, 'Oddly enough it happened that so and so were the same,' and so on. But when three such events coincide without any apparent reason for the coincidence, it seems as if there must be invisible means at work. You see, three things falling together in that manner are ten times as singular as two cases of coincidence which are distinct."

"Well, of course: what a mathematical head you have, Cytherea!"

(*DR* 146)

So, once more, we find the number three at the junction of questions of causality. But while her brother, impressed by Cytherea's facility with probabilistic calculations, may liken her to a mathematician, Hardy's own take is a little different; after the siblings list the three coincidences that prompted Cytherea's comments, the narrator describes how "From these premises, she proceeded to argue like an elderly divine on the designs of Providence which were apparent in such conjunctures" (*DR* 146).[49] He uses the language of religion rather than that of science. These may be mere *events*, rather than the Visions or Dreams of *Armadale*, yet their power nevertheless inheres in the paradoxical implications of their tripled nature.

And once you notice the pattern, you start to find threes everywhere in the novel, as though reinforcing its basic causal architecture. So, the name of Farmer Springrove's inn? The Three Tranters, naturally (a tranter is a village porter, who conveyed goods by horse and cart). Eunice Manston's profession? She was, as her husband tells us, "a third-rate actress," hence, perhaps, his erroroneous assumption that she would be riding in the "third-class" carriage (*DR* 155, 161). *Desperate Remedies* also includes no fewer than three episodes of advertising, each incorporating threes. First, when Cytherea puts in a newspaper notice seeking a position, it takes her three rounds to land the job with Miss Aldclyffe: she initially tries for a place as a governess (*DR* 22), then as a "nursery governess (*DR* 39), and finally receives her offer after advertising as a "Lady's maid" (although Miss Aldclyffe soon elevates her to companion) (*DR* 50). But while one might think this process one of trial

---

[49] Williams has counted the novel's predilection for such numbered lists (*DR* 15–16, 269, 348) as among the "ordinal obsessions" that indicate its investments in serial thinking ("Slow Fire," 23).

200   THE NUMBER SENSE

and error, grounded in the rational marketplace of meritocratic capitalism, it turns out that other forces are at work: unbeknownst to Cytherea, Edward tells his father of her desire for work, who in turn has told Miss Aldclyffe's housekeeper, who has told her mistress. As Cytherea later thinks to herself, "The whole chain of incidents that drew her there was plain, and there was no such thing as chance in the matter. It was all Edward's doing" (*DR* 66) (it turns out also to be Miss Aldclyffe's doing, intrigued as she had been by the discovery of the shared name).

The same pattern, whereby an advertisement that had apparently searched an open field emerges as a blind for a rigged process, recurs twice more. When Miss Aldclyffe places an ad for a new estate manager, she plans thereby to bring her son home without his knowledge (she had given him up into care as a baby). Since he doesn't respond to the first advertisement (despite a yield of forty-five responses), she sends him an anonymous note encouraging him to try. Ten more letters arrive, including his. After her agent fails to select him for a shortlist, Miss Aldclyffe insists on adding precisely three more candidates to be interviewed (*DR* 106). And naturally, despite her agent's preference for Edward Springrove (also on the shortlist), she selects Manston in this third round in the process. Still, the appearance of impartiality has been preserved; as Cytherea later insists (she is trying to figure out why Manston seems to have so much power over her mistress): "He was openly advertised for, and chosen from forty or fifty who answered the advertisement, without knowing whose it was" (*DR* 147). Finally, after his first wife's death comes into doubt, Manston "advertises" for the missing woman, encouraging her to return to him. He does it thrice, explaining, "there's a satisfaction in having made any attempt three several times" (*DR* 269). But it is later revealed that this open advertisement was also a cheat. Fearing discovery of her murder, Manston had decided that he must bring Eunice back to life—so he hired a woman to impersonate her, instructing her to answer only after the third ad had come out. Again, then, what seemed subject to chance processes and the doings of multiple agents is revealed to have been carefully plotted. Collectively, these tripled chains of events call to mind one of Hardy's dialect terms in the novel: *three-cunning*, used by the villagers to signify a particularly devious form of intelligence (*DR* 230).

The term is applied by Miss Aldclyffe's cook to the village clerk, Mr. Crickett. He has personal experience with threes, since, as he likes to remark, he is his wife's third husband; professing knowledge of husbands in general, his wife similarly explains, "I've had three, and I ought to know" (*DR* 151). When Farmer Springrove wonders how the clerk "could stand third" in such

CONCLUSION 201

a "list," Crickett responds by saying "Twas ordained to be." He then tells a story. The clerk recalls how Mrs. Springrove had predicted an ominous fate for him:

> "your wife will soon settle you as she did her other two: here's a glass o' rum, for I shan't see your poor face this time next year." I swallered the rum, called again next year, and said, "Mrs. Springrove, you gave me a glass o' rum last year because I was going to die—here I be alive still, you see." "Well said, clerk! Here's two glasses for you now, then," says she. "Thank you, mem," I said, and swallered the rum. Well, dang my old sides, next year I thought I'd call again and get three. And call I did. But she wouldn't give me a drop o' the commonest.

And now, as Clerk Crickett remarks, he is still alive and well, while the Farmer's wife is "moulderen in her grave." When another villager comments that he "used to think 'twas your wife's fate not to have a liven husband," the clerk responds, "Fate's nothen beside a woman's schemen!" (*DR* 121–2). Again, tripling allows for the recognition of a pattern that lets you see when the pattern is not fulfilled. And again, the number three invites questions regarding agency and causality.

Notice how in pointing to causality, and thus questions of plot, the focus on such triples also shifts attention away from the characterological issues of identity that are typically provoked by doubling, a more frequently recognized element of sensation fiction. (Comparing the twos and threes of *Armadale* highlights this contrast, as its complex array of doubles—and doubles of doubles—overlaps with the centrality of its Three Dreams; still, *Desperate Remedies* also includes among its threes both the two Cythereas and the doubling introduced by Manston's false second wife.[50]) Relatedly, while the form of doubling represented in the bigamy plot may threaten here, it proves to be a red herring: Eunice had in fact died before Manston's marriage to Cytherea took place. So instead of the simultaneity of bigamy, we have the serial experience of sequential marriages: first, second, third.[51] And, as in *Jane Eyre* (as I observed in my Introduction), the focus on numbers

---

[50] For a critical take on the doubles of *Armadale* that focuses on questions of identity, see Hensley, *Forms of Empire*, 111–26.

[51] Maia McAleavey has pointed out the reverse phenomenon: how aspects of simultaneous bigamy can hover behind the serial marriages of a realist novel like *David Copperfield* because of the Victorian belief in marriage in heaven. See McAleavey, *The Bigamy Plot: Sensation and Convention in the Victorian Novel* (Cambridge: Cambridge University Press, 2015), 193.

202   THE NUMBER SENSE

raises portents of a continuation to the sequence, which hover over the second marriage (recollect that Cytherea had earlier married Manston) concluding the novel.[52]

The "Epilogue" rounding off the book (later rechristened a "Sequel") opens with Edward and Cytherea's wedding, which is being celebrated with the ringing of the church bells—a "triple-bob-major," naturally (*DR* 377). But we also return to the clerk and his wife's many husbands. Thinking of Cytherea's earlier marriage to Manston—but doubtless also reminding readers of the fire at the heart of Hardy's plot—one of the bell-ringers remarks, "Tis no small matter for a man to play wi' fire." When the clerk answers that the case may be different for a woman, the original speaker teases him that his wife will marry again on the clerk's decease. "Well—let her, God bless her," Crickett returns, "for I'm but a poor third man, I. The Lord have mercy upon the fourth .... Ay, Teddy's [that is, Edward Springrove] got his own at last" (*DR* 377, original ellipsis). But the promised closure of that "at last" is unsettled here by the open-endedness of the clerk's previous count, with its apparition of a fourth husband, reverberating in the series of four dots that comprise the trailing ellipsis.[53] Shortly before, Cytherea had experienced what the narrator declares to be her "third and last" night of terror (on "*March the Thirtieth*," no less: 3/30) when she has a premonition—correctly—that Miss Aldclyffe is dying (*DR* 374). This scene's echo in the clerk's words also transfers some of the magic of that three, but only to imply that Edward's "last" might not be Cytherea's: *she* may live to wed a third (and last?) time.

The recognition of such ambiguities is a product of what I have called *number sense*. Let me close on my own "last" scene of threes in Hardy's novel: that in which Manston's murder of his first wife Eunice is finally discovered when he decides to move her body, which has lain hidden in the wall of one of the outbuildings on the property, to some safer location. The episode takes place in the dark, and it emerges over its course that Manston's acts are being observed not only by the woman who has been impersonating Eunice (rendered suspicious of her original's fate, she focalizes our experience of the events), but also by the detective, and finally by Miss Aldclyffe, who fears for her son. The latter two watchers, whom the false wife discovers sequentially (as do we), are unaware of the presence of the third and each

---

[52] Recall Rochester's history. Hardy's focus on women who remarry can perhaps be seen as a corrective to the many serial womanizers of both fiction and fact, including also Don Juan.

[53] Later editions regularize the punctuation here by turning the first dot into an exclamation point.

CONCLUSION 203

other; she "continue[s] on the trail of the other three" (that is, Manston, the detective, and Miss Aldclyffe) until the scene's end, in which Manston flees after attacking the detective with a spade (*DR* 349–50). As John Bayley has appreciated, the whole incident verges on the comedic. It has, I think, something of the effect of an episode from the old Scooby-Doo cartoon series. But he notes, too, that the dynamic encapsulates the novel's more general tendency to be "a parody of sequence"[54]—and (I would add) encapsulates the role played by threes in establishing this tendency: not one, not two, but *three* people are snooping on Manston and tracing his steps.

Gesturing earlier toward the disinterment scene, Bayley had described beautifully how "*Desperate Remedies* gives the impression of a gap between the plot's determined progress, and the tenor of the prose, which gropes its way forward from exploratory touch to touch, like Manston feeling his way in the dark."[55] To use number sense, though, is to recognize that "the plot's determined progress" can't be separated completely from the "touch to touch" feel of that prose: both require attunement not merely to Hardy's measured language but also to his language of measure. Number sense happens when you grope your way alongside Manston, keeping track of the experiences—and of the tally—of those three watchers, while simultaneously comparing it to other tallies by which we plot our way through the novel's action. Clarifying his comments regarding Cytherea's insistence about the improbability of a triple coincidence, Bayley reflects—seeming himself to grope for the right terms—that if it makes her sound like Sherlock Holmes, it is a version of Holmes "whose observations are as much more sensuous than his as they are inconclusive."[56] Daniel Williams wants to discriminate between two such modes in Hardy's novel: "One mode is affective, tactile, inchoate; the second rational, numerical, predictive."[57] But Bayley's "sensuous" element, which owes, as I have shown, a lot to the forces attached to the number three, suggests these ways of knowing can't be so easily divided. The ambiguity testifies as well to the vast range of significance that inheres in the word *sense* and its various cognates.[58] Its connotative reach lies behind my own use of the term; indeed, the instability famously

---

[54] Bayley, *An Essay on Hardy*, 145.
[55] Bayley, *An Essay on Hardy*, 95.
[56] Bayley, *An Essay on Hardy*, 134.
[57] Williams, "Slow Fire," 19.
[58] The classic account of this range occurs in Raymond Williams's entry on "Sensibility" in *Keywords: A Vocabulary of Culture and Society*, rev. ed. (New York: Oxford University Press, 1983), 280–3.

204 THE NUMBER SENSE

dictates the half-and-half narrative of Austen's *Sense and Sensibility* and the play of its numbers.

So while I have been arguing here that three may be especially prone to such a wobble, it is by no means singular in inviting different modes of reading. We have seen likewise how when we keep count of Juan's loves, or follow along as the "brave Tartar khan" witnesses his sons fall before him, we are learning to get a *feel* for the way the numbers work. Dickens's figures may flatten his characters, but they simultaneously manage to preserve their most intimate privacy. Trollope's ages are at once "rational [and] predictive" and "affective [and] and inchoate." As I hope I have convinced you, Dear Reader, the number sense that develops when we read nineteenth-century literature with a careful attention to its measures can help us to straddle the visceral and emotional realm of sensation and the logical and abstract realm of numbers. In today's world—one even more numerically saturated than that described in this book, and one in which the two cultures often feel even more divided—it is a faculty worth exercising.

Bibliography

Adams, Jennifer. *Pride and Prejudice: A Counting Primer.* Layton, UT: Gibbs Smith, 2011.

Agamben, Giorgio. *Homo Sacer: Sovereign Power and Bare Life.* Trans. Daniel Heller-Roazan. Stanford: Stanford University Press, 1998.

Alfano, Veronica. "Technologies of Forgetting: Phonographs, Lyric Voice, and Rossetti's Woodspurge." *Victorian Poetry* 55.2 (Summer 2017): 127–161.

Anderson, Melville B. "A Chat About George Gissing." *The Dial* 61 (June 22, 1916): 3–7.

Anderson, Walter E. "Byron's 'Don Juan' and Joyce's 'Ulysses.'" *James Joyce Quarterly* 29.4 (Summer 1992): 829–833.

Arata, Stephen D. "The Occidental Tourist: *Dracula* and the Anxiety of Reverse Colonization." *Victorian Studies* 33.4 (1990): 621–645.

Arendt, Hannah. *The Human Condition.* Chicago: University of Chicago Press, 1958.

Aristotle. *The Basic Works of Aristotle.* Ed. Richard McKeon. New York: Random House, 1941.

Auden, W. H. *The English Auden.* Ed. Edward Mendelson. London: Faber & Faber, 1986.

Austen, Jane. *Jane Austen's Letters.* Ed. Deidre Le Faye. 3rd ed. Oxford: Oxford University Press, 1997.

Austen, Jane. *Pride and Prejudice.* Ed. James Kinsley. Oxford: Oxford University Press, 1998.

Austen, Jane. *Emma.* Ed. James Kinsley. Oxford: Oxford University Press, 2003.

Austen, Jane. *Mansfield Park.* Ed. James Kinsley. Oxford: Oxford University Press, 2003.

Austen, Jane. *Northanger Abbey, Lady Susan, The Watsons, Sanditon.* Ed. James Kinsley and John Davie. Oxford: Oxford University Press, 2003.

Austen, Jane. *Persuasion.* Ed. James Kinsley. Oxford: Oxford University Press, 2004.

Austen, Jane. *Sense and Sensibility.* Ed. James Kinsley. Oxford: Oxford University Press, 2004.

Austen, Jane. *Catharine and Other Writings.* Ed. Margaret Anne Doody and Douglas Murray. Oxford: Oxford University Press, 2009.

Babb, Genie. "Victorian Roots and Branches: 'The Statistical Century' as Foundation to the Digital Humanities." *Literature Compass* 15 (2018): 1–14. Web.

Babbage, Charles. *Ninth Bridgewater Treatise.* 2nd ed. London: John Murray, 1838.

Bakhtin, M. M. "Epic and Novel." In *The Dialogic Imagination.* Ed. Michael Holquist. Austin: University of Texas Press, 1994. 3–40.

Baldridge, Cates. "Alternatives to Bourgeois Individualism in *A Tale of Two Cities.*" *Studies in English Literature* 30.4 (1990): 633–654.

Barchas, Janine. "Very Austen: Accounting for the Language of *Emma.*" *Nineteenth-Century Literature* 62.3 (2007): 303–338.

Barchas, Janine. *Matters of Fact in Jane Austen.* Baltimore: Johns Hopkins University Press, 2012.

Barrett Browning, Elizabeth. *Aurora Leigh and Other Poems.* Ed. John Robert Glorney Bolton and Julia Bolton Holloway. London: Penguin, 1995.

Barthes, Roland. *S/Z.* Trans. Richard Miller. New York: Hill & Wang, 1974.

Bayley, John. *An Essay on Hardy.* Cambridge: Cambridge University Press, 1978.

206 BIBLIOGRAPHY

Beckett, Samuel. "An Imaginative Work!" *Dublin Magazine* xi, n.s. (July–Sept. 1936): 80–81.

Beer, Gillian. *Darwin's Plots: Evolutionary Narrative in Darwin, George Eliot and Nineteenth-Century Fiction.* London: Ark, 1985.

Beer, Gillian. "The Reader's Wager: Lots, Sorts, and Futures." *Essays in Criticism* 40.2 (1990): 99–123.

Bell, David F. *Circumstances: Chance in the Literary Text.* Lincoln, NE: University of Nebraska Press, 1993.

Bevis, Matthew. "Poetry by Numbers." *Raritan* 37.2 (2017): 37–64.

Blake, William. *Blake's Poetry and Designs.* Ed. Mary Lynn Johnson and John E. Grant. New York: W. W. Norton, 1979.

Blake, William. *Complete Poetry and Prose.* Ed. David Erdman. New York: Anchor, 1988.

Blank, Paula. "Shakespeare's Equalities: Checking the Math of *King Lear.*" *Exemplaria* 15.2 (2003): 473–510.

Bloom, Paul. *Against Empathy: The Case for Rational Compassion.* New York: Ecco, 2016.

Bode, Katherine. *Reading by Numbers: Recalibrating the Literary Field.* London: Anthem, 2014.

Bowen, John. "Counting On: *A Tale of Two Cities.*" In *Charles Dickens, A Tale of Two Cities, and the French Revolution.* Ed. Colin Jones, Josephine McDonagh, and Jon Mee. London: Palgrave Macmillan, 2009. 104–125.

Boyd, Zelda. "The Language of Supposing: Modal Auxiliaries in *Sense and Sensibility.*" In *Jane Austen: New Perspectives. Women and Literature* ns. 3. Ed. Janet Todd. New York: Holmes & Meier, 1983. 142–154.

Brontë, Charlotte. *Jane Eyre.* 2nd ed. Ed. Richard J. Dunn. New York: Norton, 1987.

Brontë, Charlotte. *Selected Letters of Charlotte Brontë.* Ed. Margaret Smith. Oxford: Oxford University Press, 2007.

Brooks, Peter. *Reading for the Plot: Design and Intention in Narrative.* Cambridge, MA: Harvard University Press, 1992.

Brown, Mark William. "Language, Symbol, and 'Non-Symbolic Fact' in D. G. Rossetti's 'The Woodspurge.'" *Symbolism: An International Annual of Critical Aesthetics* 19 (2019): 243–263.

Buckle, Henry Thomas. *History of Civilization in England.* Volume 1. London: John Parker & Son, 1857.

Bulson, Eric. "Ulysses by Numbers." *Representations* 127.1 (Summer 2014): 1–32.

Burgess, Miranda. "How Wordsworth Tells: Numeration, Valuation, and Dwelling in 'We Are Seven.'" *English Language Notes* 54.1 (Spring/Summer 2016): 43–57.

Burrows, J. F. *Computation into Criticism: A Study of Jane Austen's Novels and an Experiment in Method.* Oxford: Clarendon, 1987.

Buzard, James. "*David Copperfield* and the Thresholds of Modernity." *ELH* 86.1 (Spring 2019): 223–243.

Byrne, Paula. *Jane Austen and the Theatre.* London: Bloomsbury Academic, 2007.

Byron, George Gordon. *Lord Byron: Selected Letters and Journals.* Ed. Leslie A. Marchand. Cambridge, MA: Harvard University Press, 1982.

Byron, George Gordon. *Don Juan.* Ed. T. G. Steffen, E. Steffen, and W. W. Pratt. London: Penguin, 1986.

Carlyle, Thomas. "Shooting Niagara: and After." *Macmillan's Magazine* 16 (April 1867): 64–87.

Carlyle, Thomas. *The Collected Works.* Ashburton Edition. 17 Vols. London: Chapman & Hall, 1885–6.

Carroll, Lewis. *Sylvie and Bruno Concluded.* London: MacMillan, 1893.

BIBLIOGRAPHY   207

Carroll, Lewis. *Alice in Wonderland* and *Through the Looking-Glass*. Ed. Peter Hunt. Oxford: Oxford University Press, 2009.

Case, Alison. *Plotting Women: Gender and Narration in the Eighteenth- and Nineteenth-Century British Novel*. Charlottesville, VA: University of Virginia Press, 1999.

Cervantes, Miguel de. *Don Quixote*. Trans. John Ormsby. 4 vols. New York: Dodd, Mead, & Co., 1887.

Chase, Karen. *The Victorians and Old Age*. Oxford: Oxford University Press, 2009.

Chatterjee, Ronjaunee. *Feminine Singularity: The Politics of Subjectivity in Nineteenth-Century Literature*. Stanford: Stanford University Press, 2022.

Chew, Samuel C. "The Centenary of Don Juan." *American Journal of Philology* 40 (1919): 117–152.

Choi, Tina Young. "Writing the Victorian City: Discourses of Risk, Connection, and Inevitability." *Victorian Studies* 43.4 (2001): 561–589.

Choi, Tina Young. "Natural History's Hypothetical Moments: Narratives of Contingency in Victorian Culture." *Victorian Studies* 51.2 (2009): 275–297.

Choi, Tina Young. *Victorian Contingencies: Experiments in Literature, Science, and Play*. Stanford: Stanford University Press, 2021.

Chwe, Michael Suk-Young. *Jane Austen: Game Theorist*. Princeton: Princeton University Press, 2013.

Clough, Arthur Hugh. *Clough's Selected Poems*. Ed. J. P. Phelan. London: Longman, 1995.

Cohen, Patricia Cline. *A Calculating People: The Spread of Numeracy in Early America*. New York: Routledge, 1999.

[Collins, Wilkie]. "*Autobiography* of Anthony Trollope." *Blackwood's Edinburgh Magazine* 134 (Nov. 1883): 577–596.

Collins, Wilkie. *No Name*. Ed. Virginia Blain. Oxford: Oxford University Press, 1998.

Collins, Wilkie. *Armadale*. Ed. Catherine Peters. Oxford: Oxford University Press, 2008.

Collins, Wilkie. *The Woman in White*. Ed. John Sutherland. Oxford: Oxford University Press, 2008.

Conrad, Joseph. *The Secret Agent*. Ed. John Lyon. Oxford: Oxford University Press, 2008.

Copeland, Edward. "Money." In *The Cambridge Companion to Jane Austen*. Ed. Edward Copeland and Juliet McMaster. Cambridge: Cambridge University Press, 2010. 127–143.

Craig, Sheryl. *Jane Austen and the State of the Nation*. New York: Palgrave Macmillan, 2015.

Culler, Jonathan. *Theory of the Lyric*. Cambridge, MA: Harvard University Press, 2015.

[Dallas, E. S.]. Review of *The Woman in White*. *The Times* (October 30, 1860): 6.

Dallas, E. S. *The Gay Science*. 2 vols. New York: Johnson Reprint Corporation, 1969.

Daly, Nicholas. *Literature, Technology, and Modernity, 1860–2000*. Cambridge: Cambridge University Press, 2004.

Dantzig, Tobias. *Number: The Language of Science*. Ed. Joseph Mazur. New York: Plume, 2007.

Daston, Lorraine and Peter Gallison. *Objectivity*. New York: Zone Books, 2007.

Davidoff, Lenore. *Thicker than Water: Siblings and their Relations, 1780–1820*. Oxford: Oxford University Press, 2012.

Dehaene, Stanislaus. *The Number Sense: How the Mind Creates Mathematics*. Rev. ed. Oxford: Oxford University Press, 2011.

Deresiewicz, William. *Jane Austen and the Romantic Poets*. New York: Columbia University Press, 2004.

Derrida, Jacques. *The Politics of Friendship*. Trans. George Collins. London: Verso, 2005.

208 BIBLIOGRAPHY

Desrosières, Alain. *The Politics of Large Numbers: A History of Statistical Reasoning*. Trans. Camille Naish. Cambridge, MA: Harvard University Press, 1998.

Dickens, Charles. *David Copperfield*. Ed. Nina Burgess. Oxford: Oxford University Press, 2008.

Dickens, Charles. *Dombey and Son*. Ed. Peter Fairclough. London: Penguin, 1985.

Dickens, Charles. *Little Dorrit*. Ed. John Holloway. London: Penguin, 1985.

Dickens, Charles. *Dickens' Working Notes for his Novels*. Ed. Harry Stone. Chicago: University of Chicago Press, 1987.

Dickens, Charles. *Bleak House*. Ed. Nicola Bradbury. London: Penguin, 1996.

Dickens, Charles. *Our Mutual Friend*. Ed. Michael Cotsell. Oxford: Oxford University Press, 1998.

Dickens, Charles. *Hard Times*. Ed. Paul Schlicke. Oxford: Oxford University Press, 2008.

Dickens, Charles. *A Tale of Two Cities*. Ed. Andrew Sanders. Oxford: Oxford University Press, 2008.

Donne, John. *John Donne's Poetry*. Ed. Donald R. Dickson. New York: W. W. Norton, 2007.

Dow, Gillian and Katie Halsey. "Jane Austen's Reading: The Chawton Years." *Persuasions On-Line* 30.2 (Spring 2010). Web.

Doyle, Arthur Conan. *The Memoirs of Sherlock Holmes*. Ed. Christopher Roden. Oxford: Oxford University Press, 2000.

Eliot, George. *Quarry for* Middlemarch. Ed. Anna Theresa Kitchel. Berkeley: University of California Press, 1950.

Eliot, George. *Daniel Deronda*. Ed. Graham Handley. Oxford: Oxford University Press, 1998.

Eliot, George. *Middlemarch*. Ed. David Carroll. Oxford: Oxford University Press, 1998.

Eliot, George. *The Mill on the Floss*. Ed. Gordon Haight. Oxford: Oxford University Press, 2015.

English, James F. "The Resistance to Counting, Recounted." *Representations* (January 2015). Web.

Epperly, Elizabeth R. "From the Borderlands of Decency: Madame Max Goesler." *Victorians Institute Journal* 15 (1987): 24–35.

Faulkner, Laura. "'That's Convenient, Not to Say Odd': Coincidence, Causality, and Hardy's Inconsistent Inconsistency." *Victorian Review* 37.1 (2011): 92–107.

Favret, Mary A. "Jane Austen at 25: A Life in Numbers." *English Language Notes* 46.1 (2008): 9–19.

Favret, Mary A. "A Feeling for Numbers: Representing the Scale of the War Dead." In *War and Literature*. Ed. Laura Ashe and Ian Patterson. Cambridge, UK: D. S. Brewer, 2014. 184–204.

Ferguson, Frances. *Solitude and the Sublime: Romanticism and the Aesthetics of Individuation*. New York: Routledge, 1992.

Ferguson, Frances. "Jane Austen, *Emma*, and the Impact of Form." *Modern Language Quarterly* 61.1 (2000): 157–180.

Fielding, Henry. *Tom Jones*. Ed. John Bender and Simon Stern. Oxford: Oxford University Press, 1996.

Figlerowicz, Marta. *Flat Protagonists: A Theory of Novel Character*. Oxford: Oxford University Press, 2016.

Fitz-Gerald, S. J. Adair. "Dickens and the Sandwich-Man." *Dickensian* 13.10 (1917): 266–267.

BIBLIOGRAPHY 209

Fogel, Aaron. "Wordsworth's 'We Are Seven' and Crabbe's *The Parish Register*: Poetry and Anti-Census." *Studies in Romanticism* 48 (Spring 2009): 23–65.

Forbes-Macphail, Imogen. "The Enchantress of Numbers and the Magic Noose of Poetry: Literature, Mathematics, and Mysticism in the Nineteenth Century." *Journal of Language, Literature and Culture* 60.3 (2013): 138–156.

Forster, E. M. *Aspects of the Novel*. New York: Harcourt Brace & Co., 1927.

Forster, E. M. *A Room with a View*. Intro. Wendy Moffat. London: Penguin, 2000.

Foucault, Michel. *Security, Territory, Population: Lectures at the Collège de France, 1977–78*. Trans. Graham Burchell. Ed. Michel Senellart. New York: Picador, 2009.

Fowler, Rowena. "Blougram's Wager, Guido's Odds: Browning, Chance, and Probability." *Victorian Poetry* 41.1 (2003): 11–28.

French, Tana. *The Secret Place*. London: Penguin, 2015.

Gallagher, Catherine. "The Duplicity of Doubling in *A Tale of Two Cities*." *Dickens Studies Annual* 12 (1983): 125–145.

Gallagher, Catherine. "The Rise of Fictionality." In *The Novel, Vol. 1: History, Geography, and Culture*. Ed. Franco Moretti. Princeton: Princeton University Press, 2007. 336–363.

Galton, Francis. "Measurement of Character." *Fortnightly Review* 36 (1884): 179–185.

Gardner, Martin. *The Annotated Alice*. New York: Clarkson Potter, 1960.

Gaskell, Elizabeth. *North and South*. Ed. Angus Easson. Oxford: Oxford University Press, 1998.

Gasson, Andrew. "*The Woman in White*: A Chronological Study." 2010. Web.

Gayle, N. E. "Don Juan and the Dirty Scythe of Time." *The Byron Journal* 41.1 (2013): 27–34.

Gibson, William and Bruce Sterling. *The Difference Engine*. New York: Ballantine, 1990.

Gissing, George. *Letters of George Gissing to Members of his Family*. New York: Haskell House, 1970.

Gissing, George. *The Odd Women*. Ed. Margaret Cardwell. Oxford: Oxford University Press, 2008.

Goldstone, Andrew and Ted Underwood. "The Quiet Transformations of Literary Studies: What Thirteen Thousand Scholars Could Tell Us." *New Literary History* 45.3 (2014): 359–384.

González-Díaz, Victorina. "'I *Quite* Detest the Man': Degree Adverbs, Female Language, and Jane Austen." *Language and Literature* 23.4 (2014): 310–330.

Goodlad, Lauren. *The Victorian Geopolitical Aesthetic: Realism, Sovereignty, and Transnational Experience*. Oxford: Oxford University Press, 2015.

[Greg, W. R.]. "Why are Women Redundant?" *National Review* 28 (1862): 434–460.

Grener, Adam. "The Language of Chance and the Form of *Phineas Finn*." *Genre* 50.1 (2017): 77–95.

Grener, Adam and Isabel Parker. "Dickens's Anonymous Margins: Names, Network Theory, and the Serial Novel." *Dickens Studies Annual* 50.1 (2019): 20–47.

Hacking, Ian. "Making Up People." In *Reconstructing Individualism: Autonomy, Individuality, and the Self in Western Thought*. Ed. Thomas C. Heller et al. Stanford: Stanford University Press, 1986. 222–236.

Hacking, Ian. *The Taming of Chance*. Cambridge: Cambridge University Press, 1990.

Hacking, Ian. *The Emergence of Probability: A Philosophical Study of Early Ideas about Probability, Induction and Statistical Inference*. 2nd ed. Cambridge: Cambridge University Press, 2006.

Hadley, Elaine. *Living Liberalism: Practical Citizenship in Mid-Victorian Britain*. Chicago: University of Chicago Press, 2010.

210 BIBLIOGRAPHY

Hadley, Elaine. "Nobody, Somebody, and Everybody." *Victorian Studies* 59.1 (Autumn 2016): 65–86.

Hager, Kelly and Karen Bourrier. "How Many Siblings Had Philip Pirrip?: Counting Brothers and Sisters in the Victorian Novel." *ELH* 89.1 (2022): 159–184.

Hamer, Mary. *Writing by Numbers: Trollope's Serial Fiction.* Cambridge: Cambridge University Press, 1987.

Hardy, Janice. "An Age-Old Question: How Do You Show a Character's Age?" 2019. Web.

Hardy, Thomas. *Far From the Madding Crowd.* Ed. Ronald Blythe. London: Penguin, 1985.

Hardy, Thomas. *Jude the Obscure.* Ed. C. H. Sisson. London: Penguin, 1985.

Hardy, Thomas. *Return of the Native.* Ed. Simon Gatrell. Oxford: Oxford University Press, 2008.

Hardy, Thomas. *Desperate Remedies.* Ed. Patricia Ingham. Oxford: Oxford University Press, 2009.

Harris, Jocelyn. *Jane Austen's Art of Memory.* Cambridge: Cambridge University Press, 1989.

Hart, Sarah. *Once Upon a Prime: The Wondrous Connections Between Mathematics and Literature.* New York: Flatiron, 2023.

Hartman, Geoffrey H. "Reading and Representation: Wordsworth's 'Boy of Winander.'" *European Romantic Review* 5.1 (1994): 90–100.

Heath, Kay. *Ageing by the Book: The Emergence of Midlife in Victorian Britain.* Albany, NY: SUNY, 2009.

Heath, Kay. "Trollope and Ageing." In *The Routledge Research Companion to Anthony Trollope.* Ed. Deborah Denenholz Morse, Margaret Markwick, and Mark W. Turner. New York: Routledge, 2017. 295–305.

Henderson, Andrea K. "Combinatorial Characters." In *The Palgrave Handbook of Literature and Mathematics.* Ed. Robert Tubbs, Alice Jenkins, and Nina Engelhardt. London: Palgrave Macmillan, 2021. 493–512.

Hensley, Nathan K. *Forms of Empire: The Poetics of Victorian Sovereignty.* Oxford: Oxford University Press, 2016.

Heuser, Ryan and Long Le-Khac. "Learning to Read Data: Bringing Out the Humanistic in the Digital Humanities." *Victorian Studies* 54.1 (2011): 79–86.

Higgs, Edward. *Life, Death and Statistics: Civil Registration, Censuses and the Work of the General Register Office, 1836–1952.* Hatfield: Local Population Studies, 2004.

Hilts, Victor L. "William Farr (1807–1883) and the 'Human Unit.'" *Victorian Studies* 14 (1970): 143–150.

Holmes, John. *Dante Gabriel Rossetti and the Late Victorian Sonnet Sequence: Sexuality, Belief, and the Self.* Aldershot: Ashgate, 2005.

Homer. *The Iliad.* Trans. Robert Fagles. New York: Penguin, 1990.

Houston, Natalie M. "Toward a Computational Analysis of Victorian Poetics." *Victorian Studies* 56.3 (2014): 498–510.

Hughes, Linda K. and Michael Lund. *The Victorian Serial.* Charlottesville: University Press of Virginia, 1991.

Hughes, Winifred. *The Maniac in the Cellar: Sensation Novels of the 1860s.* Princeton: Princeton University Press, 1981.

Hunt, Aeron. *Personal Business: Character and Commerce in Victorian Literature and Culture.* Charlottesville: University Press of Virginia, 2014.

Ingelow, Jean. *Songs of Seven.* Boston: Roberts Brothers, 1883.

Jaffe, Audrey. *The Affective Life of the Average Man: The Victorian Novel and the Stock-Market Graph.* Columbus: Ohio State University Press, 2010.

BIBLIOGRAPHY 211

James, Henry. "The Limitations of Dickens." *The Nation* (December 21, 1865): 786–787.

James, Henry. *The Tragic Muse*. 2 vols. New York: Scribner, 1908.

James, Henry. *The Princess Casamassima*. Ed. Derek Brewer. London: Penguin, 1987.

James, P. D. *The Private Patient*. New York: Vintage, 2009.

Johnson, Samuel. *Dictionary of the English Language*. 5th ed. London, 1785.

Jones, Lawrence O. "*Desperate Remedies* and the Victorian Sensation Novel." *Nineteenth-Century Fiction* 20.1 (June 1965): 35–50.

Joyce, James. *Ulysses*. Ed. Hans Walter Gabler. New York: Vintage, 1986.

Keats, John. *Letters of John Keats: A Selection*. Ed. Robert Gittings. Oxford: Oxford University Press, 1992.

Keegan, Bridget. "'Another Still! and Still Another!': A Poverty of Numbers in Wordsworth's 'We Are Seven' and 'The Last of the Flock.'" *Friend: Comment on Romanticism* 2.1 (1993): 13–24.

Kendrick, Walter M. "The Sensationalism of *The Woman in White*." *Nineteenth-Century Fiction* 32 (1977): 18–35.

Kendrick, Walter M. "The Sensationalism of Thomas Hardy." *Texas Studies in Literature and Language* 22.4 (1980): 484–503.

Kent, Christopher. "Probability, Reality and Sensation in the Novels of Wilkie Collins." *Dickens Studies Annual* 20 (1991): 259–280.

Kipling, Rudyard. *Kim*. Ed. Alan Sandison. Oxford: Oxford University Press, 2008.

Kittler, Friedrich. "Dracula's Legacy." *Stanford Humanities Review* 1 (1989): 143–173.

Kittler, Friedrich. *Discourse Networks 1800/1900*. Trans. Michael Metteer, with Chris Cullens. Stanford: Stanford University Press, 1990.

Kittler, Friedrich. "Number and Numeral." In *Theory, Culture & Society* 23.7/8. London, Thousand Oaks, and New Delhi: SAGE, 2006. 51–61.

Klotz, Michael. "Manufacturing Fictional Individuals: Victorian Social Statistics, the Novel, and *Great Expectations*." *Novel* 46.2 (2013): 214–233.

Knoepflemacher, U. C. *Ventures into Childland: Victorians, Fairy Tales, and Femininity*. Chicago: University of Chicago Press, 1998.

Kolb, Margaret. "Plot Circles: Hardy's Drunkards and Their Walks." *Victorian Studies* 56.4 (Summer 2014): 595–623.

Kornbluh, Anna. *The Order of Forms: Realism, Formalism, and Social Space*. Chicago: University of Chicago Presss, 2019.

Körner, T. W. *The Pleasures of Counting*. Cambridge: Cambridge University Press, 1996.

Kurnick, David. "'Numberiness.'" "Three Responses to 'Ulysses by Numbers.'" *Representations. Responses* (13 Jan. 2015). Web.

Kurnick, David. "Jane Austen, Secret Celebrity, and Mass Eroticism." *New Literary History* 52.1 (Winter 2021): 53–75.

Lamouria, Lanya. "Democracy, Terror, and Utopia in Dickens's *A Tale of Two Cities*." *Victorian Literature and Culture* 50.2 (2022): 295–324.

Langbauer, Laurie. "The Hobbledehoy in Trollope." In *Cambridge Companion to Anthony Trollope*. Ed. Carolyn Dever and Lisa Niles. Cambridge: Cambridge University Press, 2010. 113–127.

Lee, Maurice S. *Overwhelmed: Literature, Aesthetics, and the Nineteenth-Century Information Revolution*. Princeton: Princeton University Press, 2019.

Lee, Yoon Sun. "Austen's Scale-Making." *Studies in Romanticism* 52.2 (Summer 2013): 171–195.

Lesser, Wendy. "Even-Handed Oddness: George Gissing's *The Odd Women*." *The Hudson Review* 37.2 (Summer 1984): 209–220.

212 BIBLIOGRAPHY

Levi, Primo. *Survival in Auschwitz: The Nazi Assault on Humanity.* Trans. Stuart Wolf. New York: Simon & Schuster, 1996.

Levine, Caroline. *Forms: Whole, Rhythm, Hierarchy, Network.* Princeton: Princeton University Press, 2015.

Levine, Caroline. "The Enormity Effect: Realist Fiction, Literary Studies, and the Refusal to Count." *Genre* 50.1 (April 2017): 59–75.

Levinson, Marjorie. "Of Being Numerous." *Studies in Romanticism* 49.4 (Winter 2010): 633–657.

Levinson, Marjorie. "Notes and Queries on Name and Number." *Romantic Circles.* "Romantic Numbers" (April 2013). Web.

Levinson, Marjorie. *Thinking Through Poetry: Field Reports on Romantic Lyric.* Oxford: Oxford University Press, 2018.

Lukács Georg. *The Historical Novel.* Trans. Hannah and Stanley Mitchell. Lincoln: University of Nebraska Press, 1983.

Lynch, Deidre. *The Economy of Character: Novels, Market Culture, and the Business of Inner Meaning.* Chicago: University of Chicago Press, 1998.

MacKenzie, D. A. *Statistics in Britain 1865–1930: The Social Construction of Scientific Knowledge.* Edinburgh: Edinburgh University Press, 1981.

Macpherson, Sandra. *Harm's Way: Tragic Responsibility and the Novel Form.* Baltimore: Johns Hopkins University Press, 2010.

Manning, Peter J. "*Don Juan* and Byron's Imperceptiveness to the English Word." *Studies in Romanticism* 18.2 (1979): 207–233.

Markovits, Stefanie. "Form Things: Looking at Genre Through Victorian Diamonds." *Victorian Studies* 52.4 (2010): 591–619.

Markovits, Stefanie. *The Victorian Verse-Novel: Aspiring to Life.* Oxford: Oxford University Press, 2017.

Markovits, Stefanie. "Making Soldiers Count: Literature and War in the 1850s." In *Nineteenth-Century Literature in Transition: the 1850s.* Ed. Gail Marshall. Cambridge: Cambridge University Press, 2024. 179–200.

Martin, Daniel, "Wilkie Collins and Risk." In *A Companion to Sensation Fiction.* Ed. Pamela K. Gilbert. London: Blackwell, 2011. 184–195.

Maxwell, Catherine. "'Devious Symbols': Dante Gabriel Rossetti's Purgatorio." *Victorian Poetry* 31.1 (1993): 19–40.

Mayhew, Henry. *London Labour and the London Poor: A Selected Edition.* Ed. Robert Douglas-Fairhurst. Oxford: Oxford University Press, 2012.

McAleavey, Maia. *The Bigamy Plot: Sensation and Convention in the Victorian Novel.* Cambridge: Cambridge University Press, 2015.

McAleavey, Maia. "Anti-Individualism in the Victorian Family Chronicle." *Novel* 50.2 (2020): 213–234.

McCrea, Barry. *In the Company of Strangers: Family and Narrative in Dickens, Conan Doyle, Joyce and Proust.* New York: Columbia University Press, 2011.

McGann, Jerome. "Rossetti's Significant Details." *Victorian Poetry* 7.1 (1969): 41–54.

McGann, Jerome. *Don Juan in Context.* Chicago: University of Chicago Press, 1976.

McKeon, Michael, ed. *Theory of the Novel: A Historical Approach.* Baltimore: Johns Hopkins University Press, 2000.

McLane, Maureen. *Romanticism and the Human Sciences.* Cambridge: Cambridge University Press, 2000.

McLane, Maureen. "Romantic Number(s): A Brief Introduction." *Romantic Circles.* April 2013. Web.

McMurtry, Larry. *The Streets of Laredo.* New York: Simon & Schuster, 1993.

BIBLIOGRAPHY   213

Menke, Richard. *Telegraphic Realism: Victorian Fiction and Other Information Systems.* Stanford: Stanford University Press, 2008.

Menon, Tara. "Keeping Count: Direct Speech in the Nineteenth-Century British Novel." *Narrative* 27.2 (2019): 160–181.

Michie, Helena. "Rethinking Marriage: Trollope's Internal Revision." In *The Routledge Research Companion to Anthony Trollope.* Ed. Deborah Denenholz Morse, Margaret Markwick, and Mark W. Turner. New York: Routledge, 2017. 154–165.

Mill, John Stuart. *Utilitarianism.* London: Parker, Son, & Bourn, 1863.

Mill, John Stuart. *The Collected Works of John Stuart Mill.* 33 vols. Ed. J. M. Robson. Toronto: University of Toronto Press. London: Routledge & Kegan Paul, 1963–91.

Mill, John Stuart. *On Liberty.* Ed. Elizabeth Rapaport. Indianapolis: Hackett, 1978.

Miller, D. A. *The Novel and the Police.* Berkeley: University of California Press, 1988.

Miller, D. A. *Jane Austen, or, The Secret of Style.* Princeton: Princeton University Press, 2003.

Monk, Leland. *Standard Deviations: Chance and the Modern British Novel.* Stanford: Stanford University Press, 1993.

Moretti, Franco. *The Way of the World: The Bildungsroman in European Culture.* New ed. London: Verso, 2000.

Moretti, Franco. *Distant Reading.* London: Verso, 2013.

Nelson, Harland S. "Dickens's *Our Mutual Friend* and Henry Mayhew's *London Labour and the London Poor.*" *Nineteenth-Century Fiction* 20.3 (1965): 207–222.

O'Brien, Karen. "The Cultural and Literary Significance of the 1803 Essay." In Thomas Robert Malthus, *An Essay on the Principle of Population: The 1803 Edition.* Ed. Shannon Stimson. New Haven, CT: Yale University Press, 2018. 547–567.

Oppen, George. *New Collected Poems.* Ed. Michael Davidson. New York: New Directions, 2002.

Ortiz-Robles, Mario. "Hardy's Wessex and the Natural History of Chance." *Novel: A Forum on Fiction* 49.1 (2016): 82–94.

Paulos, John Allen. *Once Upon a Number: The Hidden Mathematical Logic of Stories.* New York: Basic Books, 1998.

Paxton, Amanda. "The Hard Math of Beauty: On Hopkins and 'Spectral Numbers.'" *Victorian Studies* 63.2 (2021): 246–270.

Peters, John Durham. "'The Only Proper Scale of Representation': The Politics of Statistics and Stories." *Political Communication* 18.4 (2001): 433–449.

Pettitt, Clare. *Serial Forms: The Unfinished Product of Modernity, 1815–1848.* Oxford: Oxford University Press, 2020.

Piketty, Thomas. *Capital in the Twenty-First Century.* Cambridge, MA: Harvard University Press, 2014.

Plato. *The Dialogues of Plato.* Trans. Benjamin Jowett. 3rd ed. 5 vols. Oxford: Oxford University Press, n.d.

Pool, Daniel. *What Jane Austen Ate and Charles Dickens Knew: From Fox Hunting to Whist—the Facts of Daily Life in 19th-Century England.* New York: Touchstone, 1994.

Poovey, Mary. "Figures of Arithmetic, Figures of Speech: The Discourse of Statistics in the 1830s." *Critical Inquiry* 19 (1993): 256–276.

Poovey, Mary. *Uneven Developments: The Ideological Work of Gender in Mid-Victorian England.* Chicago: University of Chicago Press, 1995.

Poovey, Mary. *A History of the Modern Fact.* Chicago: University of Chicago Press, 1998.

Porter, Theodore M. *The Rise of Statistical Thinking, 1820–1900.* Princeton: Princeton University Press, 1986.

214 BIBLIOGRAPHY

Porter, Theodore M. *Trust in Numbers: The Pursuit of Objectivity in Science and Public Life*. Princeton: Princeton University Press, 1995.

Potter, Gordon. "Byron's Numerology Revisited: *Don Juan*." *The Byron Journal* 34.2 (2007): 115–125.

Propp, Vladimir Yakovlevich. *The Russian Folktale by Vladimir Yakovlevich Propp*. Ed. and trans. Sibelan Forrester. Detroit: Wayne State University Press, 2012.

[Reynolds, G. W. M.]. *A Sequel to Don Juan*. London: Paget & Co., 1843.

Richardson, Samuel. *The History of Sir Charles Grandison*. 2nd ed. 6 vols. London, 1753–4.

Robbins, Hollis. "'We Are Seven' and the first British Census." *English Language Notes* 48.2 (2010): 201–213.

Rommel, Thomas. "'So Soft, so Sweet, so Delicately Clear.' A Computer-Assisted Analysis of Accumulated Words and Phrases in Lord Byron's Epic Poem *Don Juan*." *Literary and Linguistic Computing* 9.1 (1994): 7–12.

Rosenthal, Jesse. "The Large Novel and the Law of Large Numbers; or, Why George Eliot Hates Gambling." *ELH* 77. 3 (2010): 777–811.

Rosenthal, Jesse. "Narrative against Data." *Genre* 50.1 (2017): 1–18.

Rosenthal, Jesse. "The Untrusted Medium: Open Networks, Secret Writing, and *Little Dorrit*." *Victorian Studies* 59.2 (2017): 288–313.

Rossetti, Dante Gabriel. *The Works of Dante Gabriel Rossetti*. Ed. W. M. Rossetti. London: Ellis, 1911.

Rzepka, Charles. "Sacrificial Sites, Place-Keeping, and 'Pre-History' in Wordsworth's 'Michael.'" *European Romantic Review* 15.2 (2004): 205–213.

Schaffer, Talia. *Communities of Care: The Social Ethics of Victorian Fiction*. Princeton: Princeton University Press, 2021.

Seronsy, Cecil C. "Jane Austen's Technique." *Notes and Queries* ns 3.7 (1956): 303–305.

Shakespeare, William. *The Riverside Shakespeare*. Ed. G. Blakemore Evans. Boston: Houghton Mifflin, 1974.

Shelley, Percy Bysshe. "A Defence of Poetry." In *Shelley's Poetry and Prose*. Ed. Donald H. Reiman and Sharon B. Powers. New York: Norton, 1977. 480–508.

Shrimpton, Nicholas. "The Chronology and Political Contexts of the Palliser Novels: (i) The Internal Chronology of the Series." In *Phineas Finn*. Ed. Simon Dentith. Oxford: Oxford University Press, 2011. 570–573.

Siraganian, Lisa. *Modernism and the Meaning of Corporate Persons*. Oxford: Oxford University Press, 2020.

Small, Helen. *The Long Life*. Oxford: Oxford University Press, 2007.

Stauffer, Andrew M. *Book Traces: Nineteenth-Century Readers and the Future of the Library*. Philadelphia: University of Pennsylvania Press, 2021.

Steinlight, Emily. *Populating the Novel: Literary Form and the Politics of Surplus Life*. Ithaca: Cornell University Press, 2018.

Stevenson, Robert Louis. *Kidnapped*. Ed. Ian Duncan. Oxford: Oxford University Press, 2014.

Stewart, Susan. *Poetry and the Fate of the Senses*. Chicago: University of Chicago Press, 2002.

Stone, Wilfred. "The Play of Chance and Ego in *Daniel Deronda*." *Nineteenth-Century Literature* 53.1 (1998): 25–55.

Stoppard, Tom. *Arcadia*. London: Faber & Faber, 1993.

Stout, Daniel. "Nothing Personal: The Decapitation of Character in *A Tale of Two Cities*." *Novel: A Forum on Fiction* 41.1 (2007): 29–52.

BIBLIOGRAPHY   215

Sussman, Herbert. "Cyberpunk Meets Charles Babbage." *Victorian Studies* 38.1 (1994): 1–23.

Tennyson, Alfred (Lord). *The Poems of Tennyson*. Ed. Christopher Ricks. 2nd ed. 3 vols. Harlow: Longmans, 1987.

Thoreau, Henry David. *Walden*. New York: Thomas Crowell, 1910.

Tolstoy, Leo. *War and Peace*. Trans. Louise and Aylmer Maude. Rev. Amy Mandelker. Oxford: Oxford University Press, 2010.

Trollope, Anthony. *Framley Parsonage*. 2 vols. Leipzig: Tauchnitz, 1861.

Trollope, Anthony. *Can You Forgive Her?* Ed. Andrew Swarbrick. Oxford: Oxford University Press, 1975.

Trollope, Anthony. *The Fixed Period*. Ed. R. H. Super. Ann Arbor: University of Michigan Press, 1990.

Trollope, Anthony. *The Way We Live Now*. Ed. Frank Kermode. London: Penguin, 1994.

Trollope, Anthony. *The Small House at Allington*. Intro. A. O. J. Cockshut. New York: Knopf, 1997.

Trollope, Anthony. *An Autobiography*. Ed. Michael Sadleir and Frederick Page. Oxford: Oxford University Press, 1999.

Trollope, Anthony. *Phineas Redux*. Intro. Gregg A. Hecimovich. London: Penguin, 2003.

Trollope, Anthony. *Orley Farm*. Ed. David Skilton. Oxford: Oxford University Press, 2008.

Trollope, Anthony. *Phineas Finn*. Ed. Simon Dentith. Oxford: Oxford University Press, 2011.

Trollope, Anthony. *The Last Chronicle of Barset*. Ed. Helen Small. Oxford: Oxford University Press, 2015.

Tubbs, Robert, Alice Jenkins, and Nina Engelhardt (eds.). *The Palgrave Handbook of Literature and Mathematics*. London: Palgrave Macmillan, 2021.

Tucker, Herbert. "Trials of Fiction: Novel and Epic in the Geraint and Enid Episodes from *Idylls of the King*." *Victorian Poetry* 30.3/4 (1992): 441–461.

Twain, Mark. *Chapters from my Autobiography*, Chapter XX, *North American Review* 186 (July 5, 1907): 465–474.

Underwood, Ted, Laura McGrath, Richard Jean So, and Chad Wellmon. "Culture, Theory, Data: An Introduction," *New Literary History* 53.4–54.1 (2022-3): 519–530.

Unsigned review of *Armadale*. *Saturday Review* 21 (16 June 1866): 726–727.

Unsigned review of *The Prime Minister*. "Mr. Trollope's Prime Minister." *Examiner* (22 July 1876): 825–826.

Venn, John. *The Logic of Chance: An Essay on the Foundations and Province of the Theory of Probability*. London: Macmillan, 1866.

Verne, Jules. *Around the World in Eighty Days*. Trans. William Butcher. Oxford: Oxford University Press, 1999.

Verne, Jules. *Twenty Thousand Leagues Under the Seas*. Trans. William Butcher. Oxford: Oxford University Press, 2009.

Watt, Ian. *The Rise of the Novel: Studies in Defoe, Richardson, and Fielding*. London: Penguin, 1983.

Wells, H. G. *Mankind in the Making*. New York: Scribner's, 1904.

Wells, H. G. *The Time Machine*. Floating Press, 2009.

White, Hayden V. *The Content of the Form: Narrative Discourse and Historical Representation*. Baltimore: Johns Hopkins University Press, 1987.

Wiggins, Chris and Matthew L. Jones. *How Data Happened: A History from the Age of Reason to the Age of Algorithms*. New York: Norton, 2023.

Williams, Carolyn. *Gilbert and Sullivan: Gender, Genre, Parody*. New York: Columbia University Press, 2012.

216 BIBLIOGRAPHY

Williams, Daniel. "Slow Fire: Serial Thinking and Hardy's Genres of Induction." *Genre* 50.1 (2017): 19–38.

Williams, Raymond. *Keywords: A Vocabulary of Culture and Society*. Rev. ed. New York: Oxford University Press, 1983.

Willis, Martin. "'The Invisible Giant,' *Dracula*, and Disease." *Studies in the Novel* 39.3 (2007): 301–325.

Wollstonecraft, Mary and J. S. Mill. *A Vindication of the Rights of Woman* and *The Subjection of Women*. London: Dent, 1992.

Woloch, Alex. *The One vs. the Many: Minor Characters and the Space of the Protagonist in the Novel*. Princeton: Princeton University Press, 2003.

Womble, David A. P. "*Phineas Finn*, the Statistics of Character, and the Sensorium of Liberal Personhood." *Novel* 51.1 (2018): 17–35.

Wordsworth, William. *Lyrical Ballads, with Pastoral and Other Poems*. 3rd ed. 2 vols. London: Longman & Rees, 1802.

Wordsworth, William. *The Excursion, being a portion of The Recluse, a Poem*. London, 1814.

Wordsworth, William. *William Wordsworth: The Major Works*. Ed. Stephen Gill. Oxford: Oxford University Press, 1984.

Yeazell, Ruth Bernard. *Fictions of Modesty: Women and Courtship in the English Novel*. Chicago: University of Chicago Press, 1991.

Yeazell, Ruth Bernard. "Perspective." In *The Cambridge Companion to Prose*. Ed. D. Tyler. Cambridge: Cambridge University Press, 2021. 96–111.

Yoo, Jungmin. "More or Less than One: Reforming Character in *A Tale of Two Cities*." *Dickens Quarterly* 38.3 (Sep. 2021): 257–276.

Zeitz, Lisa M. and Peter Thoms. "Collins's Use of the Strasbourg Clock in *Armadale*." *Nineteenth-Century Literature* 45.4 (1991): 495–503.

Index

For the benefit of digital users, indexed terms that span two pages (e.g., 52–53) may, on occasion, appear on only one of those pages.

Agamben, Giorgio 83–84
adultery, *see* marriage plot
age 34–35, 36–38, 45, 76 n. 49, 81–82, 91–92, 108–109, 120–121, 133 n. 116, 134, 136, 137–156, 158–161, 165–166, 168–171, 174–176; *see also* time
agency 130 n. 111, 182, 185–186, 189–191, 194 n. 38, 200–201; *see also* chance, fate, risk, statistical fatalism
Alfano, Veronica 12–13 n. 43
Anderson, Melville B. 83–84 n. 62
Anderson, Walter E. 36–37
Arata, Stephen D. 178–179
Arendt, Hannah 190–191 n. 31
Aristotle 71–72, 102 n. 34, 156
Auden, W. H. 57
Austen, Jane 57
  Emma 60, 62–64, 71–72, 73–78, 83–84, 100 n. 24, 110–111, 114, 142
  Juvenilia 36, 40 n. 48, 64–65 n. 23, 78–79, 86, 100, 142, 165–166
  Letters 58, 60, 62–64, 79–80
  Mansfield Park 15–16, 60–61, 70–71, 73, 75, 79–80, 87–88, 89–90, 111–112
  Northanger Abbey 60 n. 13, 60–61, 77–78
  Persuasion 38 n. 40, 60, 72–73, 74–77, 100, 110, 142–143
  Pride and Prejudice 38 n. 40, 57–58, 62–64, 68, 71–72, 75–78, 88, 142
  Sanditon 62, 66, 75–76
  Sense and Sensibility 40 n. 48, 61–62, 67–72, 100, 203–204

Babb, Genie 4 n. 16
Babbage, Charles 1–2, 26–27, 38–39 n.44, 56 n. 78, 120–121 n. 89, 185–186 n. 19
Bakhtin, M. M. 154–155
Baldridge, Cates 123 n. 98
Barchas, Janine 62–64

Barrett Browning, Elizabeth 11 n. 39, 62–64 n. 25
Barthes, Roland 103–104
Bayley, John 198, 202–204
Beckett, Samuel 24
Beer, Gillian 195–196 n. 40, 197 n. 47
Bentham, Jeremy 1–2, 26–27, 65–66, 115–116
Bertillon, Alphonse 15–16 n. 50, 92, 120–121
Bevis, Matthew 1–2, 11 n. 40, 13 n. 45, 27, 28–29 n. 13, 48, 115–116 n. 71
Bildungsroman 22–24, 39–40, 113, 114 n. 64, 133–136, 184 n. 13, 184–185
Blake, William 1, 78–79, 115–116
Blank, Paula 69–70
Bloom, Harold 36–37
Bloom, Paul 44
Bourrier, Karen 182–183 n. 10
Bowen, John 99 n. 23, 115–118, 121–122 n. 93, 127 n. 107, 129–130 n. 110
Boyd, Zelda 67–68
Brontë, Charlotte 78–79
  Jane Eyre 15–19, 62 n. 18, 111–112 n. 56, 160, 201–202
Brooks, Peter 60 n. 12, 157–158
Brown, Mark William 14–15 n. 47
Buckle, Henry Thomas 6–7 n. 25, 84 n. 64, 182
Bulson, Eric 37, 41–42 n. 50, 57 n. 1
Burgess, Miranda 29–30 n. 16, 30
Burrows, J. F. 62–64
Buzard, James 118–119 n. 82
Byrne, Paula 69–70 n. 35
Byron, George Gordon 57, 59–60, 137, 171, 172–173, 179–180
  Childe Harold's Pilgrimage 33, 38
  Don Juan 32–56, 101

capitalism, *see* economics, money

218 INDEX

cardinal numbers, *see* number
Carlyle, Thomas 2–3, 97, 105–107 n. 42,
 115–116, 129–130
Carroll, Lewis
 Alice in Wonderland 4–6 n. 23, 125,
 130–136, 175
 Sylvie and Bruno Concluded 30
 Through the Looking-Glass 134, 175–176
Case, Alison 172–173 n. 94
census 1–2, 6–7, 16, 26–27, 29–30, 38,
 45–47, 59–60, 85 n. 66, 96–97, 100 n.
 25, 102; *see also* population
Cervantes, Miguel de 156–157
chance 6–7 n. 25, 32 n. 25, 73, 89, 182,
 185–186, 188–193, 193 n. 35, 195–196,
 197–200; *see also* fate, probability, risk,
 statistics
character 25–26, 91, 138–139, 163–166, 171,
 176–177
 flat versus round 91–92, 101–102,
 103–104, 109–113, 114–115, 118–119,
 120–121 n. 90, 130–136
 minor versus major 53, 55, 92–94, 99,
 101–102, 103–104, 110–111, 113–114,
 139
 see also individualism; names; singularity;
 type; novel, of plot versus of character
Chase, Karen 137–138, 169 n. 78
Chatterjee, Ronjaunee 1–2 n. 7, 18 n. 57, 21
 n. 63, 22–23 n. 65, 29–30 n. 17, 134–135
Chew, Samuel C. 41–42, 45 n. 59
Choi, Tina Young 56 n. 78, 89 n. 69, 140–141
 n. 11, 185–186 n. 19
chronicle 6–7, 41, 140, 153–154
Chwe, Michael Suk-Young 59
Clough, Arthur Hugh 3–4
Cohen, Patricia Cline 111–112 n. 56
Collins, Wilkie
 Armadale 100, 158–160, 181–182,
 185–193, 195–196, 199, 201–202
 No Name 172–173 n. 90, 186
 The Woman in White 16–17, 154–155,
 162–165, 171–174
Conrad, Joseph 120–121 n. 87
Copeland, Edward 57
counting 6–7, 12–13, 21, 25–26, 29–33,
 37–43, 46–49, 51, 57, 67–68 n. 33,
 80–81, 95–99, 102, 115–130, 134–135,
 137–166, 182–183, 194–195; *see also*
 countdown plot, matching

countdown plot 31–32, 48–50, 166–171
Craig, Sheryl 59–60 n. 9
Culler, Jonathan 154–155
cyberpunk, *see* steampunk

Dallas, E. S. 162–165, 171, 189–190 n. 29
Daly, Nicholas 163, 166 n. 70, 172 n. 87,
 185–186 n. 17, 194
Dante (Alighieri) 11–12, 14–15, 33–34,
 194–196
Dantzig, Tobias 4–6, 66–68, 69–70 n. 37,
 80–81 n. 58, 98 n. 20
Daston, Lorraine 4–6 n. 14
data 1–3, 4 n. 16, 92, 96–97, 108–109, 112,
 173–174, 190
Davidoff, Lenore 100 n. 26, 182–183 n. 10
Dehaene, Stanislaus 4–6 n. 17, 6–8, 20, 96 n.
 12, 116–117 n. 76, 130–131
democracy 2–3, 28 n. 12, 96–98, 102 n. 34,
 115–117, 125–126 n. 104, 128–130, 132,
 134–135
Deresiewicz, William 74–75
Derrida, Jacques 102 n. 34, 116–117
detective fiction 157–161, 167–168, 193, 198,
 202–203
determinism, *see* fate, statistical fatalism
Dickens, Charles 22–23, 45–46, 49, 91, 144
 n. 1, 157–158
 Bleak House 103–104
 David Copperfield 113–114, 118–119,
 121–122
 Dombey and Son 123–124, 125–126
 Hard Times 2–3, 7–8, 99, 103, 113,
 119–120, 182
 Little Dorrit 122 n. 94, 123, 127–128 n.
 108, 130
 Our Mutual Friend 92–94, 95–97, 99,
 101–104, 105–107, 110–111, 113–114,
 118–120
 A Tale of Two Cities 20, 94–95, 98–99,
 114–131, 135–136, 173–177, 185–186 n.
 15
Digital Humanities (DH) 4–6, 25, 39–40, 56
 n. 76, 62–64, 92 n. 4, 158–160 n. 53,
 182–183 n. 10
distance 20, 60–61, 73, 79–80 n. 56, 120–121,
 127–128, 167
doubles 49, 70–71, 116–117 n. 76, 135,
 201–202; *see also* matching
Dow, Gillian 66–67 n. 32

INDEX   219

Doyle, Arthur Conan (Sherlock Holmes) 60
n. 12, 157–158, 203–204
Durkheim, Emile 84 n. 64

economics 1–2, 11, 57–58, 59–60, 104–109,
200; *see also* money
Eliot, George 144–148
Daniel Deronda 38–39 n. 41, 144
Middlemarch 12–13, 85, 111–112 n. 56,
144–146
The Mill on the Floss 105–107 n. 42
English, James F. 4
Epperly, Elizabeth R. 148 n. 27

fact, *see* objectivity
Farr, William 96–97, 105–107 n. 42, 140–141
Faulkner, Laura 195–196 n. 40
fate 45–46, 84 n. 64, 181–182, 185–186,
188–193, 195–196, 200–201; *see also*
statistical fatalism
Favret, Mary A. 43–44, 48–49 n. 69, 64–65,
71–72
Ferguson, Frances 29–30 n. 16, n. 18, 38
Fielding, Henry 34–35 n. 29, 55
Figlerowicz, Marta 109–110 n. 49
Fitz–Gerald, S. J. Adair 132 n. 114
five 20, 46–48, 51, 94–95
Fogel, Aaron 29–30
Forbes–MacPhail, Imogen 56 n. 78
Forster, E. M.
Aspects of the Novel 101–102 n. 29,
110–113, 114–115, 118–119, 120–121 n.
90
A Room with a View 19–20
Foucault, Michel 28, 31
fractions 4–6, 21, 65–66, 67–70; *see also* half
French, Tana 167–168

Gallagher, Catherine 101–104, 109–110,
110–111 n. 52, 116–117 n. 76, 124
Gallison, Peter 4 n. 14
Galton, Francis 7–8 n. 29, 15–16 n. 50,
120–121
Gardner, Martin 134
Gaskell, Elizabeth 135–136
Gasson, Andrew 164 n. 65
Gayle, N. E. 35–37
genre 9, 36, 52–55, 89–90, 93, 154–155,
157–166, 193, 196 n. 42; *see also*

Bildungsroman, detective fiction, lyric,
novel, sensation fiction, steampunk
Gibson, William 38–39 n. 44, 120–121 n. 89
Gissing, George, *The Odd Women* 80–90
Goldstone, Andrew 25 n. 2
González–Díaz, Victorina 62–64
Goodlad, Lauren 171 n. 84, 187–188
Greg, W. R. 85–86
Grener, Adam 99

Hacking, Ian 1 n. 2, 21 n. 62, 84 n. 64,
115–116, 119–121, 140–141, 182, 190,
194 n. 38, 196
Hadley, Elaine 97 n. 17, 130 n. 111
Hager, Kelly 182–183 n. 10
half 21, 57, 203–204
Halsey, Katie 66–67 n. 32
Hamer, Mary 137–138
Hardy, Janice 145
Hardy, Thomas 81, 184–185
Desperate Remedies 193–204
Far From the Madding Crowd 32 n. 25,
141
Jude the Obscure 84 n. 64, 182–184
Return of the Native 105–107 n. 42,
195–196
Harris, Jocelyn 69–70 n. 35
Hart, Sarah 4–6 n. 20, 6–7 n. 25, 22–23, 47 n.
64, 64–65 n. 27, 181–182
Hartman, Geoffrey H. 76 n. 49
Heath, Kay 137–138, 148–150
Henderson, Andrea K. 94 n. 8, 96–97 n. 13,
102 n. 31, 113
Hensley, Nathan K. 26–27 n. 6, 53–54,
96–97, 99, 185–186 n. 17, 189 n. 28,
201–202 n. 50
Higgs, Edward 97 n. 14
Hilts, Victor L. 105–107 n. 42
Holmes, John 12–13 n. 43
Homer 6–7, 50 n. 70, 52–53, 55
Hughes, Linda K. 22–23 n. 65, 115 n. 69, 136
n. 124
Hughes, Winifred 185–186 n. 16
Hunt, Aeron 105, 109–110 n. 49, 125–126

individualism, individuality 25, 45–46,
83–84, 93, 100–101, 103–104, 127–128
anti–individualism 18 n. 57, 100 n. 26, 102
n. 31, 114 n. 64, 116–117 n. 78, 127, 129
n. 109

220 INDEX

individualism, individuality (*Continued*)
  see also Liberalism, names, one,
  singularity
infinity 38–39, 39–40 n. 41, 42–43, 67–68,
  156
insurance, *see* risk
Ingelow, Jean 150–151 n. 32
iteration 36–37, 38–39, 41–42, 45, 101,
  179–180

Jaffe, Audrey 16–17, 59 n. 7, 105–107 n. 41,
  119–120 n. 86
James, Henry 22–23, 118–119
  The Princess Casamassima 80–81
James, P. D. 168
Jevon, William Stanley 59 n. 7
Johnson, Samuel 62
Jones, Lawrence O. 193 n. 34, n. 35
Jones, Matthew L. 92 n. 4
Joyce, James, *Ulysses* 20, 36–37, 41–42 n. 50,
  57 n. 1, 60 n. 13, 125–126

Keats, John 27, 65–66, 120–121 n. 89
Keegan, Bridget 29–30 n. 16, 31 n. 22, 32 n.
  24
Kendrick, Walter M. 186–187 n. 22, 193–195
Kent, Christopher 16–17 n. 52, 185–186 n.
  19, 188–189
Kipling, Rudyard 125
Kittler, Friedrich 4–6, 173–174
Klotz, Michael 16–17 n. 53, 45–46, 119–120
knitting 20–21, 114–115, 120–121, 127,
  173–174
Knoepflemacher, U. C. 133 n. 116
Kornbluh, Anna 4–6 n. 23
Körner, T. W. 178
Kurnick, David 1 n. 1, 25 n. 1, 37, 42–43, 57
  n. 1

Lamouria, Lanya 98 n. 18, 114–115 n. 67,
  115–116 n. 70, 116–117 n. 78, 121–122
  n. 89, 125–126 n. 104, 129 n. 109
Langbauer, Laurie 137–138, 153–154 n. 36
Law of large numbers 21, 182–183
Lee, Maurice S. 158–160 n. 53, 172–173
Lee, Yoon Sun 60
Lesser, Wendy 80–81 n. 60, 89 n. 68
letters (alphabetic) 6–7, 94 n. 8, 98 n. 20, 110,
  111–112 n. 56
Levi, Primo 91

Levine, Caroline 25–27, 37, 46 n. 62,
  105–107 n. 41
Levinson, Marjorie 18 n. 57, 28–30, 38,
  38–39 n. 41, 45 n. 60, 50, 66–67 n. 31,
  105–107 n. 41, 109–110 n. 49
Liberalism 1–2, 28 n. 12, 83–84, 93, 97–98,
  99 n. 23, 116–117, 123 n. 98, 130 n. 111,
  134–135, 146, 147–148, 184–185
  "long family" 100, 182–183; *see also*
  population
Lukács Georg 105–107 n. 41
Lund, Michael 22–23 n. 65, 115 n. 69, 136 n.
  124
Lynch, Deidre 104, 109–110, 113 n. 63,
  120–121
lyric 22–23, 45 n. 60, 105–107 n. 41, 109–110
  n. 49, 154–156, 188–189

Macpherson, Sandra 185–186 n. 19
Manning, Peter J. 53–54 n. 76
Malthus, Thomas 1–2, 4, 26–27, 31, 32 n. 24,
  36–37 n. 33, 43, 46–47, 59–60, 71–73,
  77–79, 84 n. 64, 86 n. 67, 178–179,
  182–184; *see also* population
marriage plot 10, 18–19, 40–42, 58, 62, 62–64
  n. 25, 66–67, 80–90, 95 n. 11, 135–136,
  140–141, 143, 155, 158–160, 162–163 n.
  61, 166, 168, 193, 201–202; *see also* plot
Martin, Daniel 185–186, 190
matching 21, 29–30 n. 18, 38–39 n. 41,
  66–67, 80–81, 85, 100 n. 25, 118; *see
  also* doubles, marriage plot
mathematics 4 n. 16, 4–6, 30, 31 n. 22, 47 n.
  64, 56 n. 78, 66, 83–84 n. 62, 94 n. 8,
  173–174, 178, 194 n. 38, 197
Maxwell, Catherine 13–15
Maxwell, James Clerk 194 n. 38
Mayhew, Henry 15–16, 25–26, 41–42 n. 54,
  102, 105–110, 132, 134 n. 119
McAleavey, Maia 100 n. 26, 114 n. 64,
  201–202 n. 51
McCrea, Barry 37
McGann, Jerome 12–13 n. 43, 38–40, 41–42
McKeon, Michael 110–111 n. 52
McLane, Maureen 26–27
McMurtry, Larry 31
measurement 15–16, 33–35, 47, 108–109,
  115–116, 119–121, 127, 203–204; *see
  also* counting, meter
Menke, Richard 4–6 n. 21

Menon, Tara 110–111 n. 52
meter 4–6, 13, 22–23, 28–29 n. 13, 29–30,
    34–35, 40, 42–43, 51, 55, 156
Michie, Helena 153–154 n. 35
Mill, John Stuart 1–2, 26–27 n. 6, 65–66, 93
    n. 7, 116–117, 123 n. 98
Miller, D. A. 71–72, 122, 157–158
money 3, 11, 57–58, 68–69, 81–82, 84, 88,
    107, 113 n. 63, 118–119, 167; *see also*
    economics
Moretti, Franco 6–7, 134 n. 117

Nelson, Harland S. 102 n. 32
names 6–7, 22–23, 41, 51–55, 94, 96–97,
    98–104, 110, 143, 162–163 n. 61
narrative 6–8, 22–23, 36–37, 38–40, 49,
    77–78, 117, 127, 137–139, 153–154,
    156–158, 163, 185–186 n. 19, 186–187;
    see also plot, seriality, time
novel 6–7, 10, 25–26, 93–94, 97, 105–107 n.
    41, 109–110
    of plot versus of character 161–165
    see also Bildungsroman, character,
    detective fiction, genre, narrative,
    sensation fiction
Number
    as concept 4–6, 28–29, 66, 67–68 n. 33,
    80–81
    large versus small 21, 25–26, 28–29,
    30–31, 37–38, 43, 48, 51, 94–95,
    116–117, 178–180, 182–183, 196
    ordinal versus cardinal 4–6, 20, 38, 98 n.
    20, 133 n. 115, 199 n. 49
    see also five, half, one, three, zero

objectivity 1, 4–6 n. 14, 12–13, 59, 60–62,
    67–68, 121–122, 150–151 n. 29,
    187–188; *see also* subjectivity
O'Brien, Karen 59–60
one 18–19, 43, 127–128; *see also* singularity,
    individualism
Oppen, George 50
ordinal numbers, *see* number
Ortiz–Robles, Mario 32 n. 25

Parker, Isabel 99
Paulos, John Allen 7–8 n. 30, 92–93
Paxton, Amanda 7–8 n. 29
Peters, John Durham 4
Pettitt, Clare 22–23 n. 65, 49 n. 68, 50 n. 72

Piketty, Thomas 59
Plato 4, 66–68, 73
plot 138–139, 146–147, 155–156 n. 42,
    156–166, 176–177, 186–187, 189–194,
    195–197, 201–204; *see also* marriage
    plot, narrative
poetry *see* genre, lyric, meter
Pool, Daniel 77 n. 51
Poovey, Mary 1, 1–2 n. 7, 2–3 n. 10, 4, 16, 59,
    149–150 n. 29
population 28, 31, 84 n. 64, 85–86, 97,
    178–180, 184; *see also* census, "long
    family"
Porter, Theodore M. 149–150 n. 29
Potter, Gordon 33
probability 4 n. 16, 6–7 n. 25, 18, 21, 32 n. 25,
    185–186 n. 19, 188–189, 196–197; *see
    also* chance, statistics, law of large
    numbers, risk
Propp, Vladimir Yakovlevich 9 n. 36,
    181–182

Quetelet, Adolphe 15–16 n. 50, 182

Reynolds, G. W. M. 41–42
Richardson, Samuel 62–64, 154–155
risk 141, 185–186, 190–191, 196–197; *see
    also* probability
Robbins, Hollis 29–30 n. 16, 100 n. 25
romans-fleuves, *see* series novels
Rommel, Thomas 40
Rosenthal, Jesse 4–6 n. 16, 38–39 n. 41, 122
    n. 94
Rossetti, Dante Gabriel 11–16
Rzepka, Charles 27

Schaffer, Talia 100 n. 26
Sensation fiction 24, 97, 158–160, 162–165,
    166 n. 70, 181–182, 184–204
series novels (*romans-fleuves*) 137–138,
    150–152
seriality 22–23, 40–42, 45, 49 n. 68, 50–51,
    55, 99, 127, 136, 137–138, 170–171, 197,
    199 n. 49, 201–203
Seronsy, Cecil C. 69–70 n. 35
Shakespeare, William 43–44 n. 56, 69–70,
    142, 147–148, 163–164
Shelley, Mary 172–173
Shelley, Percy Bysshe 26–27, 156

222 INDEX

Shrimpton, Nicholas 146–148, 150–151, 164 n. 64
singularity 3, 18–19, 21, 28 n. 12, 28–29, 45–47, 53–54, 55–56, 101, 108–109, 109–110 n. 49, 116–117, 118–119, 129, 134–135, 184 n. 13; *see also* *Bildungsroman*; character, flat versus round; individualism; one
Small, Helen 154–155
sorites paradox 28–29, 96
space, *see* distance
statistics 1–3, 4 n. 16, 6–7 n. 25, 16–17, 21, 25–26, 45–46, 87–88, 92, 97, 102, 105–107, 119–120, 140–141, 149–150, 178, 182; *see also* unit, statistical fatalism
statistical fatalism 182–184, 185–186, 190–191, 195–197
Stauffer, Andrew M. 150–151 n. 32
steampunk 38–39 n. 44, 120–121 n. 89, 122 n. 95
Steinlight, Emily 84 n. 64, 98 n. 18, 118, 184
Sterling, Bruce 38–39 n. 44, 120–121 n. 89
Stevenson, Robert Louis 158–160
Stewart, Susan 42–43
Stoppard, Tom 56 n. 78
Stout, Daniel 98 n. 18, 120–121 n. 90, 123, 127–128
subjectivity 16–17, 50 n. 72, 60–62, 67–68, 97, 110–111 n. 52, 118 n. 79, 125–126; *see also* character, flat versus round; objectivity
suicide 84, 120–121 n. 87, 182–186, 193, 196
Sussman, Herbert 120–121 n. 89, 122 n. 95
sympathy 41–46, *see also* character

temporality, *see* time
Tennyson, Alfred (Lord) 9–13, 18–19, 27, 28–29 n. 13, 48, 115–116 n. 71, 188–189, 198
Thoms, Peter 185–186 n. 17
Thoreau, Henry David 108–109 n. 46
three 9–19, 181
time 7–8, 42–43, 60–61, 64–65, 75–78, 118, 127, 136, 138–139, 141, 144–156, 157–158, 162–166, 168–169, 172, 194–195
railway time 167, 172–173, 194
see also age, narrative
Tolstoy, Leo 4–6, 47

Trollope, Anthony 34–35, 35 n. 30, 137, 204
An Autobiography 137, 148, 150–151, 161, 170–171
Can You Forgive Her? 146–147 n. 24, 151
The Duke's Children 146–147, 166
The Fixed Period 169–171
Framley Parsonage 150–151
The Last Chronicle of Barset 139–140, 144, 147–148, 150–156, 166
Orley Farm 151–152, 153–154, 168–169
Phineas Finn 17, 97, 103–104 n. 38, 140–141, 146, 148–150
Phineas Redux 97, 115–116, 146, 149–150, 153–154
The Prime Minister 146–147, 166
The Small House at Allington 146–147, 152, 155
The Way We Live Now 152–154
Tucker, Herbert 11 n. 38
Twain, Mark 149–150
two, *see* doubles
type 46 n. 62, 83, 96–97, 101, 105–107, 109–110, 113, 137–138

Underwood, Ted 25 n. 2, 92 n. 4
unit 99, 105–107, 113, 115–117

Venn, John 196
Verne, Jules 167
verse, *see* lyric, meter

Watt, Ian 6–7, 93
war 6–7, 37 n. 35, 43–45, 47–56, 120–121 n. 90
Wells, H. G. 91–92, 122 n. 95, 138–139
White, Hayden V. 153–154
Wiggins, Chris 92 n. 4
Williams, Carolyn 165–166
Williams, Daniel 22–23 n. 65, 196–197, 199 n. 49, 203–204
Williams, Raymond 203–204 n. 58
Willis, Martin 178 n. 97
Wollstonecraft, Mary 111–112 n. 56
Woloch, Alex 25–26, 52–53, 94 n. 9, 98–99, 113–115, 116–117, 121–122, 122 n. 96
Woman Question 80–90
Womble, David A. P. 16–17, 97
Wordsworth, William 25–33, 37–38, 44 n. 57, 45, 48–49, 73–74, 76–77, 78–79,

96–97 n. 13, 100 n. 25, 105–107 n. 41,
108–109, 109–110 n. 49, 154–155

Yeazell, Ruth Bernard 74–75 n. 47, 149 n. 28
Yoo, Jungmin 98 n. 18, n. 19, 130 n. 111

Zeitz, Lisa M. 185–186 n. 17
Zeno's paradox 67–68, 90
zero 43, 66, 69–70 n. 37, 111–112